Viva!
Cookbook

Recipes to celebrate food, save lives and protect the planet

By Jane Easton,
Food & Cookery Coordinator, Viva!

About Jane

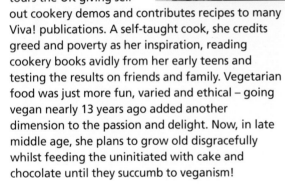

In a previous life, Jane was an English teacher and writer until she became vegan and, not long afterwards, joined the Viva! team. Jane helped create the online veganrecipeclub.org.uk, tours the UK giving sell-out cookery demos and contributes recipes to many Viva! publications. A self-taught cook, she credits greed and poverty as her inspiration, reading cookery books avidly from her early teens and testing the results on friends and family. Vegetarian food was just more fun, varied and ethical – going vegan nearly 13 years ago added another dimension to the passion and delight. Now, in late middle age, she plans to grow old disgracefully whilst feeding the uninitiated with cake and chocolate until they succumb to veganism!

Front cover photo by Chava Eichner www.flavourphotos.com, of our Strawberry Tart recipe on page 266

© Viva! 2014
Viva!, 8 York Court, Wilder Street, Bristol BS2 8QH.
T 0117 944 1000
www.viva.org.uk info@viva.org.uk
www.veganrecipeclub.org.uk for fabulous, 100% animal-free recipes and more.
ISBN: 978-0-9571874-0-5

Thanks to

Matthew Glover for his donation that helped turn the dream into a reality.

Helen Wilson – food photography and vegan cooking buddy. Previously Viva!'s Media Officer, editor of *Viva!Life* magazine and Cookery Writer – she's still part of the family but freelance. The award-winning vegan cookery and creative blog, **www.lotsofnicethings.com**, is just one of her many projects.

Juliet Gellatley (Founder & Director of Viva!) for her belief in me – as well as inspiration, encouragement, editing and the mighty task of proofing!

Tony Wardle for taking this beast of a book around publishers, for honest, down-to-earth advice, editing and for sharing his recipes.

Chava Eichner of **www.flavourphotos.com** for the stunning front cover and more.

Lucie Storrs for kindly proofing as a donation to Viva!.

Liam Nolan of Viva! for editing, proofing, techy help and humour.

Everyone in the Viva! team for your support. You work in so many ways to save animals – and you eat the cake…

Simon Parkin at **www.ethicalgraphicdesign.co.uk** for fresh and tasty design work – and for his wonderful patience with us all.

Mary, for everything, including being an ever-willing food taster.

And not forgetting **our animal friends**! Bella, Gwennie, Seren, the two Alfies (RIP) and all the others who make work and home life that bit more special.

And for **all the animals** who are not so fortunate – we do everything we can to end your suffering by changing human hearts and minds.

Contents

Recipes

Vegan basics: home-made favourites

Souperb

A bit on the side

Sweet thing

Intelligent indexes

Introduction

Welcome to the *Viva! Cookbook*.

It's got the lot – plenty of new recipes plus some indispensable old favourites. We have also included some unique sections of things we wish we'd known at the start of our vegan and cooking journeys. And of course, in line with our campaigning work to save animals, protect the environment, improve our health and help feed the world, everything in this book is 100 per cent veganlicious!

Who's it for? Anyone who likes good food, whatever their current dietary persuasion. Good food is good so get cooking! And it's aimed at all levels of cooks, from the beginner or less confident to the more kitchen savvy amongst you.

For new vegans or those cooking for them, we highly recommend our *L-Plate Vegan*, which is a splendid little guide to products, quick meal ideas and lots more. Only £1.90, it is designed to fit easily into a back pocket or handbag. Visit the Viva! Shop **www.vivashop.org.uk** or download the free online version from **www.viva.org.uk/resources/campaign-materials/guides/l-plate-vegan**

Abbreviations & weights

Recipes use both metric and imperial measurements as we are still at the conversion crossroads in the UK. Use either but it's best not to mix them up, especially if you're baking!

Recipes use a mixture of measuring cups and scales. Measuring cups (and spoon sets) are cheap to buy and make life easier. Scales – preferably digital or the old-school weights type – also make life simpler.

tsp	teaspoon (5ml)
dsp	dessertspoon (10ml)
tbsp	tablespoon (15ml)
g	gram
oz	ounce
fl oz	fluid ounce
lb	pound
K	kilo
ml	millilitre
L	litre
GF	gluten-free
WF	wheat-free
HFS	health food shops

How to use this book

Breaking the code
Each recipe is marked with appropriate symbols to help you decide if it's right for your particular needs.

 cheap as chickpeas – budget dishes. See also page 301

 fast feeds – 30 minutes or under

 going solo – cooking for one. While most recipes in the book serve four, we have included many that are easily halved or quartered. See also page 12

 gluten-free – alternatives are offered wherever possible if the dish isn't already suitable

 wheat-free – as GF

 kid-friendly – simple suggestions such as reducing salt or chilli

 freezable – all or part of the dish

 low-fat/diabetic-friendly or reduced-fat – for those who want to keep their fat intake low for either slimming or health reasons. We provide low-fat or reduced-fat alternatives for as many recipes as possible. Also, try these:
- replace oil with 2-3 squirts of oil spray when lightly frying ingredients; add a splash of stock or water if it starts to dry up
- use our recipes for Easy Mayo (page 143) and Sour Cream (page 35)
- for further information on low-fat diets for slimming and their important role in reversing or controlling diabetes and heart disease, go to Viva!Health **www.vivahealth.org.uk** and look in Resources or Campaigns. For the computer-free, please contact the office – see page 2 for details

All kitted out
Our recipes are designed specifically to assist new or inexperienced cooks, but they're equally useable by experienced cooks. Each recipe includes an equipment list because it's much quicker to get everything together beforehand rather than scrabbling for a wooden spoon while the onions are burning.

Cool combos
Each recipe also contains a list of suggested accompaniments to choose from.

Intelligent indexes
We've got the 'bits at the back' arranged to help you find dishes suitable for your particular needs. They will let you track down that gluten-free dinner party dish that you need in half an hour, find an almost instant snack for a bunch of starving teenagers, or a quick TV supper for one after a long day at work…

The veganiser: new ways with old favourites

It's much easier than you might think to eat vegan. Here are a few quick ideas…

Veganise your favourite recipes

Replace meat with veggie faux meat, tofu chunks, tempeh or cooked pulses eg

- veggie mince or whole cooked lentils replace meat mince in Martin Shaw's Chilli (page 184) and you can do the same with Spaghetti Bolognese, Shepherd's Pie and any other traditional mince dish
- tofu in Pad Thai, page 196, or Thai Curry, page 203, instead of chicken – and see *Tofu Secrets* page 22
- tempeh in Big Puff Pie, page 170
- faux chicken or beef strips for your favourite stir-fry or curry recipes
- seitan (gluten-based meat alternative) in stir-fries, roasts and much more. See pages 40-44

Cheese sauce

- Use our easy cheesy sauces on pages 139-140 to replace the traditional variety – and use them in dishes such as Mac Cheese (page 140) or cauliflower cheese

- Alternatively, Free & Easy Cheese-flavoured sauce mix is available in tubs, in the free-from ranges in large Sainsbury's, Holland & Barrett or other health food shops. It's easy to make from the tub instructions with plant milk – and adding a handful of nutritional yeast flakes plus a teaspoon or two of Dijon mustard makes it even nicer

Sausage & mash

- Use vegan sausages, bought or home-made (page 204). Mash the potatoes using vegan margarine or olive oil and serve with vegan gravy – home-made or from a tub!

Burger bliss

- Buy ready-made vegan burgers or make your own from our recipes on pages 179, 204 and 219. Eat them in a bun as usual with all your favourite trimmings

Pizza party

- Make your own (see page 215)
- Buy vegan pizza bases and add your favourite vegan toppings. Go cheese-free OR replace with vegan cheese: try hard melting cheese or cream cheese
- Take vegan cheese to your local pizzeria and ask

them to use it instead of dairy (and knock a couple of quid off the bill too!). See the list on page 17

Scrambled tofu
- It's delicious and an easy way to replace eggs (see page 126)

Cakes and other baked goods
- Lovely egg and dairy-free alternatives in our *Sweet thing* section, pages 239-282 plus vegan *Baking tips*, pages 236-237

Learn to cook a few easy basics that you can easily tweak to make different dishes

Pancakes (pages 36-39)
- Once you know how to make our lovely easy recipe you can ring the changes – vary the fillings and sauces to create savoury or sweet dishes

Sauces
- Our easy sauces liven up simple dishes. See *Back to the sauce* on pages 138-160

Wholegrains
- Brown rice, quinoa, millet and other grains are the basis of plenty of dishes, hot and cold – see page 24 for a cooking chart. Cooking a double batch allows you a quick meal the following day – a stir-fry, risotto or mixed multi-salad. They are also available ready-cooked in pouches – Merchant Gourmet, Tilda, Uncle Ben, Sainsbury's etc

Pulses: beans, peas, lentils
- Make great dips, stews, burgers and more. See cooking chart and ideas on pages 25-29

Getting enough? Vegan nutrition

Despite several generations of healthy vegans and a wealth of reputable and persuasive science, some people still worry about veganism. The simple answer is: *there is no magic ingredient in meat, fish, dairy and eggs that can't be found in a well-balanced plant-based diet.* And it's useful to turn that question on its head – people consuming typical Western, meat-based diets are more likely to succumb to Western-style diseases, such as many cancers, diabetes type 2, obesity, strokes and heart disease! The fact is that vegans tend to be less at risk of these and other degenerative diseases and are generally healthier and live longer (even when the figures are adjusted to account for the fact that we tend to be non-smokers). And yes, veganism is nutritionally sound for children and gives them the best possible start in life – several generations of healthy vegan kids all around the world are living proof. [1]

There isn't room for all our nutritional expertise here but we've included a handy little nutrition chart on pages 10-11.

Try Viva!Health **www.vivahealth.org.uk** for a wealth of nutritional fact sheets, guides and reports. These materials cover just about everything diet and nutrition-related and, of course, are all scientifically referenced, with nary an urban myth in sight!

1. See page 308

What I need each d

Number of Servings	Foods	Healthy Portion Size	To Provide
7-10	**Fruit & Vegetables to include: Dark Green Leafy Vegetables, Orange Vegetables, Fresh Fruit, Dried Fruits**		Vitamins such as Beta-carotene (makes vitamin A), Vitamins B2, B3, B5, B6, B9 (Folate), Vitamin C, Vitamin E, Vitamin K
	Fresh Fruit	1 medium piece the size of a tennis ball	
	Dried Fruit	1-1½ tablespoons or 1 golf ball	
	Green or Root Veg	2-3 tablespoons or ½ tennis ball	Minerals/trace elements such as Calcium, Iodine, Iron, Magnesium, Manganese, Phosphorus, Potassium
	Salad Veg	80g or 1 large cereal bowl	
		Note: fruit juice only counts as 1 portion per day no matter how much you drink! Smoothies using whole fruit count as a maximum 2 portions daily if you use at least 2 portions of fruit	Fibre
3-4	**Cereals & Grains (eg Wholemeal Pasta, Wholemeal Bread, Brown Rice, Oats, Rye, Buckwheat etc)**		Vitamins such as B1, B2, B3, B5, B6
	Cooked Brown Rice	2-3 heaped tablespoons or ½ teacup	Minerals/trace elements such as Calcium, Copper, Iron, Magnesium, Manganese, Phosphorus, Potassium, Zinc
	Breakfast Cereal	25g or 1 regular sized cereal bowl	
	Wholemeal Pasta	1 cup (cooked) as side dish or 2 cups as main dish	
	Wholemeal Bread	2 slices	Fibre, Energy, Protein
2-3	**Pulses (eg all types of Peas, Beans and Lentils), Nuts and Nut Butters or Seeds**		Vitamins such as B1, B2, B3, B5, B6, B9
	Peas, Beans and Lentils	½ cup (cooked)	Minerals/trace elements such as Calcium, Copper, Iron, Magnesium, Manganese, Phosphorus, Potassium, Selenium, Zinc
	Nuts or Seeds	2 tablespoons or a small handful	Fibre, Energy, Protein

Number of Servings	Foods	Healthy Portion Size	To Provide
Small amounts	**Vegetable Oil (eg Flaxseed, Hemp Seed or Rapeseed Oil, used cold; Virgin Olive Oil for cooking), Vegetable Margarines**	½ tbsp flaxseed oil or 1½ tbsp of ground flaxseeds	Vitamins such as Vitamin E (Vegetable Oils), Vitamins A & D (Fortified Margarine) Energy Essential Omega-3 and Omega-6 Fats (Flaxseed, Soya, Walnut and Hemp Oils)
At least 1	**B12 Fortified Foods (essential if vegan)** eg Fortified Soya Milk, Fortified Breakfast Cereal, Yeast Extract (Marmite, Meridian Yeast Extract with B12) or a B12 supplement		Vitamin B12

1.5-2 litres of water per day (at least eight 200ml glasses) should also be consumed as part of a healthy, balanced diet

Every Day Think Colour!
Think rainbow and brighten your meals. The chemicals that give foods their beautiful colours are also what protect your health! So take a few minutes to add colour to every meal. Here's a few ideas:

Breakfast
- Add berries, banana and ground cinnamon to your cereal
- Make a smoothie using berries, any other fruit and ground nuts with soya milk
- Add grilled tomatoes to mushrooms on wholegrain toast

Lunch
- Add salads with a vibrant mix of colours – eg rocket leaves; sliced mango; cranberries; pear; walnuts; yellow pepper; sweetcorn
- Add tomatoes and watercress to your usual sandwich
- Add more veg and any peas/beans/lentils to your soup
- Avocados are very nutritious – try with grated carrot and tomato on wholegrain bread

Evening Meal
- Add extra veg and any peas/beans/lentils to casseroles, pasta, curries and rice dishes
- Eat at least 2 veg with your main meal

Snacks
- Snack on a high protein food such as mixed unsalted nuts or seeds with fresh or dried fruit – any you enjoy. (The protein slows down the release of the fruit sugars and that's what your body and brain loves!)
- Raw carrots or celery dipped in hummus or guacamole
- Handful of cherry tomatoes

Rainbow Reminder:
The more colours you add to your food – the more health boosting nutrients you eat!

Every Day Think Smell!
Herbs and spices are packed with antioxidants which fight many diseases including heart disease, strokes, diabetes, some cancers and some of the effects of ageing. You only need small amounts of herbs and spices to boost the flavour of your food and your health. Use what you enjoy, here's a few examples:

Black pepper, caraway, cardamon, cayenne, chilli pepper, cinnamon, coriander, cumin, garlic, ginger, juniper berries, mustard, nutmeg, oregano, peppermint, rosemary, sage, saffron, turmeric, thyme

Adapted from Viva!'s wallchart by Juliet Gellatley.

Going solo: cooking for one

Some tried and tested suggestions:

- Many of our recipes are suitable for halving or quartering – see the 🅐 symbol and *Themed indexes* on page 302
- Make a half or full-sized dish and freeze the leftovers – or just eat it for lunch or supper the next day! Many of our recipes are suitable for freezing. See *Chill out* opposite
- If you aren't already a member of a local veggie or vegan group, consider joining one. Not only will you meet friendly, like-minded folk, they often do pot luck suppers and meals out so you get to try lots of dishes
- Try regular 'bring a dish' evenings with friends/family – book a DVD and you've got a cheap, fun night in!
- Make friends with your favourite local takeaway(s) – Chinese, Indian, Thai and other outlets usually have great options for those nights when you don't want to cook. Just make sure they understand what to omit – eg no fish sauce in Thai/Vietnamese food, no egg/oyster sauce in Chinese fried rice, no butter/cream/yoghurt in Indian food
- Find a 'weigh-your-own' shop in your area if possible; that way you can buy small quantities of dried goods such as spices, grains, nuts and pulses. Not only will it help your cash flow, it means fresher goods. Many independent health food stores sell some loose goods
- Find someone to split an internet order to save postage – many offer free postage on orders over a certain value

Chill out: freezing food to save time and money

Label and date everything

This may sound obvious but it's easy to forget… meaning that you end up with mysterious boxes. That's great if you like a culinary challenge but keeping a sheet of labels and a pen near your plastic container stash might make life easier. (We speak from experience!)

Pastry

Home-made – make a double batch so there is some left over for another time.

Some of us just don't make pastry, so shop-bought – vegan shortcrust, vegan puff and vegan filo (JusRol, Sainsbury's and other brands) are always worth keeping in the freezer.

Pesto

Vegan pesto keeps well in the fridge but if you don't use it that often, simply freeze what's left of the jar in ice cube trays and transfer to a small plastic bag.

Pulses – beans, lentils and peas

For the time-strapped, a huge range of pre-cooked beans and lentils are sold in tins and packets and, of course, there are frozen peas and edamame (fresh soya beans) too. They are cheap, nutritious, tasty and versatile. However, cooking your own is an even cheaper option. They freeze very well indeed so if you

have a pressure cooker or even just a large saucepan, it's worth producing a big batch so you can freeze them in small portions. Large beans/chickpeas take about 15 minutes at high in a pressure cooker! See also *Feel the pulse*, pages 25-29.

Soup
Most soup freezes very well.

Soya milk and other milk alternatives
Soya, almond and coconut are the most popular although there are plenty more types. Some are available in 250ml or 500ml cartons. Plant milks of most types can be frozen in smaller portions but may need a quick whisk after defrosting.

Stews, curries, casseroles
These usually freeze very well and having a small stash of frozen leftovers means you have a ready-made basis to create other dishes, eg:
- left-over chilli can be heated and rolled in tortillas/wraps/pancakes or layered in filo pastry and baked (Martin Shaw's Classic Chilli, page 184)
- dry curries or lentil dahl can be wrapped in pastry to make samosas – filo, shortcrust or puff. For example, Old School Lentil & Potato Curry, page 191

Stock
Home-made: for the really frugal or eco-cooks amongst you, save home-made stock in ice cube trays then transfer to a plastic bag. Defrost as many cubes as you need – they will melt quickly in the pan when you cook with them. Alternatively, just use Marigold vegan bouillon (red or purple tub) or vegan stock cubes – for more information see the *L-Plate Vegan*, details page 6.

Tofu
See *Tofu secrets*, pages 22-23.

Vegetables and fruit
Many freeze well, although there are a few exceptions, particularly those with a high water content such as strawberries and uncooked mushrooms. Cooked mushrooms work in frozen meals, however. Shop bought frozen veg and fruit are also a nutritious and budget option.

Wine, sherry, beer and cider
A little booze cheers up gravies, soups and sauces no end. Freezing leftover booze (is there such a thing?!) in ice cube trays does work; just pop a cube or two into the recipe and let it cook in. For more information about vegan-friendly booze, see the *L-Plate Vegan* (page 6).

Shopping and the vegan food cupboard

The range of vegan foods is expanding all the time and there are plenty of places to buy them:

- Large supermarket branches: free-from shelves (not all vegan so check labels), ethnic, organic and vegetarian sections are particularly useful but vegan options aren't limited to those. Most major supermarkets also offer vegan lists and/or label own-brand products, eg Co-op, M&S, Sainsbury's, Tesco and Waitrose. Labelling tends to be quite random although it is improving in places
- Independent food manufacturers offer product information via websites or customer services, eg Merchant Gourmet, Thai Taste, Discovery Foods
- Health food shops: Holland & Barrett and independents
- Ethnic grocers: Oriental, Indian etc
- Delicatessens: these often offer a good range, including chilled snacks, salads etc
- Online stores: the range is growing all the time; they are great places to find the best vegan cheeses, chocolates and more – see page 21. Not only dedicated vegan stores but also Ocado, Amazon and others offer an increasingly large range of items

For a much more comprehensive list of products and stockists, check out Viva!'s *L-Plate Vegan* Guide. See page 6 for details.

Vegan or allergen-free?

If an item contains no animal ingredients but the packaging states 'may contain traces of milk/egg' etc… this means the item is most likely vegan. Why? Because companies who make a variety of foods have to clean the production lines between different batches of foods containing potential allergen triggers such as nuts, soya and dairy. A chocolate manufacturer may make a batch of non-vegan milk chocolate then clean the line and make a batch of vegan dark chocolate! Although the lines are cleaned scrupulously, there is always the risk of microscopic traces and companies have a legal obligation to warn allergy sufferers about possible cross-contamination.

From an ethical point of view, most vegan groups agree that this is an acceptable compromise. While it is undoubtedly better to support dedicated vegan companies, it isn't always practical. Being able to buy items from mainstream companies widens the choice of products available to vegans – and in turn, reduces animal suffering and environmental damage. As ever, when in doubt, check with the manufacturer.

Vegan alternatives

Vegetables, fruit, wholegrains, pulses, nuts and seeds are inherently vegan so we don't list them. That covers a lot of food but there is plenty more!

Meat alternatives

These range from the more natural/minimally processed such as tofu, seitan and tempeh – each used in other countries for millennia – to the more modern, processed types such as sausages, burgers, chunks and strips. All have their uses and they each work in some dishes better than others. Some people – often meat-eaters – suggest that the use of such alternatives is a kind of 'cheating' but we would argue that they are a useful alternative and why not use them if you like them? Others dislike over-processed food like TVP. The bottom line is that it's always best to use a food closest to its origins, eg tofu or tempeh, for obvious reasons. On the other hand, processed foods like veggie burgers, mince and sausages are great for an occasional treat and a useful crossover food for mixed vegan/meaty families and friends. They also work very well on a barbecue. You choose!

At the time of writing, Quorn is not vegan. Cauldron and Linda McCartney feature some vegan products in their ranges – check labels and websites. Vegan brands to look out for include Fry's; V-Bites/Redwood; Vegetarian Choice; Sainsbury's Meat-free (some) and more – see the *L-Plate Vegan* (page 6).

Seitan/gluten – see pages 40-44 for brands and simple home-made versions. It's a tasty, traditional product with good texture made from vital gluten flour (largely wheat protein with little starch).

Tempeh is made from fermented soya beans and sold in slabs or flavoured rashers. It originates from Indonesia where it is often used in a coconut-based curry. Doctor Tempeh makes a traditional curry in tins (health food shops).

Tofu is made from soya beans and comes in various flavours and types. We use different types of tofu in many of our recipes. See also *Tofu secrets*, pages 22-23.

TVP (textured vegetable protein) is made from defatted soya. It comes in mince or chunks and is often the basis of commercial veggie sausages, burgers etc. It often contains wheat. It can also be bought dried, then soaked in hot stock and added to stews, chillies etc.

- Frozen veggie mince brands include Fry's, Linda McCartney Vegemince, Sainsbury's Meat-free, Tesco Meet the Alternative, V-Bites Gourmet Meat Free Mince and Vegusto
- Quorn mince is not vegan
- Some items made from TVP are vegan, others not! See the *L-Plate Vegan,* page 6

Vegan dairy alternatives

Cheese
Whenever you see 'cheese' in this book, it means a vegan version.

There is currently nothing vegan that tastes like Brie (although given all those inventive vegans out there, who knows what the future may bring?). However, there are some good alternatives to many conventional cheese flavours. Depending on the brand, they may contain soya, nuts, rice, wheat or lupin flour – or a combination of some of these. Some are GF, eg Cheezly

- Vegan hard cheeses are not identical to dairy cheeses but some come quite close. Some melt better than others and work quite well on pizzas
- Try different brands – there are big differences
- Vegan cream cheese is almost identical to the dairy variety

Brands to look for: Mozzarisella, Sheese, Tesco, Tofutti, V-Bites (Cheezly), Veganic, Vegusto – with more appearing all the time!

Engevita Nutritional Yeast Flakes make a great condiment, sprinkled on pasta dishes. Or use them to make some of the cheesy-style sauces in our recipe section, such as on pages 139-140 (not to be confused with brewer's yeast).

Also…
- Try our Cream Cheese recipe on page 34
- Try Creamy Baked Cheesecake with Three Variations, page 259

Cream, dairy-free
Any mention of cream here means a vegan type.

To find out why vegans and others don't use dairy, see **www.whitelies.org.uk**.

Single cream
Provamel, Alpro, Oatly, Ecomil Cuisine.

Double/whipping cream

Soya Too, Soya Whip, Rice Whip, Cocos Whip – all whip up well with an electric beater. Soyatoo and Schlagfix's Whiptop (large branches of Tesco) come in squirty cans. All nice – depending on your personal taste.

Sour cream

Tofutti Sour Supreme – or try our simple low-fat Sour Cream recipe on page 35.

Ice cream

Booja Booja Stuff in a Tub, Razzle Dazzle, Bessant & Dury, Swedish Glace, Food Heaven, Tofutti.

Margarine

Biona – top of *Ethical Consumer* magazine's list. HFS
M&S Sunflower Spread
Pure (Soya or Sunflower) – supermarkets
Suma – also high up on the *Ethical Consumer* list. HFS
Tesco Free From
Vitalite – supermarkets.

Mayonnaise

Plamil, Solesse, Tiger Tiger, Mayola – or make our Easy Mayo on page 143 – cheap, quick and low fat too!

Milk

Most of our recipes state 'soya milk' but other delicious, healthy plant milks can be used, eg almond, hemp, rice and pouring coconut like Kara and Koko – widely available from almost all supermarkets and health shops.

   Fortified plant milks are a good source of calcium, B12 and sometimes other vitamins. Use them in tea and coffee (see page 19) as well as on cereal and in cooking – just as you would cow's milk. Some are creamier than others, particularly soya and coconut, but it's all down to personal taste. And remember that we all get a new set of taste buds every few weeks so you'll get used to the slight differences in taste.

Yoghurt

Alpro, Co-yo, Granovita, Joya, Provamel, Sojade, Tesco, V-Bites – and probably new brands soon also! Vegan yoghurt tends to be soya, coconut or even pea-based and comes in plain and flavoured varieties. Or try making it at home, see our recipes on pages 32-33.

Egg alternatives

- Tofu is often used to replace eggs, eg mayo page 143, French toast page 91 and scramble, page 126
- Baking: a range of ingredients are used to bind cakes etc depending on the consistency needed
  - Flax meal (ground flaxseeds or linseeds – same thing!)
  - Commercial egg replacer
  - Mashed banana, apple sauce or cooked and mashed sweet potato
  - Soya or gram (chickpea) flour
  - Cornflour, eg to thicken vegan lemon curd
  - The Vegg – an eggy-tasting product that can be used in different ways

Some soya milks curdle in coffee. Here are a few tips:

1 Fresh soya milk is less likely to curdle than longlife
2 Heat the soya milk first but don't boil it
   • Fresh coffee: pour in hot soya milk then add the coffee last
   • Instant coffee: pour in hot soya milk, then hot water then whisk in the coffee granules
3 Most coffee outlets, such as Costa, sell wonderful soya lattes, soya cappucinos and the like (which don't curdle!). They tend to use Alpro soya milk

Other stuff

Chocolate

Most milk and white chocolate is made from cow's milk. However, there is a growing range of excellent vegan alternatives, milk and white-style as well as dark. For the widest selection – including bars, truffles, drops, alternatives to Mars/Snickers/Bounty/Milky Way and others, try **www.vivashop.org.uk/chocolates**. Otherwise, look in health food shops, delis or large supermarket branches (Waitrose, large Sainsbury's, Tesco etc).

Plain/dark chocolate is often dairy free but check it contains no butterfat, skimmed milk, cream or whey. It is widely available from supermarkets and health stores. Keep your eye out for new varieties and check existing brands carefully as manufacturers sometimes change their recipe! As ever, consult the *L-Plate Vegan* for brands, page 6.

Custard

● Ready-made: Provamel and Alpro in cartons
● Powder: Birds and supermarket own-brand custard powders in tubs are vegan. Use less soya milk than it says on the packet – 420ml/¾ pint instead of 560ml/1 pint, or use a bit more custard powder if you want a pint! NB many custard powders in packets (ie not in tubs) contain milk products so always read the labels
● Soya Dessert: a cross between a dessert and custard, assorted flavours – Alpro and Provamel

Nuts and seeds

They can be used whole or ground in a spice grinder – many types of dishes, savoury, sweet and sauces. High in minerals, vitamins and protein – and good quality fat – they should be eaten in small quantities. See page 10.

Nut and seed butters
- **Nut**: almond, cashew, peanut etc, eg Meridian brand
- **Seed**: hemp, pumpkin, sunflower and tahini – sesame seed paste, used in hummus
- **Bought**: available in good supermarkets or HFS
- **Home made**: it's not difficult and can be made with raw or roasted nuts. There are several good YouTube videos to show you how. However, it's important to use a good quality food processor with a big engine, eg Magimix – cheaper models won't hack it

Oils
- Extra virgin olive oil or unrefined (cold-pressed) rapeseed oil are best for general cooking, eg frying onions or stir-frying
- Refined oils such as plain vegetable (rapeseed) are best for deep-frying or baking. However, Clearspring Sunflower Oil for Frying is unrefined so a bit more expensive but is mild-tasting and also works for frying or baking. See *Baking tips* on page 236
- Cold-pressed oils such as olive, hazelnut, walnut and sesame are best in salad dressings or stir-frying. Don't use them for deep-frying as this destroys their health benefits as well as being expensive
- For omega-3s, the best source is flaxseed (linseed) oil and it is also found to a lesser degree in rapeseed, walnut, hemp and mixed omega-3 oils. Use for salad dressings as heat destroys omega-3. Store in a cool dark place

Keep all oils to a minimum and use a vegan-friendly oil spray like Fry Light or Filippo Berio wherever possible to reduce fat intake. Or make your own. In a sterilised spray bottle, mix 2 tbsp rapeseed or olive oil with 180 ml filtered water. Shake well before use. If the mister spray clogs up, clean it with a toothpick or pin. Store in the fridge and use quickly to prevent bacteria forming.

Quinoa
Pronounced 'keen-wah'. An ancient grain which is now very popular. High in complete protein and a good source of iron, it can be found in large branches of major supermarkets as well as health food shops – and takes only 15-20 minutes to cook. See page 24 (*Wholegrain know-how*) and page 124 (Quinoa Pilaf). The time-strapped can buy ready-cooked quinoa and other grains in pouches, eg Merchant Gourmet, Morrison, Sainsbury's, Tilda and Uncle Ben.

Soya sauce

Use the best you can afford – it really does make a difference. Shoyu or tamari types are the best and tamari is also gluten and wheat-free. Essential, Clearspring, Sanchi and Kikoman are all good brands.

Stock

Instant stock cubes or powder give an oomph and depth of flavour to lots of dishes. Go easy, as many of them have a high salt content, and ensure they are vegan. Some supermarket brands are good while others stick in whey and the like so read the labels.

Our personal favourite is Marigold – red and purple tubs are vegan but not the orange.

Vital gluten

A type of flour used to make seitan – see pages 40-44.

Is it vegan?

Please note: while dedicated vegan companies such as Plamil, V-Bites, Fry's, Vegusto etc are completely reliable, other companies may change their vegan products from time to time. We can only go by what they tell us at the time of publication – you may need to check with suppliers.

Stockists

Supermarkets continue to improve in leaps and bounds. Waitrose and Sainsbury's (and Ocado online) are particularly good even if their labelling is inconsistent. Holland & Barrett carries a pretty good range and most of the big supermarket chains will send you their vegan list by post or email – but not Morrison, Lidl or Aldi at the time of writing. However, Lidl and Aldi's vegan labelling is improving. Independent HFS tend to have a much better range as a rule.

Online shopping is a godsend as you can receive a host of vegan food and other animal-free goodies in the post! It may be worth checking out the minimum order and perhaps splitting it with someone?

Our very own **www.vivashop.org.uk** sells books, vegan confectionery and many other treats – and there are other outlets too.

www.alternativestores.com
www.animalaid.org.uk
www.goodnessdirect.co.uk
www.honest-to-goodness.org.uk
www.vegan.co.uk
www.vegancross.com
www.veganstore.co.uk
www.veggiestuff.com

And to accompany the dishes you make, check out the Viva! Wine Club, which sells over 200 vegan wines as well as ciders, beers and spirits. And to get the lowdown on all vegan booze, see the *L-Plate Vegan* guide – details on page 6. Cheers!
www.viva.org.uk/wineshop

Tofu secrets

Also known as bean curd, tofu is made from soya beans. Soya milk is coagulated – set – using a process not unlike the way dairy milk is made into cheese. Tofu comes in several varieties, from very soft to firm and also in several flavours. This cookbook contains lots of easy tofu recipes – check out the *Index by ingredient* on page 299.

If you would like to try making your own tofu, go to **www.veganrecipeclub.org.uk** and search 'home-made tofu'. It's really not difficult. Otherwise it's easy to buy!

Silken tofu

Usually sold in tetra packs (long-life) although there are some fresh varieties. It is available from most large supermarkets, Oriental grocers and health food shops. Leftovers should be stored in an airtight container in the fridge and can be added to fruit smoothies or blended into soup. Soft and blancmange-like in texture, it is best used in desserts, savoury flans or other dishes where a creamy consistency is needed – not stir-fried. It also makes great sauces and mayo: see pages 35 (Sour Cream), 140 (Cheesy Sauce), 143 (Easy Mayo).

Plain firm tofu

White in colour, it is sold in chill cabinets at supermarkets, health food shops and Oriental supermarkets. Leftovers should be stored in fresh water in a covered container in the fridge. Change the water daily and it will last for 3-4 days.

To cook plain tofu: press as much of the water out as possible. Place the opened tofu in a colander, put a plate on the top then weigh it down with something heavy, eg tins of food. Leave it for 10 minutes or so then mop up the excess liquid with paper kitchen towel

Weigh down the tofu with something heavy

Mop up excess liquid with a kitchen towel

or a clean tea towel. Chop into cubes or long thin 'steaks' and fry in hot oil in a good non-stick pan until golden brown. Season with garlic, grated ginger, tamari or shoyu.

Freezing? Firm tofu freezes well, becoming more chewy in texture – especially good in casseroles and stews. Before you freeze, extract as much water as possible. Place the tofu in a colander over the sink, cover with kitchen paper or a clean cloth and weigh down with tins or weights for at least 20 minutes. Cut into chunks, store in a plastic sealable box and defrost a few hours before you need it. Pat off the excess moisture with some kitchen towel or a clean tea towel. Fry it up, drizzle with soya sauce and then add to your recipe a few minutes before serving. For the time-strapped, Cauldron marinated fried pieces or deep-fried tofu from Oriental grocers work very well in many dishes – add just before serving and heat through gently.

Flavoured tofu – also sold in chill cabinets – comes in the following varieties. The range may well increase as tofu becomes more mainstream. Such varieties come without liquid – simply store in an airtight container in the fridge for a few days.

- **Fried tofu**. Found in Oriental supermarkets, the pieces look like small golden pillows and work best in well-flavoured dishes such as Thai curries or other South East Asian meals, eg Vietnamese, Chinese, Burmese. They can be chopped up with scissors
- **Marinated tofu pieces.** These are deep fried and delicious. They can be eaten raw in a salad or tossed into a hot dish like stir-fry or pasta sauce just before serving
- **Smoked tofu.** It can be eaten raw or stir-fried to make it crispier. It is great added to pasta or rice dishes and also nice in salads, thinly sliced or diced – try it with avocado slices and a home-made vinaigrette, for example. Smoked tofu can be bought in its natural smoked state or else flavoured with sesame seeds or with almonds and sesame seeds together
- **Tofu rosso**. This is a red-coloured very firm tofu, flavoured with sundried tomatoes and herbs. It is delicious cold in salads, thinly sliced in a sandwich or cubed and added to a hot pasta or rice dish just before serving
- **Tofu basil**. Green and basil-flavoured. Use like Tofu rosso

Tofu manufacturers

There are other brands, but these are the most common:

- Cauldron
- Clear Spot
- Demeter Taifun: fresh silken tofu, smoked tofu (several varieties), Tofu Rosso, Tofu Basil. Available in good health food shops and many are sold in Waitrose
- Dragonfly
- Mori-nu, Morinaga, Blue Dragon and Clearspring (silken tofu) in long-life packs – a great food cupboard stand-by. Usually sold in the larger branches of the larger supermarkets as well as Oriental grocers and health food shops
- Unicurd plain firm tofu, regular or organic, is available from Oriental supermarkets
- Viana: a range of tofu and other quality products. Independents or online stores

Other tofu
Unlabelled tofu is also available in Oriental stores – firm, silken and deep-fried. The quality of this tofu is usually excellent and it is also cheaper, although its provenance isn't always clear (eg whether it is GM or not).

Wholegrain know-how

Forget Atkins and all those crazy diets – we need carbs for good health but in the form of wholegrains, not over-refined and processed foods. Wholegrains should be our main source of energy and are a fantastic natural source of fibre and other nutrients. Brown rice, stoneground wholemeal bread, jumbo oats and the like taste different from their white and processed counterparts – think of them as a different food entirely. They also fill you up – they have a low-GI which means that they keep your blood sugar stable for longer. That in turn means you are less likely to start reaching for cakes mid-morning!

Cooking times for wholegrains

The chart below uses cups – a cup of raw grains will give 3-4 servings but if you use grams/ounces, the ratio of dried grains to liquid is still the same: eg 225g of Basmati brown rice will need 2-2½ times liquid, ie 450-560ml. When in doubt, use the minimum amount of liquid and add more hot water/stock if it starts to dry out.

Grains per 1 cup	Fluid (water or stock)	Cooking time (ordinary pan)
Barley (wholegrain)*	3 cups	30-40 minutes
Basmati rice (brown)	2-2½ cups	25-30 minutes
Brown rice (long grain)	2½-3 cups	20-30 minutes
Brown rice (short grain)	2½-3 cups	30-40 minutes
Buckwheat (pre-roasted is nicest)	2 cups	10-15 minutes
Bulghur (cracked wheat) wholemeal variety only	2 cups	10-15 minutes or less: soak in boiling water/stock, depending on coarseness
Corn	Use fresh, frozen or tinned	Fresh cobs take a few minutes: frozen or tinned just need heating up
Cornmeal/polenta	3-3½ cups	20-30 minutes, depending on coarseness
Couscous, wholemeal only	See bulghur	See bulghur
Millet	2 cups	20-35 minutes
Oats	2 cups	10-15 minutes for jumbo, less for porridge oats
Quinoa	2 cups +	15-20 minutes
Wild Rice	3½ cups	40-55 minutes (less for quick-cook variety, which is about 30)

*Pearl barley is partly refined but still contains some natural bran etc. Avoid quick pearl barley, which is refined.

Pressure cooking grains

Pressure cook only dense grains like brown rice or barley. Brown rice takes about 13-15 minutes at high pressure, barley a little longer. Softer grains such as quinoa or buckwheat are best cooked in an ordinary pan. Cracked wheat – bulghur and couscous – can just be soaked in hot water/stock without cooking.

Feel the pulse: beans, lentils and peas

High in protein, vitamins and minerals, low in fat, cholesterol-free, and a good source of fibre – pulses are disease-busting little miracles. They are also very cheap, particularly if bought dried. Their adaptability to a wide range of dishes is why they are one of the world's key food staples.

A mighty wind?

If you are sensitive to pulses, we suggest two things to help:

1 Extended soak (see page 26).
2 Do what traditional Japanese cooks do: cook beans with a piece of dried kombu sea vegetable – available from good health food shops. It makes them easier to digest as well as softening them and reducing cooking time. Discard the kombu after cooking – or blend it in soup.

Tinned pulses (or cartons)

These are still full of nutrients and very convenient as they are already cooked. Most types are available but not split lentils or split peas. They are sold in tins or cartons, usually 400g/14oz. Mixed beans are also available, ideal for salads. Drain and rinse all tinned pulses thoroughly, and try to buy unsalted/ unsweetened varieties wherever possible.

Types of pulses

This isn't a comprehensive list, but will give you a good start. Try ethnic shops or any shop with a good foreign section for more variety.

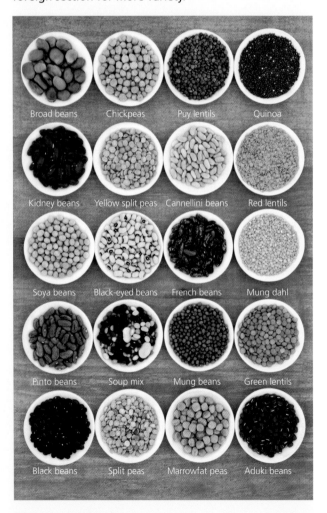

Broad beans — Chickpeas — Puy lentils — Quinoa

Kidney beans — Yellow split peas — Cannellini beans — Red lentils

Soya beans — Black-eyed beans — French beans — Mung dahl

Pinto beans — Soup mix — Mung beans — Green lentils

Black beans — Split peas — Marrowfat peas — Aduki beans

Cooking your own: dried

The cheapest way to buy pulses is dried, especially if you want to use organic produce.

Ensure that they are cooked within the best before date on the packet, or use a shop with a high turnover. Old beans are tougher and take longer to cook.

Soak all pulses (not split lentils) overnight if possible, for a minimum of eight hours in a cool place – particularly important in hot weather. Drain away the soaking water from the pulses and rinse well. Cook in fresh water, in either an ordinary saucepan or pressure cooker.

Soaking is essential before cooking larger, dried pulses.

- Overnight cold soak – make sure you add plenty of water to the pulses as they expand massively! Cover and keep in a cool place
- Extended soak. If you find it hard to digest pulses (especially the larger beans), soak them for 2-3 days. Leave them in a cool place, near the sink if possible. That will remind you to change the water twice daily until the beans are just starting to germinate (sprout). This breaks down the sugars that can lead to bloating. Then cook them as usual
- Lentils. Soaking isn't necessary for whole lentils, but may make them more digestible. It also reduces cooking time (and fuel use) quite substantially. 1-2 hours soaking is sufficient, but you can leave them overnight if it's easier. Split lentils don't need soaking at all but split peas will benefit

Whichever method you use:
- Avoid old beans – they take much longer to cook and are likely to be very chewy and indigestible
- **Never sprout larger beans for salad, especially kidney beans. They must be boiled for at least 15 minutes to remove a naturally-occurring toxin**

- Wash all pulses thoroughly, especially lentils, to get rid of small stones, dust and other debris – use a colander with small holes or a sieve
- Drain the soaking water and rinse well before cooking in fresh water
- Boil until tender

Freezing pulses

If you cook one portion of pulses you might as well cook more. So, if you have freezer space, cook bigger batches and freeze in meal-size portions – use clean small plastic bags or boxes with lids. To freeze the equivalent of a tin of drained pulses, use a 400g/14oz clean empty tin as a guide, fill about three-quarters full, then transfer the contents to a bag or box. Defrost as usual, or in a microwave.

Other frozen pulses

Peas, broad beans and fresh soya beans (edamame) are sold in most supermarkets and are very useful freezer stand-bys – quick, fresh and full of protein and other nutrients. Fresh soya beans are a beautiful bright green colour and are delicious as a side dish or in salads or stir-fries. Find them in large supermarkets, Oriental stores or some health food shops.

Sprouting

Buy ready-made sprouts from health food shops or large supermarkets. They range from traditional Chinese-style beansprouts to alfalfa, radish and mixed bean sprouts.

Or sprout your own! It's easy and very cheap to do so – for simple instructions check out the Vegan Recipe Club's article: **www.veganrecipeclub.org.uk/super-sprouts**

Cooking

The chart below gives approximate times for ordinary cooking. These times depend on the age of the beans. Properly cooked beans should be tender but not too mushy.

Type of dried pulse	Soaking time	Cooking time (ordinary pan)
Split lentils	No soaking required	15-30 minutes
Split peas	2 hours minimum	20-35 minutes
Whole lentils	2 hours minimum	20-30 minutes
Whole lentils	Unsoaked – but see note re digestibility	25-40 minutes
Mung/aduki beans	2 hours minimum	25-40 minutes
Black-eyed beans	6-8 hours or overnight	30-60 minutes
Flageolet /kidney/ cannellini/pinto/black beans	6-8 hours or overnight	1-1¼ hours
Chickpeas and other large beans	6-8 hours or overnight	1-1½ hours
Soya beans	12 hours minimum	1½-3 hours

Pressure cooking pulses

Times will vary slightly, depending on the brand, so check the handbook beforehand. Always soak large beans for at least 8 hours. Large beans such as kidney or chickpeas take 15-17 minutes to cook at the high setting. Don't pressure cook whole lentils for freezing as they go mushy. However, you can pressure cook them as part of a soup or other dish with a soft texture.

Important Safety Tip

While pulses are one of the most healthy and unprocessed foods available, there are a few important guidelines to follow:

- Rinse beans and change the water if soaking longer than overnight
- Cook beans thoroughly. Most large dried beans contain a naturally occurring toxin called lectin or phytohaemagglutinin. This is naturally destroyed in cooking but is likely to trigger nasty food poisoning if it is not done. Lectin is contained in kidney beans, cannellini beans, black beans, haricot beans and butter beans. Soya beans don't contain lectin, but do need to be soaked and cooked thoroughly
- Boil such beans vigorously for 15 minutes before you reduce to a simmer. However, pressure cooking or ordinary boiling is fine
- Do NOT cook raw beans in a crockpot/slow cooker as this increases their toxicity! However, it IS safe to add pre-cooked beans to a crockpot or oven casserole, stew etc

NB Whole or split lentils, chickpeas, mung beans and aduki beans are safe to sprout.

Global pulse – ideas and recipes using beans, peas or lentils

Caribbean
- Black bean salad made from cooked black beans, fresh chilli, garlic, pineapple, mango and lime juice

Indian Sub-Continent
- Chana Aloo (chickpea and potato curry)
- Lentil & Potato Curry on page 191 (or traditional dahl), using red split lentils or mung dahl (smaller, yellow split lentils)
- Muttar Panir (pea and curd cheese curry). Replace the curd cheese with cubed and fried plain firm tofu

Italy
- Aubergine & Bean Stew with Red Wine with chickpeas or butterbeans, page 167
- Minestrone – traditional Italian vegetable soup with added white beans – haricot or cannellini, page 59

Mexico
- Martin Shaw's Classic Chilli, page 184
- Quesadillas, page 198
- Enchiladas – two options:
  - Tortillas or wraps filled with the chilli recipe as above
  - Superfast version. Heat up a jar of fajita sauce (eg Discovery brand), mash in some cooked pinto or kidney beans and stir in some chopped red pepper

Whichever Mexican dish you choose, try serving it with our Sour Cream recipe, page 35

Middle East/North Africa
- Hummus and falafel – these form the basis of many a quick meal. Both are widely available – try them together with couscous or Quinoa Pilaf page 124 and a drizzle of plain soya yoghurt and sweet chilli sauce
- Falafel and hummus with other Middle Eastern mezze (side dishes)

Africa
- African Slow & Sweet Potato Stew with Red Beans, page 163

Spain
- Spanish Chickpea & Potato Stew, page 212

Vegan basics

Classic dishes that can be used in a multitude of ways. There are plenty of vegan dairy and meat alternatives in the shops of course – but it's fun (and cheaper) to make your own sometimes. (And so far there are no ready-made vegan pancakes!).

once you have your own starter culture

Yoghurt

This basic recipe also has variations – see below. It's nice – I gave some to a very sceptical Indian friend whose mum made traditional milk yoghurt and he was so pleasantly surprised, he went off to make his own batch.

You need a starter culture – a little ready-made, plain, live vegan yoghurt (see page 18). Once you have made the first batch, you can make another in a day or two using some of your own yoghurt as starter culture. Eventually, if your home-made batches start to weaken, you will need to buy some more ready-made vegan yoghurt as a fresh starter.

- 600ml/generous 1pt unsweetened soya milk
- 1/3 tsp agar agar powder or flakes
- 2 tsp sugar
- 1½ tbsp tapioca flour/starch (same thing)
- 4 tbsp/¼ cup of starter culture, ie plain, live vegan yoghurt (Sojade, Alpro or Tesco) or home-made. See page 19 for stockists

Optional: 1-2 tsp agave syrup OR ½-1 tsp lemon juice, depending on whether you want the yoghurt a little sweeter or tarter. Fresh, chopped fruit of your choice can also be added just before serving if you prefer a sweeter yoghurt

1 If the flask smells musty, get rid of the smell:
- soak flask in medium-hot water and 1 tbsp bicarbonate of soda
- soak the delicate plastic and rubber screw top in a small bowl of warm water with 2 tsp bicarbonate
- leave both parts to soak for at least 30 minutes, wash in warm soapy water then rinse thoroughly in cold

2 Sterilise the flask by pouring just-boiled water inside. Empty the water and set aside. Drain all items and place upside down on a clean tea towel.

3 Heat the soya milk to boiling in a saucepan. Add the agar agar, tapioca starch and sugar. Whisk vigorously so there are no lumps.

4 When the milk boils, turn off the heat.

5 Cover and leave to cool for a few minutes – it should be warm to your fingers but not too hot. Add the starter culture and gently stir in.

6 Pour the mixture into flask, screw on lid and leave in a cool place.

7 Eight hours later (or next day), see if yoghurt has set. If not, seal up and leave longer. Whisk until smooth and glossy. Taste and add either agave or lemon juice if desired, mixing in any additions well.

8 Transfer to clean glass or other airtight container(s) and store in the fridge.

ALL KITTED OUT

- Medium-hot water
- Kettle – to sterilise equipment
- 1 tsp bicarbonate of soda
- 1 medium saucepan
- 1 teaspoon
- 1 whisk
- A medium-large vacuum flask – a wide-mouthed food flask is best

Thicker Yoghurt, Greek-style

- A batch of yoghurt as above

1 Place yoghurt in centre of muslin, pull corners together, tie it into a bag with string and suspend somewhere cool (I tied it to my mixer taps and let it drip into the sink). Place a container beneath to contain drips.
2 After a couple of hours, untie and check thickness.
3 If necessary, reform the bag and hang for a further half hour or so.
4 Whisk until smooth and glossy. Taste. Sweeten with a little agave syrup or sugar if too sour. Alternatively, add ½-1 tsp lemon juice if a slightly tarter yoghurt is desired.

ALL KITTED OUT

Equipment as above plus:
- a large square of clean muslin
- string long enough to tie around the muslin bag and suspend it

Ricotta-style Soft Cheese

1 Do the same as for Greek-style yoghurt but hang for several hours. This will make a tangy cheese that can be used in the following ways:
- Desserts: sweeten with agave syrup or sugar for desserts that traditionally use ricotta
- Savoury: season with chopped chives, garlic etc to make a low-fat spread – great with crackers or oat cakes
- Lasagne: season with herbs, nutmeg and salt

£ cheaper than the shop-bought variety
halve or quarter the recipe

Cream Cheese

Spread on bagels or crackers for a quick snack. Vegan cream cheese is friendlier to cows and the environment than the dairy version. It's also cholesterol-free and with half the fat, it's friendlier to your waistline too!

- 3½ tbsp cashew butter OR 5 tbsp raw cashews, finely ground
- 1 pack firm silken tofu (approximately 300-350g, eg Nori-mu or Clearspring brand)
- 4½ tsp lemon juice
- ½ tsp salt
- ½-1 tsp agave syrup

1 Place tofu in a clean tea towel, gather ends together and squeeze to extract most of the water.

2 Crumble into a food processor with remaining ingredients and process for several minutes until the mixture is smooth. If necessary, stop and use spatula to scrape down sides of processor.

3 Use immediately or place in an airtight container and refrigerate. It firms up with refrigeration and will keep for 2-3 days.

ALL KITTED OUT

- Clean tea towel
- Grinder (if making your own cashew powder)
- Scissors
- Measuring spoons
- Food processor
- Spatula
- Container with air-tight lid

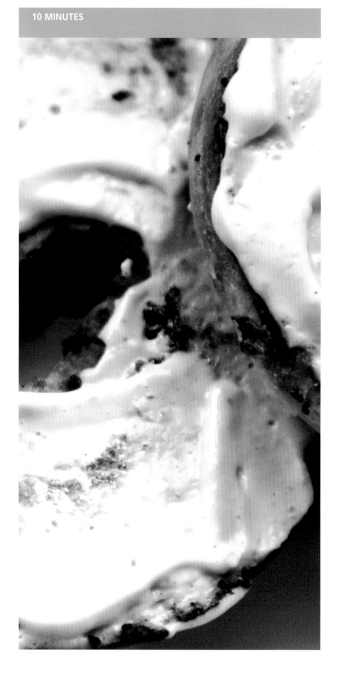

halve or quarter the recipe
will need to be whizzed on defrosting

Sour Cream

Good in dishes such as mushroom stroganoff (see page 207 for our Smoky Mexican version) or other Mexican dishes (see pages 184, 198, 216).

- 350g firm silken tofu, drained (packs range from 300-350g)
- 2 tbsp lemon juice
- 1 tbsp mild-tasting vegetable oil – plain (rapeseed) is the best. Add 1-2 tbsp more if you want it thicker

- 1 tsp cider vinegar
- 1 tsp sugar or agave syrup
- ½ tsp salt

1 Whizz silken tofu until smooth and creamy and no longer grainy.
2 Add remaining ingredients and whizz again to mix.
3 Taste and adjust flavourings as necessary – more lemon juice, salt etc.

ALL KITTED OUT

- Scissors
- Hand blender or food processor
- Measuring spoons
- Air-tight container, eg jar or plastic container with lid

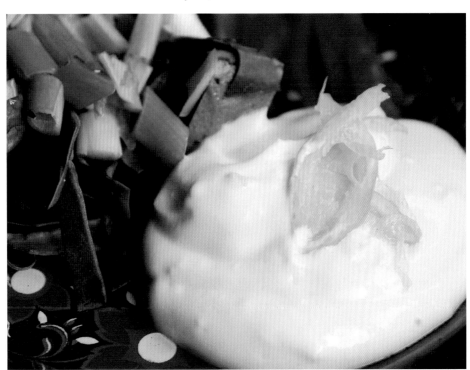

gf wf replace flour and baking powder with GF equivalents. Gram flour is already GF
❄ batter and cooked pancakes both freeze well | 🍳 use oil spray to fry
Diabetic-friendly. Use all fine wholemeal flour and use oil spray to fry
● Sweet: serve with sliced banana or blueberries and a drizzle of agave or other syrup   ● Savoury: cook additions in oil spray and avoid oily or coconut options

Perfect Pancakes

These recipes can be adapted to fit many dishes.

Basic Batter

This old Viva! favourite from our *Martin Shaw Cooks Veggie Guide* is the best pancake/crêpe recipe we've found – all that and vegan too! For a quicker meal, make the batter the night before – it takes only 5 minutes with a whisk or hand blender. Cover and store in the fridge until you need it. Remember to get the frying pan really hot before frying the first pancake.

● 175ml/6fl oz soya milk
● 175ml/6fl oz water
● 175g/6oz plain or self-raising flour*
● 2 tbsp chickpea flour (also called besan or gram flour)
● 1 tsp baking powder (½ tsp if using self-raising flour)

● 1 tbsp sunflower oil
● Pinch of salt
● Additional oil or oil spray for frying
● Sweet or savoury options of your choice
* Choose either all white flour OR half each of fine wholemeal and white

1 Pre-heat oven to 160°C/300°F/Gas Mark 3.
2 Sieve dry ingredients, especially the gram flour.
3 Blend all ingredients (except the additional oil/oil spray for frying) until smooth. Alternatively, add liquid a little at a time and whisk by hand until lump free.
4 Heat frying pan until a droplet of water spits off it. This helps to avoid the 'first pancake is rubbish' syndrome! Add small amount of oil or oil spray. Drain off any excess.
5 Using ladle, pour batter mixture into frying pan and swirl so bottom is thinly covered.
6 Fry one side for about a minute. Loosen edges with a spatula or fish slice and turn pancake – flip if you dare.
7 Fry other side for a minute or until done – as frying pan gets hotter, it will take less time.
8 Remove pancake and keep warm in the oven covered with tinfoil.
9 Add more oil to pan as and when necessary.
10 Repeat steps 4 to 7 until mixture is used up. Serve hot.

ALL KITTED OUT

● Oven tray
● Scales
● Sieve
● Measuring spoons
● Measuring jug
● Mixing bowl
● Whisk or hand blender
● Ladle or large spoon
● Frying pan – non-stick or one that is well-seasoned and heavy-bottomed
● Fish slice and metal spatula

COOL COMBOS: SWEET

● Blueberry & Orange Sauce, page 284
● Sliced banana with vegan chocolate spread (such as Plamil)
● Maple syrup, with or without banana
● Lemon and sugar
● Jam with dairy-free cream
● Ice cream (vegan of course!)

COOL COMBOS: SAVOURY

● Coconut Parsnip with Red Beans, Lime & Ginger, page 104
● Mushroom slices fried in vegan margarine or oil/oil spray with a little garlic
● Mushrooms cooked as above with finely chopped spinach fried in – add a pinch of nutmeg, some soya sauce or salt

● Ratatouille – home-made or from a tin
● Any vegetable combo, red peppers, onion, garlic, sweetcorn – lightly steamed or fried and topped with a suitable sauce from *Back to the Sauce* pages 138-60

gf use GF flour mixed with 1 tsp baking powder plus 1 tbsp flax meal (ground flaxseed) mixed with 3 tbsp hot water | wf use WF or GF flour | omit chilli
batter and cooked pancakes each freeze well
use oil spray to fry and use all fine wholemeal flour

Padma Pancakes – Indian-style

These are a bit of a hybrid – crêpe meets Indian sub-continental spice! Gram flour gives them a lovely yellow colour and they're easy to make. They work with gluten-free flour also.

- 100g/3½oz gram (chickpea or besan) flour plus an extra 2 tbsp
- 75g/2½oz self-raising white flour OR fine wholemeal self-raising – OR half and half
- ½ tsp ground fenugreek OR asafoetida powder *

- 1 tsp turmeric
- ¼ tsp salt
- 350ml/12fl oz water
- 1 tbsp oil
- 1 small red chilli, de-seeded and chopped fine
- Oil or oil spray to fry

* a pungent but not hot spice, often used in dahl and other split lentil recipes. It is sometimes labelled 'hing' in Asian grocers

1 Pre-heat oven to 160°C/300°F/Gas Mark 3.
2 Sieve flours, spices and salt into medium-large bowl – plus 1 tsp if using GF version.
3 Make a hole in the flour and slowly whisk in water and oil until a smooth batter forms – a stick blender will do the job quickly. Add the flaxmeal mixture now if using the GF version.
4 Add chopped chilli.
5 Set aside, covered, for at least 30 minutes or overnight.
6 Pre-heat oven to a low setting so cooked pancakes can be kept warm.
7 Cook as stages 4-10 in previous recipe and repeat until all batter has been used.

ALL KITTED OUT

- Chopping board
- Knife
- Oven tray
- Scales
- Sieve
- Measuring spoons
- Measuring jug
- Mixing bowl
- Whisk or hand blender
- Ladle or large spoon
- Frying pan – non-stick or similar
- Fish slice and metal spatula

COOL COMBOS

- Old School Lentil & Potato Curry, page 191
- Grilled Aubergine & Coriander Chutney, page 118
- Yoghurt Dip, made with bought vegan yoghurt or with our recipe on page 32. Use it plain or mix in a little grated cucumber and chopped mint

Praise seitan!
Vegan meaty wonders...

No vegan cookbook would be complete without a nod to seitan (pronounced like Old Nick's name!). The Japanese name is seitan whereas the Chinese tend to call it gluten – and yes, this delicious meat alternative is made from gluten, the protein-rich heart of wheat and has been used for thousands of years in the Orient, often to feed Buddhist vegetarian monks. Indeed, some Chinese restaurants still have a Buddhist veggie menu where gluten – along with tofu, mushrooms and other delights – is used instead of animal foods.

Clearly, seitan is not for the gluten or wheat intolerant but it is a very versatile product. It is very rich so is a great occasional treat that can be used to make everything from 'wheatballs' to pepperoni to roasts. It also freezes well. Divide it up into small pieces, slices or balls, then freeze in small portions.

We have given you just two recipes and a handful of ideas to use it in other dishes, but we know your imagination will take you to further culinary zones. Plus there is plenty more seitanic inspiration out there on the web!

Where can I buy it?

Ready-made – this is a good idea if you haven't tried it before.
- Yakso and Lima sell seitan in jars
- Coronation brand gluten (including Mock Duck and Mock Chicken) is sold cheaply in tins from Chinese, Korean and other Oriental stores
- Granovita Mock Duck is sold in Holland & Barrett and other health food stores

Each of these varieties comes in a savoury stock, is easily shredded and therefore works well in stir-fries, Chinese mock duck pancakes and savoury pies.

Home-made

Making it yourself is the nicest (and cheapest) option as it means the flavours can be added to fit your needs. It's also possible to make a chewier, 'meatier' version, especially if it's baked.

Vital wheat gluten (also known as gluten flour) is the basis of all recipes. Some health food shops are beginning to stock it – otherwise try online. Suma wholesale added it to their range recently. Prices vary a bit so if you get a liking for seitan, it's worth buying a larger bag to save money and postage.

It also freezes well – it is best divided into small pieces, slices or balls and frozen in small portions.
www.realfoods.co.uk
www.honest-to-goodness.org.uk
www.lowcarbmegastore.com
www.veggiestuff.com
www.vegancross.com

How do I cook it?

Seitan can be simmered in broth or poached in the oven in foil, depending on the kind of texture you prefer. (Ready-made seitan can be fried, baked or poached.)

Basic Simmered Seitan: meatballs, loaves, slices & steaks

Seitan mix

- 225g/8oz/1½ cups vital wheat gluten (also known as gluten flour)
- 120g/4oz/½ cup nutritional yeast flakes (eg Engevita)
- 2 tbsp plain flour or tapioca flour
- 2-3 tbsp soya sauce
- 1 tbsp tomato puree
- 1 tbsp oil, olive or plain vegetable
- 2 large cloves garlic, crushed OR 1 heaped tsp garlic powder/granules
- 1 tsp lemon zest

- 225-250ml/8-9fl oz/1 cup + cold water or cold vegan stock (if using bouillon or stock cubes, dissolve them in a little hot water then top up with cold)

Optional

- Dried or fresh herbs, eg ½ tsp allspice, 1 tsp paprika, ½ tsp chilli, 1 tsp mixed herbs – experiment!

Stock

- 3L/5 pints COLD strong vegan stock (see notes on stock above)
- 60ml/2fl oz/4 tbsp soya sauce

1 Combine the first 3 ingredients in a large mixing bowl. In a small bowl, mix the purée, the soya sauce, oil, garlic and lemon zest. Add this to the dry ingredients then gradually mix in the smaller quantity of stock about a cup at a time with a wooden spoon or spatula. Start to mix everything together with your hands so all the dry bits round the edge of the bowl are incorporated into the ball of dough. Continue adding the liquid until everything is integrated and a thick dough has formed.

2 Knead the dough for 3-5 minutes or until the dough is elastic and easy to handle. Now roll it into a rough log shape and form it into the shape you want to use
   a 6 large slices (use a knife)
   b meatballs/chunks (use your hands to shape)

3 Pour the stock/soya sauce into a large saucepan with a lid and then place the seitan pieces in carefully. Bring to the boil then reduce to a simmer/rolling boil. Cook the large pieces for 30 minutes, the meatballs/chunks for 20. Turn over and repeat the cooking for these times. Make sure the seitan is covered with liquid at all times. Taste to see that the stock is strong enough – you can always add a dash or so of soya sauce but remember that the seitan can be seasoned in cooking so you don't want it too salty.

4 Remove seitan from heat, and let it cool in the stock.

5 When it is cool, divide it into portions with stock – plastic boxes with lids are good. Keep some aside for using within the next 3 days and freeze anything else, also in the stock. Any leftover stock can be used for soups, stews, gravy etc.

Spicy Seitan Sausage

This recipe makes two large spicy sausages, resembling pepperoni or chorizo, and tastes good sliced thinly on pizza or in small chunks added to a hearty aubergine stew – or whatever else you fancy. One of the Viva! crew adds it to vegan mac(aroni) cheese!

It might seem like a lot of ingredients but most of this is in the flavouring – and while onion and garlic powder might seem artificial, they are absorbed better into the mixture.

- 1 cup vital gluten flour
- ½ cup nutritional yeast flakes (Engevita, health food shops)
- 3 tbsp tapioca flour/starch (health food stores or Oriental supermarkets)
- 1 tsp garlic powder/granules
- 1 tsp onion powder/granules
- 2 tsp smoked paprika
- 1 tsp ground fennel seed
- ½ tsp whole fennel seeds
- ½ tsp allspice
- ½ tsp cayenne or mild chilli powder
- ½ tsp salt
- ¼ tsp black pepper
- ¾ cup water
- 2 tbsp tomato sauce or puree
- 2 tbsp olive oil
- 2 tbsp soya sauce, preferably shoyu or tamari type
- 1 tsp liquid smoke (currently online, eg Amazon. If you can't get it, use another ½ tsp smoked paprika)

1 Pre-heat the oven to 180°C/350°F/Gas Mark 4. Fill a small but fairly deep baking tray – about 23cm/9 inches long – with about 1cm/½ inch of water.

2 In a mixing bowl, sieve the vital gluten and tapioca flour and add the rest of the dry ingredients. In a smaller bowl, mix the water and other liquid ingredients well. Stir this into the dry ingredients and mix in very well. Knead the mixture thoroughly for 2-3 minutes.

3 Divide the mixture into two even-sized logs. Roll them into fat sausages about 18cm/7 inches long. Wrap them in tinfoil so they are completely sealed on the edge and at both ends.

4 Bake the logs for 30 minutes, then turn over and bake for another 30 minutes. Unwrap and let them cool for about 15 minutes then transfer to the fridge in the foil and let them firm up for about 1-2 hours. The sausages can be left intact or else thinly sliced with a bread knife or cut into chunks. Freeze some or all.

5 Use as it is, eg on a pizza, or fry up as needed. Keep tightly wrapped in the fridge and use within 3-4 days. It will freeze for about a month.

COOL COMBOS

- Aubergine & Bean Stew with Red Wine, page 167
- Spanish Chickpea & Potato Stew, page 212
- Speedy Pizza, page 215

Souperb

A bowl of soup can be served as a starter or a light meal, depending on the recipe. Adding cooked pulses such as beans, peas or lentils bulks up a basic soup as well as adding protein, iron and other goodies. Throw in some good quality bread and a salad on the side and you have a feast!

easily halved or quartered to serve two or one
use a GF stock such as Marigold or some of the Kallo range

Cheesy Broccoli Soup

This variant on the traditional Broccoli and Stilton soup is very nice indeed – quick, too.

- 2 tbsp olive oil
- 4 spring onions, finely sliced
- 350g/12oz broccoli, florets and stalks cut into small pieces
- 400ml/14fl oz strong vegetable stock
- ½ tsp mixed dried herbs or 2 tsp fresh parsley, chopped
- 60g/2oz vegan blue cheese or any strong-tasting vegan cheese. Vegusto Piquant is good
- 400ml/14fl oz soya milk
- Salt and freshly ground black pepper
- Pinch freshly grated nutmeg

1 Fry off spring onions in oil until softened. Add in broccoli florets and herbs.
2 Add stock, bring to boil then reduce heat. Simmer for 20 minutes.
3 Add soya milk, nutmeg and seasoning. Blend, taste and season as necessary.
4 Grate cheese and mix in well.
5 If too thick, add a dash more stock or soya milk until desired consistency is achieved. Serve hot.

gf wf use a GF stock such as Marigold or some of the Kallo range

Chilled Avocado Soup

This delicious summer soup looks beautiful and sophisticated but is very easy to make. If you can grow lovage in a pot or garden, go for it. It's fast-growing and adds a unique flavour to this dish.

- 2 large ripe avocados or 3 smaller ones – use the ready-to-eat variety
- 480ml/17fl oz cloudy apple juice
- Dash of white wine or dry cider (1-2 tbsp)
- 240-480ml/9-17fl oz water, depending on size of avocados and how thick you want the soup. Start small and add gradually!
- 1 tsp lemon zest – plus a little more for garnish
- Juice of 1-2 lemons, depending on size and taste. Add gradually and taste as you go

- 1-2 tsp vegan bouillon, eg Marigold red tub
- Handful of chopped lovage (the nicest) or parsley. Keep a few sprigs for garnish
- Centre stalks of a head of celery, chopped finely
- Salt and black pepper to taste

1 Slice the avocados in half, remove the stones and remove all the flesh with a spoon.
2 Process the flesh with some of the water and lemon juice plus all the apple juice, lemon zest, bouillon, herbs and celery. Blend until smooth.
3 Taste and add more water/lemon juice as desired. Season with salt and pepper.
4 Chill for about half an hour – it needs to be cool but not too cold or the taste won't come through so well.
5 Garnish with a little lemon zest and chopped herbs and serve.

ALL KITTED OUT

- Chopping board
- Knife
- Hand blender/food processor
- Measuring spoons
- Measuring jug
- Medium-large saucepan with lid
- Wooden spoon
- Bowl and lid to cover
- Zester

gf wf use tamari soya sauce
❄ give it a good whisk while re-heating
£ use value mushrooms

Cream of Mushroom Soup

Use Luxury Two-mushroom Sauce on page 146 and add the following:

- 420ml/15fl oz unsweetened soya or almond milk
- ½ tsp paprika

Alternatively, split the recipe in half so you keep half as sauce and use the other half for soup. In that case, halve the soya milk and paprika.

Use Luxury Two-mushroom Sauce on page 146

ALL KITTED OUT

- Kettle of hot water
- Measuring jug
- Scissors
- Chopping board
- Knife
- Measuring spoons
- Medium-large saucepan with lid
- Wooden spoon
- Blender if using

(♥) if ground cashews used

gf wf use GF stock such as Marigold bouillon or some of the Kallo range

Cream of Tomato Soup

A rich creamy soup that does it dairy-free! It's also the closest we've found to a certain famous brand in a tin…

- Oil spray OR 1 tsp olive oil
- 1 onion
- 3 cloves of garlic
- 2 medium sweet potatoes, peeled and chopped into medium small chunks
- 2 tins of plum tomatoes
- 250ml/9fl oz water
- 1-2 tsp vegan bouillon powder or 2 Green Oxo

- A handful of fresh basil OR ½ tsp dried basil
- 1 or 2 handfuls of cashew nuts ground fine OR 2 tbsp cashew butter, eg Meridian brand
- Sea salt
- Black pepper

1 In a medium-large saucepan, heat the oil or oil spray. Sauté the onion in the oil until it starts to soften. Add garlic and sweet potato pieces. Sauté for another 2-3 minutes, adding a little water to stop it sticking if necessary.

2 Add the tomatoes, water and bouillon/stock cubes to the saucepan. Add the herbs.

3 Bring to the boil then reduce heat and simmer for 10-15 minutes or until potatoes are soft.

4 Blend soup, adding the ground nuts or nut butter.

5 Bring to the boil and add a little more stock if it is too thick. Taste for seasoning, adding salt if desired.

ALL KITTED OUT

- Chopping board
- Knife
- Garlic crusher
- Vegetable peeler
- Measuring jug
- Measuring spoons
- Medium-large saucepan
- Wooden spoon
- Hand blender or food processor

gf wf use GF stock such as Marigold vegan bouillon or some of the Kallo range
❄ if pressure-cooked

Harira, Middle Eastern Aromatic Soup

Try it with a green salad and wholemeal bread for an even more substantial feast – or check out our COOL COMBO suggestions below. It is low-fat but deceptively rich tasting for you calorie counters – result!

Stage I
- 1 medium large chopped onion
- 1L hot vegan stock
- 1 tsp ground cinnamon
- 1 tsp turmeric
- 1 tbsp fresh ginger, grated
- Large pinch mild chilli powder or cayenne
- 1 large carrot, scrubbed and diced
- 1-2 stalks celery, diced
- 1 tin of chopped tomatoes
- 2 medium potatoes, scrubbed and diced
- Pinch of saffron

Stage II
- 1 tin brown lentils, rinsed and drained well OR 1 cup home-cooked – about 225-240g/8-9oz
- 1 tin chickpeas, rinsed and drained well OR 1 cup home-cooked, as lentils
- 1-2 tbsp finely chopped fresh coriander
- 1 tbsp fresh lemon juice
- Salt and freshly ground black pepper to taste
- Lemon wedges to serve

1 In a soup pan, simmer chopped onion in one cup of the hot stock for 10 minutes.
2 Add the cinnamon, turmeric, ginger and chilli/cayenne to the pot along with the carrots, celery and another cup of stock. Cook for 2-3 minutes.
3 Add the rest of the stock, bring to boil then lower heat, cover and simmer for 5 minutes.
4 Add the tomatoes and potatoes and continue to cook, covered, for 15-20 minutes, until the potatoes are tender.
5 Crumble in the saffron.
6 Stir in lentils, chickpeas, coriander, lemon, salt and pepper.
7 Reheat and serve with lemon wedges.

ALL KITTED OUT
- Vegetable scrubbing brush
- Kettle of hot water
- Measuring spoons
- Measuring jug
- Chopping board
- Knife
- Tin opener
- Large saucepan
- Wooden spoon
- Ladle
- Lemon squeezer

COOL COMBOS
- Herby Potato Salad, page 84
- Savoury Scones, page 95
- Bread: wholemeal, rye, wholemeal soda, wholemeal pitta, sundried tomato or olive bread

Alternative methods to stovetop cooking

Pressure up?
The soup can be made in a pressure cooker (12 minutes on high).

Pressure down?
Use a slow cooker (8 hours on low).

Either way, cook only Stage I ingredients. Then:
- add the cooked chickpeas and lentils right at the end, heating through for about five minutes so they don't become mushy
- season, then add the fresh coriander and lemon juice just before serving

£ if pressure-cooked
gf wf use GF stock
low if oil spray and low fat options used (ie not soya cream)

Jerusalem Artichoke Soup

A slightly nutty-flavoured, creamy soup that is very easy to make and absolutely lovely.

- 1 tbsp olive oil or 2 squirts of oil spray
- 1 large leek cut in half lengthways, then into small chunks. (Soak chunks to loosen dirt, wash thoroughly in running water, then drain)
- 350g/12½oz Jerusalem artichokes. Soak to loosen dirt, scrub well and remove any black bits then chop into small chunks
- 1 medium carrot, scrubbed (peeled if necessary) and grated
- ¼ tsp nutmeg
- ½ tsp oregano
- ½ tsp black pepper
- 1 tsp yeast extract (eg Marmite)
- 1L/35fl oz hot vegetable stock – home-made or from bouillon powder/stock cube
- Salt to taste (remember yeast extract and cubes/bouillon will add salt)

Optional: 2-3 tbsp soya milk, single soya cream (eg Alpro), or plain yoghurt

1 In a medium-large saucepan, heat the oil and sauté the leek for 3 minutes, stirring occasionally.
2 Add the Jerusalem artichoke pieces and sauté for 3-4 minutes, as above.
3 Add the carrot, nutmeg, oregano and black pepper and stir in.
4 Add the yeast extract and stir in, followed by the hot stock. Stir well to ensure the yeast extract is dissolved.
5 Cook for 30-40 minutes or until the artichokes are soft. Alternatively, cook in a pressure cooker for 15 minutes on the high setting.
6 Blend until smooth and creamy. Stir in soya milk or other options if using. Taste, adjust seasoning if necessary and serve.

ALL KITTED OUT

- Chopping board
- Knife
- Vegetable brush
- Sieve
- Measuring spoons
- Measuring jug
- Kettle of hot water
- Large saucepan or pressure cooker
- Wooden spoon
- Blender or food processor

COOL COMBOS

- Big Mushroom Burger, page 89
- Avocado & Walnut Toast with Tomato, page 88
- Tofu 'Egg' Mayo & salad on rolls or sandwiches, page 120
- Tofu Burgerettes, page 219, on rolls with green/tomato salad

gf wf use GF stock
if oil spray used

Lentil & Tomato Soup with Herbs

This soup recipe is a big favourite with everyone. Tasty, simple to make, cheap and very comforting – what's not to like? It's also a great way to sneak vegetables into the diet of fussy eaters – just blend before serving!

- 1 tbsp olive oil or a little oil spray
- 1 onion, chopped
- 2 or more garlic cloves, crushed
- 200g/7oz red lentils OR 2 tins cooked lentils (green or brown)
- 2 bay leaves
- 1 tsp mixed dried herbs
- 1 medium carrot, grated
- 1 tin chopped tomatoes
- 1 tbsp tomato purée

- 1.25L/2½ pints hot stock
- Salt and black pepper to taste

Options:
- Finely chopped red pepper or celery
- Greens: finely chopped cabbage/spinach/swede/ Brussels sprouts
- Potato: use one medium large potato and cut into small dice so it cooks quickly
- Splash of wine, any colour

1 Heat oil/oil spray in a large pan and gently fry onion and garlic for a few minutes until the onion is soft.

2 Add lentils, bay leaves, mixed herbs, grated carrot, tomatoes and tomato puree plus stock to the pan. Add any other vegetables you want from the options list at this stage too. If using tinned lentils, rinse them well and reduce salt.

3 Give everything a good stir, bring to the boil and cook for 5 minutes, stirring regularly.

4 Reduce heat and simmer for 20 minutes until soup is thickened and the lentils are cooked.

5 Adjust seasoning if necessary and blend if you wish.

6 Serve with crusty bread, hummus or other dip and green salad for a more filling meal.

COOL COMBOS
- Savoury Scones, page 95
- Tofu Burgerettes, page 219, in small rolls or pitta halves, with mixed salad and vegan mayo
- Vegan Chick'n Caesar Salad, page 227
- Tofu 'Egg' Mayo, page 120, on rolls or sandwiches

gf wf use rice or GF pasta
halve the oil or replace with oil spray; use nutritional yeast flakes (not vegan cheese)

Minestrone

A classic recipe that is easy to make. Like most soups, it is even nicer the next day.

- 2 tbsp olive oil
- 1 small red onion
- 3 cloves garlic, crushed
- 2 medium potatoes, peeled and chopped (leave skins on if possible)
- 3 carrots, diced
- 2 small courgettes, chopped into semi-circular pieces
- 1½ tins tomatoes – plum or chopped (if using whole, chop in the pan)
- ½ tsp dried sage OR 1 tbsp fresh
- 1 heaped tsp dried basil OR a handful of fresh
- ½ tsp dried oregano
- 2 tbsp chopped fresh parsley
- ½ tin cannellini or white haricot beans
- 100g/3oz frozen peas or French beans
- Handful of broken spaghetti or small pasta shapes
- 1L strong hot stock (eg made with 2 Green Oxo or 4 heaped tsp Marigold red tub)
- Salt and black pepper

To serve: sprinkle with grated V-Bites Cheezly Hard Italian-style vegan cheese or nutritional yeast flakes

1 Prepare the vegetables as described above. Heat the oil in a large saucepan and sauté the onion, garlic, potatoes and carrots for a few minutes until the onion is soft.
2 Add the courgettes, tomatoes, stock and herbs; bring to the boil then simmer for 15 minutes.
3 Add the white beans, the peas/French beans and pasta. Simmer for another 10 minutes or until the pasta is *al dente* (cooked but with a bite).
4 Taste and season. Serve with warm crusty bread and one of the serving options shown if liked.

ALL KITTED OUT

- Kettle of hot water
- Chopping board
- Peeler
- Knife
- Measuring spoons
- Measuring jug
- Tin opener
- Large saucepan with well-fitting lid
- Wooden spoon
- Ladle

gf wf use tamari soya sauce and GF miso (most misos are suitable except Mugi, Hatcho and Mame. These often contain barley so are not GF)
for older children. Go easy on the miso and soya sauce as they are salty
the basic soup can be frozen. Add the miso paste to defrosted, re-heated soup – along with any options you fancy

Miso Soup

Good for the body and soul, miso soup can be made as a thin vegetable soup or a meal in a bowl, depending on what you add to it. It's a delicious Japanese soup – comforting and nourishing. Find most Japanese ingredients at large supermarkets or all of them online at Amazon, Goodness Direct and others (see *Stockists*, page 21).

Dashi (Basic stock)
- 1.5L/just under 2 pints home-made vegetable stock or water
- 5-6 small dried or fresh shiitake mushrooms
- 2 tbsp mirin (rice wine) or medium sherry
- 1 strip kombu sea vegetable

Soup
- ½ a daikon, diced (long white radish, also known as mooli – available from Indian and Chinese grocers). Alternatively, use half a small swede
- 1 stick celery, finely chopped
- 1 large carrot, finely diced or sliced on largest section of grater
- 1 small head broccoli or similar green vegetable, sliced into small pieces
- Small bunch of spring onions, sliced into 2cm/1 inch pieces
- 2-3 tbsp shoyu or tamari soya sauce – add gradually as it's very salty

- 1 tsp grated fresh root ginger
- Just before serving: 2 tsp medium-brown or dark brown miso per person

Options
Choose one or more of these if you want more bulk and/or nutrition – add just before serving and heat through well.
- Cooked brown rice, about one cup
- Cooked noodles – wholemeal, udon or buckwheat (soba)
- Tofu chunks
- Cooked pulses, about one cup. Choose from chick peas, whole lentils or aduki beans
- Nori flakes. NB Nori is the dark-coloured wrap on sushi, but is also crumbled to make a delicious condiment. You can crumble the large sheets yourself or buy packets of 'nori sprinkles'

1 Put the 4 dashi ingredients (stock/water, mushrooms, mirin and kombu) into a a large pan suitable for soup.
2 Bring to boil and simmer for 15 minutes.
3 Meanwhile, prepare vegetables and other ingredients. Chop into small pieces and set aside.
4 After stock has cooked 15 minutes, you have two choices
   a. remove the kombu and discard
   b. OR blend it with some of the stock then return to soup pan (it is full of nutrients)
5 Add vegetables, ginger and soya sauce to the soup and simmer for 5-7 minutes, or until vegetables are just tender and no more.
6 Remove from heat.
7 Put one helping of miso into each soup bowl. Mix with a little cold water until it is a smooth paste.
8 Add 1-2 ladles of hot soup to each bowl, stirring in with the miso paste.
9 Add some of the options if desired and stir well in to the hot soup.

ALL KITTED OUT
- Wooden spoon
- Chopping board
- Vegetable peeler
- Vegetable brush
- Knife
- Scissors
- Measuring jug
- Measuring spoons
- Blender/food processor
- Large saucepan
- Ladle

COOL COMBOS
- Joe's Chestnut Rice, page 123, topped with Greens & Garlic, page 103
- Vegetable Tempura, page 228
- Butternut Squash with Garlic & Aduki Beans, page 172

- Miso is a paste made from soya beans and used for stocks and soups in Japanese cooking
- Sea vegetables were once part of a traditional British diet and are still widely used in Japan. They are rich in calcium, iodine and other important nutrients but are far less polluted than fish because they are lower down the food chain

gf wf use GF stock
if oil spray used

Pauper's Gourmet Potato & Green Soup

Delicious yet frugal. This lovely, simple recipe is a great way of using up whatever is in your veg box or fridge because it works with different combinations of the onion family as well as different greens!

- 1 tbsp olive oil or oil spray
- Onion flavouring. Choose from ONE of these:
  - 1 large leek, peeled and chopped
  - 4 large shallots, peeled and chopped
  - 1 medium white onion, peeled and chopped
- 700g/1½lb potatoes, peeled and diced
- Greens. Choose from ONE of these. Use 130g – 2-3 good handfuls

- young nettle leaves
- finely shredded spring greens
- spinach
- watercress
- 900ml/1¾ pints hot stock
- 2-3 tbsp dairy-free milk, eg soya or oat
- Salt and lots of black pepper

Optional garnishes
- Dairy-free yoghurt
- Finely chopped parsley or watercress

1 In a large saucepan, heat the oil and sauté whichever type of onion you are using.
2 Turn down heat and cover – cook for 5 minutes until the onion is translucent but not brown.
3 Add a little stock if necessary to prevent sticking.
4 Add the potatoes and cook, covered, for 5-10 minutes.
5 Stir from time to time, adding a little stock to prevent sticking.
6 Stir in rest of stock and bring to the boil.
7 Cover pan and leave to simmer on a low heat for about 20-25 minutes or until the potatoes are cooked.
8 About 5 minutes from the end, add the greens of your choice.
9 Add non-dairy milk to soup and blend everything thoroughly.
10 Season to taste.
11 Serve the soup hot in bowls, each with a swirl of yoghurt and herb garnish if using.

ALL KITTED OUT

- Kettle
- Rubber gloves and plastic bag for nettle option
- Medium-large saucepan with lid
- Chopping board
- Knife
- Vegetable peeler
- Colander
- Measuring jug
- Measuring spoons
- Wooden spoon

COOL COMBOS

- Savoury Scones, page 95
- Speedy Pizza, page 215

Grasp the nettle!

Make friends with nettles – they taste great, are free and a rich source of nutrients. Just remember that they are best March to early July. Use the youngest leaves, choose the top leaves and wear rubber gloves to pick and wash – they lose their sting once cooked.

gf wf use GF stock

Quick Cream of Watercress Soup

A very nice variation on a traditional recipe. It is faster than usual because it is thickened with creamy, protein-rich white beans instead of potato.

- 1 tbsp vegan margarine (eg Pure, Vitalite, Suma or Biona)
- 2 tsp olive oil
- 1 onion, peeled and chopped roughly
- 1 large bunch of watercress OR 2 bags ready-washed watercress – keep a few small sprigs for garnish
- 500ml/18fl oz strong hot stock – use 2 Green Oxo or 2 tsp vegan bouillon powder such as Marigold

- 2 tsp dried parsley OR 1 handful of fresh, chopped roughly
- 2 tins of white beans, eg buttterbean, haricot, cannellini
- 1 pinch nutmeg
- Dash of soya milk or soya cream – or other unsweetened, plain plant milk such as coconut or rice
- Salt and lots of black pepper

1 In a medium-large saucepan, heat the margarine. When it is melted, add the oil. Fry the onion gently in the fat until it is translucent (softened but not brown).

2 Add the watercress and sauté for another few minutes.

3 Add the stock, parsley, beans and nutmeg. Bring to the boil then simmer for 15-20 minutes.

4 Blend until smooth. Taste and season – add more salt/pepper/nutmeg as desired. Add the soya milk or soya cream at this point.

5 Add the watercress sprigs just before serving.

Budget tip

For bargain haricot beans, rinse value baked beans thoroughly under cold water in a colander to get rid of the tomato sauce.

easily halved or quartered to serve two or one
gf wf use GF stock such as Marigold vegan bouillon or some of the Kallo range
go easy on the chilli
use oil spray to roast the squash

Roasted Butternut Squash Soup with Rosemary & Chilli

I first ate this at the River Station Café in Bristol and was so impressed that I went home and created my own version! It is a very easy but elegant soup that looks and tastes delicious; you can do other things while the squash is roasting – or even roast it the day before you need it. Use as much or as little chilli as you like. If you are really spice-sensitive, omit it altogether and serve hot pepper sauce (like Tabasco) on the side for the chilli-lovers.

- 1-2 tbsp olive oil OR a few squirts of oil spray plus tinfoil to cover the squash in the oven
- 1 large butternut squash
- 1 long sprig fresh rosemary
- ½-1 fresh green chilli

- 1.5L/generous 2½ pints hot strong vegetable stock, either home-made or from vegan bouillon/stock cubes
- Salt and black pepper

Options: Half a tin/120g cooked white beans – haricot, butterbean or cannellini – and see budget tip on page 64

1 Pre-heat the oven to 180°C/350°F/Gas Mark 4.
2 Scrub the squash, slice in half and scoop out the seeds. Leave the skin on – it will soften during the roasting process. Some like to leave it in the soup, others prefer to peel it off – it's up to you, but it will blend in pretty well.
3 Roughly chop into medium chunks.
4 Drizzle the olive oil/oil spray on a large roasting tray and place the chunks of squash on it, turning over to coat each piece. If using oil spray, cover the roasting tray with foil.
5 Place in the oven and bake for 45-60 minutes until soft.
6 Place all ingredients (except for the salt and pepper) into a medium-large saucepan and bring to the boil.
7 If using unblended pulses, add now. Reduce the heat to a simmer and cook for about 20-30 minutes, or until you can taste the rosemary without it being too overpowering.
8 Remove the rosemary sprig. If blending pulses, add now and blend the soup until it is smooth. Taste and adjust seasoning if necessary.

if you have the spices already! | if pressure cooked
use GF vegan bouillon or cubes such as Marigold vegan or some of the Kallo range
freezes well (without the 'to serve' options)
if oil spray and reduced fat coconut milk used. However, it's not suitable for low fat or diabetes diets

Spicy Coconut & Lentil Soup

A rich and creamy soup with a spicy kick that is almost a main meal.

- 2 tbsp plain oil (not olive) or oil spray
- 2 red onions, finely chopped
- 1 small green chilli, deseeded and finely sliced
- 2 garlic cloves, crushed or chopped
- 1 tsp lemongrass paste – sold in jars, or grind your own from a fresh stalk
- 3 large dried kaffir lime leaves
- 200g/7oz red lentils, rinsed and drained in a sieve

- 1 tsp ground coriander
- 1 tsp paprika
- 400ml/14fl oz coconut milk – the reduced fat variety if possible
- 900ml/1½ pints vegan stock

To serve
- Juice of 1 lime
- 3 spring onions, chopped
- 20g/¾oz fresh coriander – one good handful! – chopped fine
- Salt and freshly ground black pepper

1 Heat oil/oil spray in the large saucepan or pressure cooker then add onions, chilli, garlic and lemongrass.
2 Cook for 5 minutes or until onions have softened. Add lentils, lime leaves, spices, coconut milk and the stock. Stir.
3 Bring to boil, stir, reduce heat and simmer for 30 minutes or until lentils are mushy. Cover, but stir occasionally. Alternatively, pressure cook on high for 15 minutes.
4 Meanwhile, prepare the 'to serve' ingredients.
5 Add lime juice, spring onions and fresh coriander, reserving some for garnish.
6 Season and serve with garnish.

ALL KITTED OUT

- Chopping board
- Knife
- Garlic crusher if using
- Scales
- Sieve to wash lentils
- Measuring spoons
- Kettle if making stock from bouillon/cubes
- Measuring jug
- Tin opener
- Large saucepan with lid or pressure cooker
- Wooden spoon
- Lemon squeezer

COOL COMBOS

- Tropical Rice Salad with Sesame Orange Dressing, page 86
- Edamame Fuji, page 100
- Oriental Vegetable Fan Wraps with Spring Onion Tufts, page 192

gf wf use GF vegan stock and tamari soya sauce
if oil spray and reduced fat coconut milk used. Not suitable for those on a low-fat or diabetes diet however

Thai Banana Soup

One of the earliest Viva! website recipes – fast, fragrant, fantastic. Other parts of the world use fruit in savoury dishes for a marvellous taste, so do give this a try! Adapted with thanks from *Thai* by Jackum Brown.

- 1 tbsp plain vegetable oil/ 2 squirts of oil spray
- 50g/2oz spring onions (including green tops), sliced
- 25g/1oz garlic, sliced
- 200ml/7fl oz coconut milk – reduced fat if possible
- 400ml/14fl oz hot vegan stock
- ¼ tsp ground pepper
- 3 tsp soya sauce – shoyu or tamari
- ¼ tsp salt
- ½ tsp sugar OR 1 tsp agave syrup

- 1 large banana (just ripe), peeled and cut on the diagonal into thin slices
- 1 large fresh red chilli, sliced obliquely. (Be careful to remove seeds if you don't like very hot food – and don't touch your eyes after preparing!)

To garnish
- Fresh coriander leaves
- 2 limes, quartered
- Spring onion strips

1 Heat oil/oil spray in saucepan and fry the sliced spring onion and garlic quite fast. Add a little water if it starts to stick.

2 Add all the other ingredients in order, and cook for five minutes.

3 Serve as it is or blend. To blend, set aside about a quarter of the banana and chilli slices, then whizz the rest with a hand blender or food processor until smooth

4 Return blended mixture to the pan, add reserved banana and chilli and warm through for three minutes.

5 Serve hot, garnished with coriander leaves, lime quarters and spring onion strips.

ALL KITTED OUT
- Chopping board
- Knife
- Kettle (hot water for stock)
- Measuring spoons
- Measuring jug
- Tin opener
- Medium saucepan
- Wooden spoon
- Blender/food processor if desired
- Soup ladle

COOL COMBOS
- Oriental Vegetable Fan Wraps with Spring Onion Tufts, page 192
- Joe's Chestnut Rice, page 123, topped with Spinach Citron, page 116
- Pad Thai, page 196
- Tropical Rice Salad with Sesame Orange Dressing, page 86

A bit on the side

In this section you will find small meals or side dishes to accompany a larger meal. Alternatively, you might want to combine a few to make a complete meal. Our Cool Combo sections for each recipe offer suggestions for mixing and matching.

Avocado, Fennel & Grapefruit Salad

A tangy and delicious mixture of flavours that seem to bring out the best in each other! Also, fast to make.

- 1 medium-sized ripe avocado chopped into wedges or cubes
- 1 fennel, sliced very thinly
- 1 red grapefruit
- 1 tbsp fresh chopped mint
- Juice of half a lime
- 1 tbsp olive oil
- Black pepper, freshly ground

1 Peel grapefruit and remove pith with a sharp knife. Chop into segments then chunks.

2 Place avocado, fennel and grapefruit in a bowl.

3 Sprinkle with mint, lime juice and olive oil.

4 Toss carefully so avocado doesn't break up.

5 Cover for 5-10 minutes to let the flavours party a little.

6 Just before serving, sprinkle with black pepper.

ALL KITTED OUT

- Chopping board
- Knife
- Measuring spoons
- Lemon squeezer
- Serving bowl and a cover (a plate or saucepan lid will do)

use white haricot beans - or see tip page 64

Cauliflower & Flageolet Bean Antipasto (Chilled Marinated Salad)

A special yet easy way to serve cauliflower – the flageolet beans are a pretty pale green colour that go well with the other ingredients. If you can't find them, substitute with white haricot beans.

Stage I

- 180ml/6fl oz extra virgin olive oil
- 180ml/6fl oz red wine or balsamic vinegar
- 120ml/4fl oz water
- 2 medium cloves of crushed garlic
- ½ tsp salt
- ½ tsp whole black peppercorns
- 2 bay leaves
- 1 medium cauliflower, broken into bite-sized florets

Stage II

- 1 small red onion, chopped fine
- 1 large handful of parsley, chopped. Flat leaf or curly is fine
- 5 fresh basil leaves, torn
- 1 large carrot, coarsely grated
- 1 tin of flageolet or haricot beans, drained and rinsed (or equivalent home-cooked, 240g/generous 8oz)

1 Place all ingredients from Stage I in a medium saucepan.
2 Bring to boil and simmer gently for about 5 minutes or until cauliflower is just tender – it should be *al dente* (have a little bite).
3 Remove from heat and set aside in a bowl to cool then cover and chill in fridge.
4 Before serving, prepare ingredients for Stage II.
5 Mix cauliflower mixture with Stage II ingredients in an attractive bowl and serve.

ALL KITTED OUT

- Chopping board
- Knife
- Measuring spoons
- Measuring jug
- Garlic crusher
- Saucepan
- Container with lid to marinate salad in fridge
- Tin opener
- Serving bowl and spoon

COOL COMBOS

- Speedy Pizza, page 215
- Socca Pizza with Cream Cheese, Sundried Tomatoes & Artichoke Hearts, page 211
- Vegan Chick'n Caesar Salad, page 227
- Muffaletta Stuffed Loaf, page 92
- Potato Salad with Creamy Wholegrain Mustard Dressing, page 85
- Savoury Scones, page 95
- Crusty fresh bread – white or wholemeal

Coleslaw Central

Three versions of the popular salad.

Traditional Coleslaw

Grate white cabbage – about a small handful per person. Grate in some carrot and add finely chopped mild onion, if liked, eg spring or red. Thin down some vegan mayo with a little soya or rice milk, add to grated vegetables, season with salt and black pepper and mix well so evenly coated.

Celeriac & Seed Slaw

Celeriac has a tangy taste, somewhat like celery, but it is a root and has a root vegetable texture. In its unpeeled state it also resembles a Doctor Who alien… but no need to hide behind the sofa!

- 2 tbsp sunflower seeds
- 2 tbsp pumpkin seeds
- 1 tsp shoyu or tamari soya sauce
- 100ml/3½oz plain vegan yoghurt
- 3 tbsp vegan mayonnaise – bought, see page 18 OR Easy Mayo, page 143
- 4 tbsp soya or rice milk
- 1 small celeriac, grated fine (about 300-350g/10-12oz after peeling). Alternatively, substitute some of the celeriac with grated carrots, 75g/3½oz or thereabouts
- 1 clove garlic, crushed
- Salt and black pepper

1 Dry-fry the seeds in a frying pan, stirring constantly to prevent burning. When lightly browned, stir in soya sauce to coat everything.

2 Remove from heat, place in a dish and set aside.

3 Grate celeriac by hand or with a food processor – use small holes or it may be chewy.

4 Mix together vegan yoghurt, mayo and milk to make a smooth sauce. Add crushed garlic and stir well.

5 Mix together grated celeriac and mayo sauce and stir to combine.

6 Sprinkle in seeds and stir again.

7 Chill for 20-30 minutes.

ALL KITTED OUT

- Frying pan
- Wooden or plastic spatula/ fish slice
- Dish for hot seeds to cool
- Chopping board
- Knife
- Vegetable peeler
- Grater or small hole attachment on a food processor
- Measuring spoons
- Serving bowl and spoon

Carrot & Beetroot Slaw

This slaw makes excellent use of beetroot – and uses vinaigrette rather than the usual mayo dressing.

- 2-3 carrots – about 200g/7oz
- 1 beetroot – about 200g/7oz
- 100g/3½oz raisins or other dried fruit of your choice – try chopped dates, unsulphured apricots or even figs
- 2 tbsp cider vinegar
- 2 tbsp olive oil
- Salt and black pepper

1 Wash/scrub all ingredients as necessary.
2 Top and tail carrots and beetroot. Remove any rough skin but don't peel unless the skins are old and manky!
3 Grate carrots and beetroot together by hand (rubber gloves prevent purple hands) or use medium-holed grater in a food processor.
4 Mix together grated vegetables with raisins in bowl.
5 In a jug or bowl, stir together cider vinegar and olive oil. Pour over slaw, mix, season and serve.

ALL KITTED OUT

- Scales
- Vegetable scrubbing brush
- Rubber gloves if grating by hand
- Vegetable peeler
- Knife
- Grater or grater attachments with food processor
- Measuring spoons
- Bowl
- Jug

COOL COMBOS

- Vegan Chick'n Caesar Salad, page 227
- Muffaletta Stuffed Loaf, page 92
- Burgers of any type eg 179, 204 or 219
- Mixed salad platters

Luscious Two Pear Salad with Balsamic Dressing

Simple and pretty to look at as well as delicious.

- 2 large ripe pears, peeled and chopped into long slices if not too mushy. Otherwise chop into chunks. Comice or Anjou varieties are particularly nice
- 2 large ripe but firm avocado pears, stones removed. Chop into long slices or into chunks if too mushy
- ¼ small red onion OR 2 spring onions, chopped into pieces
- 1 large bunch rocket OR a bunch of watercress, washed, drained and chopped roughly
- 5 large lettuce leaves, eg Cos, washed, drained and shredded

Dressing
- 1 tbsp balsamic vinegar
- 1 tbsp lime juice
- 5 tbsp olive oil
- Salt and pepper

1 Make dressing in a jar or bowl.
2 Arrange rocket and lettuce on a large plate or dish.
3 Alternate pear and avocado slices/chunks on the top.
4 Scatter onion pieces over top.
5 Drizzle with dressing and serve immediately.

ALL KITTED OUT
- Chopping board
- Knife
- Measuring spoons
- Colander
- Jar with lid or bowl to make dressing
- Serving dish and spoon

COOL COMBOS
- Smoky Black Bean Cakes & Sausages, page 204
- Tofu Burgerettes, page 219
- Muffaletta Stuffed Loaf, page 92

with bargain mangos!
omit the chilli or serve on the side for the heat lovers

Mango Salsa

Just divine. Great with any Mexican-style dish or as a salad in its own right.

- 1 large ripe mango, peeled and chopped as fine as possible without it becoming too mushy
- 1 medium tomato, chopped fine
- Half red onion, chopped fine
- 1 large handful fresh chopped coriander
- 1 tbsp lime juice (or more to taste)
- Salt
- Black pepper

Optional:

- a little chilli powder or little chopped, de-seeded green chilli
- half a tin of kidney or pinto beans (approximately 120g cooked beans)

1 Mix all the ingredients in a bowl.
2 Chill in the fridge.

ALL KITTED OUT

- Chopping board
- Knife
- Measuring spoons
- Serving bowl and spoon

COOL COMBOS

- Smoky Black Bean Cakes, page 204
- Quesadilla with Guacamole, page 198
- Time-is-Tight Tacos, page 216
- Quinoa Pilaf, page 124
- Caribbean Coconut Wild Rice, page 175
- Martin Shaw's Classic Chilli, page 184

£ use value mushrooms
gf wf use tamari soya sauce

Marinated Mushroom Salad

A remarkably simple yet nice side dish.

- 800g/1lb 12oz mushrooms, sliced
- 4 tbsp shoyu or tamari soya sauce
- 6 tbsp olive oil
- Fresh dill, chopped – about 3-4 tbsp

1 Wipe mushrooms.
2 Slice and place in a bowl.
3 Make marinade by mixing the soya sauce and olive oil.
4 Pour marinade over sliced mushrooms and mix well to coat.
5 Stir in dill and marinate for two hours.

ALL KITTED OUT

- Chopping board
- Knife
- Measuring spoons
- Bowl and lid/plate to cover

COOL COMBOS

- Socca Pizza with Cream Cheese, Sundried Tomatoes & Artichoke Hearts, page 211
- Herby Potato Salad, page 84
- Cauliflower & Flageolet Bean Antipasto, page 76
- Muffaletta Stuffed Loaf, page 92
- Quinoa Pilaf, page 124
- Joe's Chestnut Rice, page 123

use Easy Mayo, page 143

Potato Salad: Two Variations
Herby Potato Salad

Simple and satisfying.

Salad

- 800g/1lb 12oz firm waxy potatoes – peel if old, or scrub/scrape new potatoes if in season
- Salt & pepper
- 1 small red onion or 3 spring onions
- 1 small handful of fresh chives

Dressing

- 1 tbsp cider vinegar
- 3 tbsp oil
- 4-5 tbsp vegan mayo OR 3 tbsp vegan mayo + 2 tbsp vegan yoghurt. Use bought mayo, page 18, OR make our Easy Mayo, page 143

1 Boil potatoes in lightly salted water until tender.

2 Allow to cool and chop into small-medium pieces.

3 Make dressing by mixing everything in a clean, lidded jar or whisk with a fork in a jug/small bowl.

4 Chop chives with scissors.

5 Mix dressing, onion and chives thoroughly with potatoes to coat. Season with a little salt and some fresh black pepper.

6 Serve in a nice bowl.

ALL KITTED OUT

- Medium or large saucepan with lid
- Colander
- Knife
- Chopping board
- Scissors
- Measuring spoons
- Clean jar with well-fitting lid/fork, jug or small bowl
- Serving bowl and spoon

COOL COMBOS

- Cauliflower and Flageolet Bean Antipasto, page 76
- Muffaletta Stuffed Loaf, page 92
- Middle Eastern Baked Cauliflower, page 111
- Tofu Burgerettes, page 219
- Mixed salad platter of your choice

use Easy Mayo recipe page 143

Potato Salad with Creamy Wholegrain Mustard Dressing

Simple, quick and good.

Salad

- 800g/1lb 12oz firm waxy potatoes – peel if old, scrub and scrape if new
- Salt & pepper
- 2 tbsp fresh parsley – flat leaf is nice but the curly will do also. Or chives, chopped with scissors

Dressing

- 4-5 tbsp vegan mayo – bought (see page 18) OR Easy Mayo, page 143
- 2 tsp wholegrain mustard
- 1-2 tbsp soya or rice milk to thin down if liked

1 Boil potatoes until tender. Drain.

2 Allow to cool, chop into small-medium pieces.

3 Meanwhile, make dressing by mixing everything thoroughly in a bowl.

4 Chop parsley as fine as possible.

5 Coat potatoes with the dressing and fresh herbs. Season with salt and pepper and mix everything well.

6 Serve in a nice bowl.

ALL KITTED OUT

- Medium saucepan with lid
- Colander
- Measuring spoons
- Chopping board
- Knife
- Small bowl and spoon/fork
- Serving bowl and spoon

COOL COMBOS

- Cauliflower and Flageolet Bean Antipasto, page 76
- Muffaletta Stuffed Loaf, page 92
- Middle Eastern Baked Cauliflower, page 111
- Tofu Burgerettes, page 219
- Mixed salad platter of your choice

gf wf use tamari soya sauce

Tropical Rice Salad with Sesame Orange Dressing

A truly superior version of rice salad! The dressing is particularly gorgeous.

- Cooked rice: 450g/1lb brown long grain or brown basmati
- Uncooked rice: 200g/7oz brown long grain or basmati rice simmered in water with 1 tsp vegan bouillon powder (eg Marigold red tub OR Kallo OR 1 Green Oxo)

Salad

- 1 thick slice of fresh ripe pineapple, cored and cut into medium cubes OR half a mango, peeled and cubed (unsweetened tinned pineapple will do at a pinch)
- 1 small, ripe avocado, peeled, stone removed and chopped into medium cubes
- 2 spring onions, chopped + 3 more left whole for decoration
- ½ stalk celery, finely chopped
- ½ pack bean sprouts, washed and drained
- 1 tbsp raisins (omit these if you hate them – but try experimenting with chopped apricots)

- 2 tbsp whole peanuts
- 2 tbsp toasted cashew pieces
- 1 tbsp sesame seeds
- ½ red pepper, sliced very thinly
- ½ yellow or orange pepper, sliced very thinly

Dressing

- 40ml/2 tbsp + 2 tsp plain vegetable oil
- 1½ tbsp toasted sesame oil
- 60ml/4 tbsp fresh orange or pineapple juice
- 1 small garlic clove, crushed
- 1 tsp grated fresh ginger root
- 1 good pinch of chilli flakes or powder
- 1 tbsp shoyu or tamari soya sauce
- Pinch of salt
- 1 tbsp cider vinegar

1 If using leftover cold rice or pre-cooked from a sachet, go to 4.

2 Put rice in pan and add water to cover by about 2cm/1 inch), sprinkle in bouillon or stock cube and bring to boil.

3 Simmer for 25-30 minutes. The rice should be tender but not sloppy. If it starts to dry up, add a little hot water.

4 Meanwhile, dry fry cashews and sesame seeds in non-stick frying pan over a medium heat, turning continuously with a spatula. Nuts and seeds should be a light golden colour, not black. Remove from pan and set aside until needed.

5 Prepare rest of the salad ingredients.

6 Make dressing in a screw top jar and shake to blend.

7 Rice should be cooked but free of liquid – if not, drain then cool.

8 Once cooled, add all salad ingredients. Pour on dressing and mix well. Serve in an attractive bowl and garnish with the leftover spring onions.

Cheat's Tip

Use 1-2 packets of pre-cooked brown rice in a sachet for a very quick dish.

ALL KITTED OUT

- Medium saucepan with lid
- Small frying pan
- Wooden or plastic spatula
- Chopping board
- Knife
- Vegetable peeler
- Colander
- Measuring spoons
- Measuring jug
- Garlic crusher
- Grater
- Clean jar or other container with secure lid
- Serving bowl and spoon

COOL COMBOS

- Oriental Vegetable Fan Wraps with Spring Onion Tufts, page 192
- Edamame Fuji, page 100
- Spinach Citron, page 116

gf wf use gluten-free bread
use Easy Mayo, page 143. Not suitable for a low-fat/diabetes diet

Avocado & Walnut Toast with Tomato and Coriander

A taste of sunshine…

- 2 slices of toast, made with good wholegrain bread
- Vegan mayonnaise – bought, see page 18. Alternatively, make Easy Mayo, page 143, or Maca Mayo, page 148
- Slices or chunks of ripe avocado
- Fresh lime juice
- Salt and freshly ground black pepper
- ½ a tomato, sliced OR a few ripe cherry tomatoes, halved
- A few roasted walnut pieces
- Fresh coriander leaves

1 Make toast and spread it with mayonnaise.
2 Arrange avocado on it in a thick layer.
3 Sprinkle lightly with lime juice and salt.
4 Tuck some halves of cherry tomato among avocado and top with a few walnut pieces.
5 Add more salt and pepper to taste, top with coriander leaves and eat.

ALL KITTED OUT

- Chopping board
- Knife
- Bread knife if using unsliced bread
- Table knife
- Lemon squeezer

COOL COMBOS

- Cauliflower & Flageolet Bean Antipasto, page 76

gf wf use GF rolls and tamari soya sauce
use oil spray

Big Mushroom Burger

If you like mushrooms, this really delivers the goods.

- One very large flat mushroom, stalk removed
- 2 tsp olive oil
- 2 tsp shoyu or tamari soya sauce
- One large bread roll

- Green salad for garnish
- 1 thin slice of beef tomato or other variety
- Vegan mayonnaise – bought, see page 18 OR Easy Mayo, see page 143
- Fresh black pepper to taste

1 Heat oil in a non-stick frying pan or wok.
2 Gently fry whole mushroom.
3 Turn over when first side is cooked.
4 Slice open roll and spread with vegan mayo.
5 When mushroom is cooked and juicy, add a splash of shoyu to pan, making sure mushroom soaks it up.
6 Place mushroom in roll, add salad and tomato and a sprinkle of black pepper.

ALL KITTED OUT

- Chopping board
- Knife
- Large frying pan or wok
- Teaspoon

COOL COMBOS

- Either of our potato salad recipes, page 84 and page 85
- Spiced Roasties with Lime, page 115
- Carrot & Beetroot Slaw, page 80

gf use gluten-free bread
wf use wheat-free bread, preferably white or light wholemeal
use oil spray to fry the slices

French Toast

This is the vegan version of French toast or what some folk call 'eggy bread'! Eat it UK style with a dollop of tomato or brown sauce. In North America it is served with cinnamon and drizzled with maple syrup – on its own or as part of a huge cooked breakfast. Whatever, it's a great way to use up slightly stale bread.

- ½ a pack of firm silken tofu (approximately 175g/6oz)
- 120ml/4fl oz soya milk
- 1 tbsp vegetable oil (not olive) plus more oil/oil spray for frying
- 1 tbsp nutritional yeast flakes (Marigold's Engevita brand, sold in health food stores or good delis)

- 4-6 slices of bread (depending on size of loaf), medium thick – good quality white is best but other types are okay

To serve (optional): maple syrup and cinnamon powder

1 Blend tofu until almost smooth. Add soya milk, oil and yeast flakes and blend again.

2 Heat a non-stick frying pan until hot. Coat with a little oil – about 2 tsp – or a couple of squirts of oil spray.

3 Depending on size of pan, coat 1-2 slices of bread in mixture and place them in it.

4 Cook for several minutes on each side until crispy, golden and not soggy.

5 Repeat process until mixture is used up.

6 Serve hot.

ALL KITTED OUT

- Scissors
- Bowl or large mixing jug
- Measuring spoons
- Blender/food processor – hand blender is best
- Non-stick frying pan
- Fish slice

COOL COMBOS

- As part of a full vegan English breakfast! Sausages, rashers, baked beans, mushrooms, hash browns, or any combination of these

Leftover silken tofu can be blended with a little plant milk, banana and other fruit to make a smoothie. Store the tofu in an air-tight container in the fridge for up to three days.

use a ciabatta or large roll and reduce filling quantities
gf wf ● use a large round gluten-free loaf or similar ● use tempeh or plain tofu (not smoked or ready-made marinated pieces)
go easy on the olives
● use tempeh or smoked tofu plus a low-fat salad dressing ● use the White Bean & Roast Garlic Dip option in Filling B

Muffaletta Stuffed Loaf with a Choice of Two Fillings

Pronounced 'Moofaletta', this is the ultimate sandwich! Basically, you stuff a large round loaf with lots of goodies then cut into wedges. It makes a great centrepiece at a picnic or a garden lunch – or just as a treat at home.

- 1 large round loaf – granary or malted

Stage I
Mix together in a bowl and set aside:

- 1 avocado, chopped into chunks
- 1 large tomato, thinly sliced
- 1 large handful of green leaves – eg rocket or any other salad leaves of your choice

Plus ONE of these mixed in with the salad above

- 1 pack of smoked tofu, cubed small
- 1 pack of tempeh, cubed small
- 1 pack of Cauldron marinated tofu pieces

Now choose between Filling A or Filling B!

Filling A
- 1 large carrot, grated
- 1 large red, orange or yellow pepper, diced

- Half a tin of artichoke hearts, drained and chopped into quarters
- 6 sundried tomatoes, chopped into small pieces with scissors
- 1 tbsp capers, rinsed and drained
- 4 tbsp finely chopped fresh herbs, eg basil and/or parsley
- 6 pitted green or black olives
- Half a bunch spring onions, chopped fine
- 2 tbsp vinaigrette dressing – use low fat if possible

Filling B
- A portion of Italian Olive Dip, page 119, OR White Bean & Roast Garlic Dip, page 121 – or for a quick filling, use shop-bought plain or roasted onion hummus
- 1 large red, orange or yellow pepper, diced
- 1 large carrot, grated

- Oil spray

1 If using smoked tofu or tempeh, lightly fry in a frying pan until golden. Let it cool and add it to the Stage 1 ingredients. If using ready-cooked tofu pieces, go to step 2.

2 Now make Filling A or B. Place ingredients in a bowl and mix well. If using Filling A, add a little vinaigrette.

3 Make a single horizontal slice through loaf, about two thirds from the bottom with one third for a lid. Scrape a lot of the bread from the bottom half and a little from the lid to make a hollow.

4 Spoon your chosen filling into the bottom half then top with the Stage I mixture. Place bread 'lid' on top.

5 Eat – or even better, wrap with foil and chill for an hour or so before eating.

6 Cut into wedges before serving.

ALL KITTED OUT
- Chopping board
- Knife
- Bread knife
- Frying pan
- Spatula/fish slice
- Small bowl
- Tin opener
- Scissors
- Measuring spoons
- Grater
- Tin foil

COOL COMBOS
- Vegan Chick'n Caesar Salad, page 227
- Luscious Two Pear Salad, page 81
- Carrot & Beetroot Slaw, page 80
- Cauliflower & Flageolet Bean Antipasto Salad, page 76
- Herby Potato Salad, page 84
- Potato Salad with Creamy Wholegrain Mustard Dressing, page 85
- Marinated Mushrooms, page 83

make half a batch. Freeze some or just eat them the next day, warmed through
use GF flour and add ½ tsp extra baking powder
defrost then warm through in a medium oven

Savoury Scones

These little beauties are a doddle to make. Try them hot from the oven with soups or stews – or grill with melting dairy-free cheese and strips of moist sundried tomato or roasted red pepper.

- 1 tbsp flax meal (ground flaxseed) mixed with 3 tbsp warm water and set aside. See note below
- 225g/8oz self-raising flour
- 1 tsp baking powder
- 45g/1½oz vegan margarine, plus extra for greasing

- 1 tbsp dried mixed herbs
- 3 tbsp nutritional yeast flakes OR 2 tbsp grated dairy-free cheese
- ¼ tsp salt
- A pinch of black pepper
- 150ml/5fl oz soya milk, plus extra for glazing

1 Preheat oven to 220°C/425°F/Gas Mark 7.
2 Mix the flax meal/water together and set aside. Measure everything else out.
3 Sift flour and baking powder into a large bowl and rub in margarine until mixture resembles breadcrumbs.
4 Add herbs, yeast flakes/vegan cheese, salt and pepper and mix together thoroughly.
5 Make a well in middle of mixture and slowly pour in soya milk plus flax meal mix, stirring with a metal spoon. Bring mixture together until it forms a dough.
6 On a clean work surface or well-scrubbed chopping board, knead dough for a couple of minutes. Sprinkle a little flour if it sticks to the surface. Roll out to a 2.5cm/1 inch thickness and, using a fluted 9cm/3 inch cutter or drinking glass of same size, cut rounds from the dough.
7 Place rounds on a greased and floured non-stick baking tray and brush tops with soya milk.
8 Bake for 12-15 minutes in oven and serve immediately. If using later, leave to cool on a rack then transfer to an air-tight container.

ALL KITTED OUT

- Scales
- Sieve
- Mixing bowl
- Measuring spoons
- Measuring jug
- Chopping board
- Metal spoon
- Grater if using vegan cheese
- Non-stick baking tray
- Pastry brush
- Cookie cutters, cup or glass to cut out scones

COOL COMBOS

- Pauper's Gourmet Potato & Green Soup, page 63
- Roasted Butternut Squash Soup with Rosemary & Chilli, page 67
- Viva!'s Very Moorish Moroccan Stew, page 232
- Italian Olive Dip, page 119

Flaxseeds and linseeds are the same thing. Flax meal, aka ground flaxseed, is ready-ground for you and is sold in some large supermarkets and many health food shops. Alternatively, grind up flaxseeds until fine in an electric spice or coffee grinder. Store in the fridge in an airtight container.

Braised Fennel with Ginger & Lime

Another simple and lovely way with vegetables.

- 2-3 heads of fennel (ie 2 large or 3 small heads)
- 1 thumb-sized piece of ginger, grated
- 2 tbsp olive oil
- 1-2 tbsp white wine
- Salt and black pepper
- Lime wedges

1 Prepare fennel by chopping off bases and removing any tough stalks. If there are any fronds on the stalks, keep for garnish.

2 Chop rest of fennel into long thin pieces.

3 Heat oil and sauté the fennel. Add ginger and mix in well and sauté for another minute or two.

4 Cover, add wine and cook for about 20-30 minutes on a low heat, until fennel is tender and slightly caramelised (sticky and golden brown).

5 Stir occasionally to ensure it doesn't burn or stick to the pan.

6 Season with salt and pepper and eat with juice from lime wedges.

ALL KITTED OUT

- Chopping board
- Knife
- Medium-sized heavy bottomed saucepan with lid
- Measuring spoons
- Grater

COOL COMBOS

- Joe's Chestnut Rice, page 123
- Oven-roasted Tofu Mediterranean, page 195
- Chinese Red Bean Burgers, page 179, with Fragrant Coconut Sauce, page 144
- Butternut Squash with Garlic & Aduki Beans, page 172

this might be a good way to make them lovers of greens!

Cabbage with Sesame & Marmalade

The tanginess of the marmalade plus sesame oil gives a pleasant lift to the humble cabbage. Any dark green cabbage works but we particularly like Savoy or January King varieties.

- 200g/7oz cabbage, shredded quite fine
- 2 tbsp toasted sesame oil
- 4 tbsp bitter orange marmalade
- 1 tbsp water
- Salt & pepper to taste.

Optional: 1 tbsp toasted sesame seeds

1 Steam or boil cabbage. If boiling, cook in tiny bit of water that remains on the cabbage after washing to prevent vitamin loss and mushiness!

2 Heat oil in small saucepan, mix in marmalade so it melts. Add a little water to thin the glaze. Mix in sesame seeds if using.

3 Mix glaze throughout cooked cabbage and serve hot.

ALL KITTED OUT

- Chopping board
- Knife
- Colander
- Steamer
- Measuring spoons

COOL COMBOS

- Roast dinners, eg Chestnut Pâté en Crôute, page 176
- Joe's Chestnut Rice, page 123
- Quinoa Pilaf, page 124

if cauliflower is in season

Cauliflower Dijon

A simple, elegant take on steamed cauliflower! It looks particularly stylish made with the bright green variety that my greengrocer told me is called Romanesco – see picture.

- 1 medium-large cauliflower OR Romanesco
- 1 tsp vegan margarine
- 1 shallot, finely chopped OR 1 tbsp finely chopped red onion
- 30g/1oz cashew pieces OR 4 tbsp cashew butter

- 150ml/5fl oz water
- 1 tsp Dijon mustard
- 2 tsp capers, rinsed and drained
- Salt and black pepper

1 In large pan of boiling salted water, cook cauliflower florets or steam the whole head to impress - this will take a bit longer.

2 Meanwhile, in a small saucepan, melt margarine and sauté shallot/red onion until browned. Set aside.

3 If using cashew pieces, grind to a fine powder and add to a small saucepan with the water. Otherwise, add cashew butter and water to a small saucepan.

4 Bring nut/water mix gently to boil until it starts to thicken. Add shallot/red onion mixture.

5 Add mustard and capers. Season to taste.

6 Place cauliflower in a serving dish and pour sauce over.

7 Serve hot.

ALL KITTED OUT

- Chopping board
- Knife
- Measuring spoons
- Measuring jug
- Grinder (if using cashew pieces)
- Large saucepan or steamer, depending on whether you cook the cauliflower whole or in florets
- Colander
- Small saucepan
- Wooden spoon
- Serving dish

COOL COMBOS

- Herby Potato Salad, page 84
- Oven-roasted Tofu Mediterranean, page 195
- Quinoa Pilaf, page 124

Edamame Fuji

This simple dish made from edamame – fresh soya beans – will give you a bit of a Zen-like zing!

Beans are sold frozen in large supermarkets such as Tesco and Waitrose, or else you'll find them in good health food shops and Oriental grocers. If they are in their pods (my local Korean grocer sells them like this), allow two handfuls per person, steam and serve them whole with the lime wedges. If shelled, one handful per person.

- Edamame beans – 1 or 2 handfuls per person
- 1 lime wedge per person (allow 4 wedges per lime)
- Sea salt

1 Lightly steam the beans until just tender – 3-5 minutes or according to packet instructions.
2 Serve hot with a wedge of lime and sea salt on the side.
3 Eat with a light sprinkling of salt and a squeeze of lime juice.

ALL KITTED OUT

- Steamer
- Knife
- Chopping board

COOL COMBOS

- Joe's Chestnut Rice, page 123
- Butternut Squash with Garlic & Aduki Beans, page 172
- Chinese Red Bean Burgers, page 179, with Fragrant Coconut Sauce, page 144
- Vegetable Tempura, page 228
- Any stir-fry of your choice

halve or quarter the quantities
use less oil

Green Beans with Tomatoes & Herbs

Green beans can be expensive - and not good on air miles. The frozen variety is at least much cheaper and a good freezer staple for Thai curries and dishes like this. And like most frozen veg and fruit, it may well contain more nutrients.

- 250g/9oz green beans
- 4 large salad tomatoes
- 1-2 fat cloves garlic, crushed
- 2-3 tbsp olive oil
- 5 fresh basil leaves, chopped
- Salt and black pepper

1 Top and tail beans and steam until tender – check after 5 minutes.

2 Meanwhile, cut tomatoes into quarters and fry lightly in olive oil with garlic.

3 Add fresh basil at the end, stir into green beans and season. Serve hot or cold.

ALL KITTED OUT

- Chopping board
- Knife
- Colander
- Steamer
- Garlic crusher
- Wok or frying pan
- Spatula or fish slice

COOL COMBOS

- Any wholegrain dish, eg Quinoa Pilaf, page 124
- Oven-roasted Tofu Mediterranean, page 195
- Tofu Frittata with Curly Kale, page 220
- Tony's Leek & Almond Pie, page 223

gf wf use tamari soya sauce
reduce soya sauce or use a reduced salt variety
use oil spray instead of oil

Greens & Garlic Combinations

Garlic works well with just about any greens: curly kale, spring greens, dark green cabbage, sliced Brussels sprouts, Swiss chard or broccoli. Rocket is another delightful addition. Garlic and soya sauce are a good way to introduce the green-phobic to the joys of such vegetables… the salt in the sauce helps the tastebuds, apparently!

- 1 tbsp olive oil or oil spray
- 2 large cloves garlic, peeled and crushed
- Greens: eg a bag of spring greens, ½ a dark green cabbage or enough of any green vegetable to serve 3-4. If using a tougher-leaved green such as cabbage or kale, shred stalks fine to enable speedy cooking

- 1 tbsp shoyu or tamari soya sauce
- Black pepper

Optional: a large bunch of rocket – added to quick-cooking greens like spinach or chard

1 Heat wok until hot then add both oils.
2 Lightly fry garlic then add greens, stirring to coat.
3 Cook for a couple of minutes or until greens are tender but not mushy. Add dash of water if they start to stick.
4 Add soya sauce, mix in and serve immediately with a sprinkling of fresh black pepper.

ALL KITTED OUT
- Chopping board
- Knife
- Colander
- Garlic crusher
- Wok
- Measuring spoons
- Wooden or plastic spatula for wok

COOL COMBOS
- Oven-roasted Tofu Mediterranean, page 195
- Joe's Chestnut Rice, page 123, or any wholegrain dish
- Old School Lentil & Potato Curry, page 191, with Padma Pancakes, page 39
- Middle Eastern Spicy Filo Rolls, page 187
- Any stir-fry or noodle dish

Garlic Broccoli

- 1½ large heads broccoli, chopped into florets – about 600g/1lb 5oz
- 2 tsp sesame oil
- 1 tbsp vegetable oil
- 6 large cloves garlic, chopped

- 240ml/1 cup strong vegetable stock (use 1 tsp vegan bouillon such as Marigold red or purple tub)
- 1-2 tbsp soya sauce
- 1½ tbsp cornflour

1 Prepare and steam broccoli for 5 minutes so it retains its 'bite'.
2 Meanwhile, heat the oils in small saucepan on medium. Add garlic, stirring until it starts to soften.
3 Add stock and soya sauce. Stir well.
4 Put cornflour in a small bowl and mix to a paste with splash of water. Add to saucepan with other ingredients.
5 Stir sauce, turn heat down and allow to thicken. Pour over broccoli immediately and serve.

ALL KITTED OUT
- Steamer
- Small saucepan
- Wooden spoon
- Chopping board
- Knife
- Vegetable peeler
- Measuring spoon
- Garlic crusher
- Measuring jug

Coconut Parsnip with Red Beans, Lime & Ginger

You need never again stare at the unused parsnips in your fridge because here's a stunningly quick way to use them. Red beans look particularly pretty but the dish works well with black beans too.

- 1 tbsp plain oil (not olive)
- Parsnips, 700-800g/1lb 8oz-1lb 12oz, peeled and chopped into medium chunks
- 2 cloves garlic, crushed
- 5cm/2 inch piece of ginger, grated – about 1 tbsp grated
- Half a large red chilli, deseeded and chopped fine
- 1 tsp cumin powder

- 100ml/3 generous fl oz coconut milk
- 1 lime, zested and squeezed – at least 1 tbsp juice
- Half a tin of red or pink beans: aduki, kidney or pinto – about 120g/4oz home-cooked
- Salt and pepper to taste
- 2 tbsp finely chopped fresh coriander

1 Put parsnip pieces on to steam – about 15 minutes, but test with a sharp knife after 10. You want neither hard and woody nor mushy.

2 Meanwhile, heat oil in a medium heavy-bottomed saucepan.

3 Lightly cook garlic, chilli and ginger for 1-2 minutes. Add cumin powder and cook for a further minute, stirring well. Take off the heat and set aside.

4 When parsnips are cooked, add to the pan with garlic mixture and heat through, gently stirring.

5 Add coconut milk and heat to a simmer. Add lime zest, lime juice and beans. Stir in well, ensuring they are heated through. Check seasoning.

6 Sprinkle with fresh coriander and serve immediately.

ALL KITTED OUT

- Chopping board
- Knife
- Vegetable peeler
- Steamer
- Garlic crusher
- Grater
- Tin opener
- Lemon squeezer
- Measuring spoons
- Measuring jug
- Medium heavy-bottomed saucepan
- Wooden spoon

COOL COMBOS

- Greens & Garlic, page 103
- Old School Lentil & Potato Curry, page 191
- Smoky Black Bean Cakes & Sausages, page 204
- Joe's Chestnut Rice, page 123

reduce oil and add more soya milk and yoghurt

Mash It Up
Mash with Cumin Seeds & Yoghurt

The gently spiced flavour makes a nice change from traditional mash.

- 900g/2lb potatoes
- 2 tbsp olive oil
- 150ml/5fl oz plain vegan yoghurt – bought or home-made page 32
- 1½ tsp cumin seeds
- Salt and black pepper
- Fresh parsley or coriander for garnish

1 Put a pan of water on to heat.
2 Meanwhile, peel potatoes and cut into small, but not tiny, chunks.
3 Salt the water and add potatoes, cooking at medium boil for 10-15 minutes.
4 Meanwhile, dry-fry cumin seeds in frying pan until brown. Stir continuously so they don't burn.
5 When potatoes are tender, drain, mash with a potato masher* and mix in oil and yoghurt until creamy.
6 Stir in the cumin seeds.
7 Season with black pepper and garnish.
8 Serve hot.

ALL KITTED OUT
- Chopping board
- Knife
- Vegetable peeler
- Medium-large saucepan with lid
- Measuring jug
- Measuring spoons
- Frying pan, preferably non-stick
- Spatula
- Potato masher

COOL COMBOS
- Martin Shaw's Classic Chilli, page 184
- Middle Eastern Filo Rolls, page 187
- Viva!'s Very Moorish Moroccan Stew, page 232
- Spinach Citron, page 116
- Greens & Garlic, page 103

*Never blend or food-process potatoes – for some strange reason they become glutinous and revolting. Old-fashioned hand mashers do the job nicely!

halve or quarter the quantities, depending on how many days you want to eat mash
use soya milk and 1 tsp of margarine or oil

Mixed Rooty Mash

Mash doesn't have to be made from traditional white potatoes, lovely though that is! This recipe uses carrots and squash but works with other combinations: sweet potato and swede, parsnip and swede or the traditional 'neeps and tatties' of Burns' Night fame – otherwise known as swede and potato!

- 110g/4oz carrots
- ½ medium butternut squash – about 500g/generous 1lb
- Soya milk

- 1-2 tbsp vegan margarine (eg Pure) or olive oil
- Salt and pepper

1 Scrub or peel carrots. Youngish carrots are best scrubbed – old ones may need to be peeled. Chop into small pieces.

2 Carefully cut squash in half lengthways, scraping out seeds with a spoon.

3 Peel skin off one half with a potato peeler and chop into small chunks.

4 Place carrot and squash in a saucepan and cover with water. Bring to boil, turn down and simmer on medium for around 20 minutes, or until very soft. Alternatively, steam until tender.

5 Using a colander, drain vegetables then return to saucepan.

6 With a potato masher, mash until smooth and creamy, adding a dash of soya milk. Add a little margarine or olive oil if desired.

7 Mash until mixture reaches desired consistency. Add salt and pepper to taste.

ALL KITTED OUT

- Vegetable peeler
- Colander
- Chopping board
- Knife
- Steamer or saucepan

COOL COMBOS

- Chestnut Pâté en Croûte, page 176
- Big Puff Pie, page 170
- Rose's Onion Gravy, page 153
- Vegan sausages, gravy and greens – bought or home-made, eg page 204

easily made in smaller portions but perhaps cook another dish in the oven to utilise the heat?

Middle Eastern Baked Cauliflower

This is quick to prepare and most of the cooking time is done in the oven, freeing you up to do other things. If possible, optimise the oven by cooking other things at the same time!

- 1 medium cauliflower, divided into florets
- 1 red onion, sliced
- 70g/2½oz sultanas or raisins
- 90g/3oz green olives, pitted and cut in half lengthways
- 110g/4oz cooked chickpeas (approximately half a tin, drained and rinsed)

- ½ tsp saffron strands, infused in 3 tbsp of boiling water – in a small bowl or jug
- 3 tbsp extra virgin olive oil
- 2 bay leaves
- Salt and pepper
- 4 tbsp parsley, roughly chopped – any type

1 Preheat oven to 200°C/400°F/Gas Mark 6.
2 Toss together all ingredients (except the parsley) in a large oven-proof dish and distribute evenly. Cover with foil and bake for 40-50 minutes.
3 Halfway through cooking, remove from oven, lift off foil and stir. Re-cover and return to finish until cauliflower is tender but not soft.
4 Remove foil and leave to cool before stirring in chopped parsley. Adjust seasoning and serve at room temperature.
5 Serve with one or more of the following:
- Plain vegan yoghurt
- Harissa sauce – a spicy sauce sold in jars from large supermarkets, health food shops or ethnic grocers
- Tahini sauce (3 tbsp tahini thinned with 1 tbsp water)

ALL KITTED OUT

- Oven-proof dish
- Tinfoil
- Chopping board
- Knife
- Scales
- Measuring spoons
- Small bowl or jug

COOL COMBOS

- Use as an alternative filling in Padma Pancakes, page 39
- Middle Eastern Spicy Filo Rolls, page 187

Mustard Glazed Carrots

This recipe is the vegan alternative to honey-glazed carrots! It uses agave syrup – sold in health food shops as well as large supermarket branches.

- 600g/1lb 5oz carrots, peeled and cut into strips

Glaze
- 4 tbsp olive oil
- 2 tsp wholegrain mustard
- 2 tbsp agave syrup
- Salt and pepper

1 Pre-heat oven to 200°C/400°F/Gas Mark 6.
2 Mix all glaze ingredients together in a bowl.
3 Arrange carrots in a large oven dish, pour glaze over and mix to coat. Season with salt and pepper to taste.
4 Roast for around 45 minutes, until carrots are golden and cooked.

COOL COMBOS

- Mixed Rooty Mash, page 108
- Chestnut Paté en Croûte, page 176
- Vegan sausage etc – bought or home-made, eg page 204 – with Rose's Onion Gravy, page 153

halve the oil or use oil spray

Red Veg

A quick and delicious recipe for red cabbage – and a great way to get those all-important coloured vegetables into your diet!

- Quarter of a medium red cabbage, shredded by hand or with a food processor – use the large round holes
- 1 medium red onion, chopped fine

- Half a firm but ripe pear, chopped into thin slices. Only peel if the skin is tough
- 2 tbsp oil
- 1 tsp cinnamon
- Salt to taste

1 Heat medium wok or large frying pan for a minute or two.
2 Add oil and when hot, add cabbage and onion.
3 Sauté until almost tender then add pear slices and cinnamon.
4 Cook for another minute or two then add salt to taste.
5 Serve hot.

ALL KITTED OUT

- Chopping board
- Knife
- Grater or food processor
- Measuring spoons
- Wooden spoon
- Wok or large saucepan

COOL COMBOS

- Butternut Squash with Garlic-thyme Aduki Beans, page 172
- Mash with Cumin Seeds & Yoghurt, page 107
- Veggie Roast dinners – eg Chestnut Pâté en Crôute, page 176
- Vegan sausage and mash, bought sausages or home-made page 204

*if bargain olives used

Sautéed Squash with Olive Tapenade & Cannellini Beans

Steaming the squash or pumpkin is much quicker than roasting or baking, yet the flavour is rich – and the rest of the prep can be done while the squash is cooking. The recipe can be transformed easily into a more substantial dish by increasing quantities and serving with sauce and salad.

- 1 medium squash or pumpkin, eg butternut or acorn – 500-600g/1lb 2oz-1lb 5oz peeled and seeded squash, cut into medium chunks
- 100g/3oz mixed green and black pitted olives (or use one type if that is all you have)
- 2 tbsp olive oil

- 120g/4oz cooked cannellini beans, tinned or home-cooked
- 2 tbsp finely chopped parsley – any type
- 1 lemon, zested
- Black pepper
- 1 tbsp olive oil OR a few squirts of oil spray
- 1 clove garlic (or more if preferred)

1 Steam squash chunks until tender – 15-25 minutes.
2 Meanwhile, chop olives and parsley and mix thoroughly with the 2 tbsp olive oil, cannellini beans and lemon zest. Add a dash of water if too thick.
3 In large frying pan, heat 1 tbsp olive oil or oil spray. Cook crushed garlic gently until starting to turn translucent then toss the hot cooked squash in the mix.
4 Mix in olive tapenade, add black pepper and serve hot.

ALL KITTED OUT

- Chopping board
- Knife
- Vegetable peeler
- Steamer
- Measuring spoons
- Tin opener
- Zester or grater
- Frying pan
- Wooden or plastic spatula

COOL COMBOS

- Oven-roasted Tofu Mediterranean, page 195
- Quinoa Pilaf, page 124
- Viva!'s Very Moorish Moroccan Stew, page 232
- Socca Pizza with Cream Cheese, Sundried Tomatoes & Artichoke Hearts, page 211

gf wf just check the curry paste is suitable
use a very mild curry paste
using cold leftover potatoes

Spiced Roasties with Lime

This roast potato dish is simple but nonetheless has a bit of a gourmet feel, especially served with a chunk of lime and sprinkling of fresh coriander. NB Geo curry pastes are vegan. Many of Patak's are too, just check that no cream or yoghurt have been added. Their lactic acid is vegan in origin.

- 900g/2lb potatoes, peeled and chopped roughly into medium pieces – approximately 5 x 2.5cm/2 x 1 inch

- 2-4 tsp mild vegan curry paste OR mix same quantity of curry powder with 1-2 tsp plain oil
- 4 tbsp plain vegetable oil
- Salt to taste
- Juice of 1 lime
- 1-2 tbsp chopped fresh coriander

1 Pre-heat oven to 230°C/450°F/Gas Mark 8.

2 Meanwhile, parboil the potatoes for about 5-7 minutes. Drain and mop excess moisture with kitchen paper.

2 Using a metal roasting tray, toss potato chunks in curry paste, oil and salt.

3 Spread evenly across tray and place in oven.

4 Roast for 25-30 minutes, turning halfway through. Test with a toothpick or sharp knife to see if they are cooked. If not, return to oven for another 5-10 minutes. Reduce oven temperature if they are getting too brown.

5 Transfer to a serving dish and sprinkle with the lime juice and coriander. Serve hot.

Fry cold leftover potatoes for a super-fast version. Simply fry in a little hot oil until light golden brown then stir in the curry paste so the potatoes are coated evenly. Season, then sprinkle with the lime juice and coriander.

ALL KITTED OUT

- Metal roasting tray with high sides
- Vegetable peeler
- Colander
- Large saucepan to parboil potatoes
- Kitchen towel
- Measuring spoons
- Chopping board
- Knife
- Lemon squeezer
- Serving dish and spoon

COOL COMBOS

- Quick Aubergine Curry, page 200
- Tofu Burgerettes, page 219
- Viva!'s Very Moorish Moroccan Stew, page 232

if you can get them to eat slightly tart greens, that is!
use oil spray

Spinach Citron

A quick and tangy recipe.

- 1 tbsp olive oil or oil spray
- 1 bag (approximately 250g) baby spinach leaves. If using larger leaves, chop roughly and remove any tough stalks
- 2 cloves garlic, chopped fine
- Juice of half a lemon or lime – approximately 1 tbsp or a little more according to taste
- Salt and black pepper

1 Wash and drain spinach.
2 Heat olive oil in a wok or large frying pan.
3 Gently fry garlic without over-browning.
4 Add spinach a little at a time and cook until just wilted.
5 Add lemon juice and season to taste.
6 Serve immediately.

ALL KITTED OUT

- Colander
- Chopping board and knife (if using larger leaves)
- Measuring spoons
- Garlic crusher
- Lemon squeezer
- Wok or large frying pan
- Spatula

COOL COMBOS

- Joe's Chestnut Rice, page 123
- Coconut Parsnip with Red Beans, Lime & Ginger, page 104
- Old School Lentil & Potato Curry, page 191

... just reduce quantities to serve one person

Tony's Asparagus Gratinée

- 2 bunches of asparagus – allow 5-6 large spears per person, more if thin
- 2-3 handfuls of nutritional yeast flakes (Marigold Engevita brand, available from health food shops) OR a few handfuls of grated, melting vegan cheese (see page 17)

- 1-2 tbsp extra virgin olive oil
- Salt and ground black pepper

1 Snap each spear about three quarters of the way down the stalk or where the woody bit stops – it should break off easily.

2 Steam asparagus (preferably) or boil until cooked but still firm – about 7-10 minutes. Meanwhile, pre-heat grill.

3 Spread tinfoil over bottom of grill pan and place spears on it, side by side.

4 Sprinkle 2-3 handfuls of nutritional yeast flakes or grated cheese over then drizzle with olive oil.

5 Grill on full until gratinée is golden – about 2-3 minutes.

6 Transfer to individual serving plates, scraping any residue from the tinfoil. Season with a little salt and black pepper.

7 Serve with nice bread as a first course or with new potatoes and salad.

ALL KITTED OUT

- Chopping board
- Knife
- Colander
- Steamer or saucepan
- Grill pan
- Tinfoil

COOL COMBOS

- Oven-baked Tofu Mediterranean, page 195
- Tony's Leek & Almond Pie, page 223
- Big Mushroom Burger, page 89
- Big green and tomato salads
- Herby Potato Salad, page 84

Grilled Aubergine & Coriander Chutney

Is it a chutney, is it a pâté? Whatever it is, it's very good and pretty easy to make – just get everything ready and keep a close watch on the grill!

- 2 large aubergines or equivalent. It's usually cheaper to buy value aubergines (individual or in a bag), even if they're smaller
- 50ml olive oil – generous 3 tbsp
- 55g/2oz red lentils
- 100ml/generous 3fl oz water
- 2 cloves garlic, peeled
- 1-2 small red chilli peppers, deseeded and roughly chopped
- 1 tsp tamarind paste
- 60g/2oz chopped fresh coriander
- 1 tsp salt
- 2 tomatoes, roughly chopped

1 Pre-heat grill to high.

2 Put the lentils on to cook – about 10-15 minutes.

3 Slice aubergines in half and brush with olive oil. Place on tin foil and grill for 10 minutes, watching carefully. Remove from grill, turn over and score through each piece of aubergine with a knife and brush with olive oil

4 Grill for a further 10 minutes, or until aubergine is tender throughout (test by cutting into each piece with a knife). Chop roughly.

5 Check lentils. They should be just tender. Drain.

6 Blend lentils, garlic, chilli peppers, aubergine, tamarind and coriander using a hand blender or food processor, retaining some texture. Add remaining oil and mix by hand.

7 Spoon mixture into a bowl and stir in chopped tomatoes to serve.

Salting aubergines? No need – modern aubergines have had the bitterness bred out of them, happy little things! However, adding a bit of salt to them before frying does stop them soaking up oil like a sponge…

ALL KITTED OUT

- Fish slice or spatula to turn aubergines
- Wooden spoon
- Sieve/colander to drain lentils
- Chopping board
- Kettle
- Knife
- Scales
- Grill pan
- Tinfoil
- Measuring spoons
- Blender (hand or goblet) or food processor

COOL COMBOS

- Old School Lentil & Potato Curry, page 191
- Padma Pancakes, page 39
- Smoky Black Bean Cakes & Sausages, page 204
- Mash with Cumin Seeds & Yoghurt, page 107

Italian Olive Dip

This is so good and super-quick! Hunt for bargain olives and roasted red peppers if you're on a budget. The recipe will keep in the fridge for 2-3 days in an airtight container.

- 110g/4oz pitted green olives
- 30g/1oz pitted black olives
- 3 large roasted red peppers (found alongside sundried tomatoes in supermarkets). If stored in brine, drain and rinse. If in oil, omit the olive oil from this recipe
- 3-4 pickled onions
- 2 tbsp capers
- 1 medium clove garlic, chopped
- 1 tsp dried oregano
- Black pepper
- 2 tsp fresh lemon juice
- 2 tbsp olive oil

1 Blend all ingredients together but retain some texture, to make a rough pâté.

ALL KITTED OUT

- Measuring spoons
- Lemon squeezer
- Blender (hand or goblet) or food processor
- Serving dish (or air-tight container if using at a later date)

COOL COMBOS

- Muffaletta Stuffed Loaf, page 92
- White Bean & Roast Garlic Dip, page 121, and good bread
- Any sandwich
- Crudités (raw vegetable sticks)

gf wf use GF bread
use Easy Mayo page 143

Tofu 'Egg' Mayo

An excellent vegan version of this classic sandwich filling – and with the added bonus of being both cruelty and cholesterol-free! With thanks to Sue Daniels of Leicester Veggies and Vegans, ace vegan cook and star Viva! Supporter. Check out her Facebook recipes on 'Veggie Sue' too!

- 1 block (225-250g) firm tofu, crumbled quite fine so it resembles ricotta
- 1 small red onion OR 4-6 spring onions, chopped fine
- 1-2 tsp wholegrain mustard, according to taste
- ½-1 tsp turmeric
- 3 tbsp vegan mayo – bought or Easy Mayo, page 143
- Salt and pepper to taste
- Large handful of chopped chives (use scissors) or cress

1 Mix all ingredients together in a bowl.
2 Serve on wholemeal bread, topped with chives or cress.

ALL KITTED OUT

- Chopping board
- Knife
- Measuring spoons
- Bowl
- Fork and spoon

omit oil or reduce to 2 tsp

White Bean & Roast Garlic Dip

The roast garlic adds cooking time to this recipe – so it's best made on days when using the oven for other things. Make a batch – other roast garlic bulbs can be squeezed into soups, stews and such for added flavour and will keep in the fridge for up to three days. Once the garlic is roasted, it only takes a few minutes to make the dip.

- 1 bulb of garlic
- 1 tin cooked white beans – eg haricot or cannellini – drained and rinsed (or approximately 240g home-cooked)
- ½ tsp dried thyme
- 2 tsp lemon juice
- 1½ tbsp extra virgin olive oil
- Salt and black pepper

1 Preheat oven to 200°C/400°F/Gas Mark 6.
2 Roll garlic bulb in olive oil and wrap loosely in tinfoil.
3 Place on a baking tray and bake in oven for 45 minutes.
4 Check for softness – if it feels squidgy, it's done. Set aside to cool.
5 When cool enough to handle, slice off top quarter and squeeze out the puree.
6 Blend the beans, thyme, lemon juice and squeezed garlic purée until smooth.
7 Season with salt and pepper.

ALL KITTED OUT

- Tinfoil
- Oven tray
- Chopping board
- Knife
- Lemon squeezer
- Measuring spoons
- Blender or food processor

COOL COMBOS

- As part of the Muffaletta Stuffed Loaf filling options, page 92
- Ciabatta, rocket and roasted pepper sandwich
- Crackers, Ryvita or rice cakes
- Raw vegetable sticks (crudités)

gf wf use tamari soya sauce and GF stock

Joe's Chestnut Rice

Chestnuts give the rice a slightly sweet and nutty taste. Try with either dried or vacuum-packed varieties. You can buy the dried sort in good health food shops or delis. Although the packets aren't cheap, they go a long way as this recipe only calls for a handful per batch and they last for ages stored in a jar. Leftovers from the vacuum-packed variety can be frozen for another day. It's easy to vary this in other ways too. Try frying up onion and garlic and adding to the rice, adding toasted nuts/seeds, using different herbs and spices… you get the picture!

Thanks to the late Joe Beales for this recipe and so much vegan food inspiration.

- 250g/8oz brown rice – any type
- 1 tsp vegan bouillon powder or ½ a vegan stock cube
- 6-8 whole chestnuts – dried or ready-cooked in a vacuum pack

- 500ml/18fl oz hot water (make sure you have some more left in the kettle in case the rice starts to dry up too early)
- A little soya sauce to serve if desired

1 Wash and drain rice in a sieve then place in a medium saucepan.

2 Add bouillon/crumbled stock cube and water.

3 If using dried chestnuts add now as they need to cook with the rice. If using vacuum-packed, add a few minutes before the end of cooking to heat through.

4 Bring to boil and simmer, covered, for 25-30 minutes. Check occasionally to ensure the rice hasn't stuck – add a little hot water if necessary.

5 Rice should be tender but not mushy and liquid should have been absorbed. If still sloppy, remove lid and turn up heat for a few minutes to reduce liquid, stirring occasionally to prevent sticking.

6 Add soya sauce if desired and serve hot.

ALL KITTED OUT

- Scales
- Measuring spoons
- Sieve
- Medium heavy-bottomed saucepan with well-fitting lid
- Wooden spoon

COOL COMBOS

This versatile dish goes with lots of things – below are a few of the most obvious. It's also great with the ubiquitous stir-fried veg and tofu plus a simple sauce – see pages 137-160 for ideas.

- Oven-roasted Tofu Mediterranean, page 195
- Vegetable Tempura, page 228
- Gado Gado, page 183
- Chinese Red Bean Burgers, page 179

omit the oil and cook the onion and garlic in the liquid instead

Quinoa Pilaf

Not only is the wholegrain quinoa – pronounced 'keen-wah' – high in protein, it is also a good source of iron, containing more than spinach or other green leafy vegetables. This recipe is a useful basic so get improvising! Try adding mushrooms (fresh or dried porcini), garlic or mange tout – in fact, just about any vegetables you like that will cook in the time. Experiment with other fresh herbs too – parsley, coriander, marjoram and chervil all work well. For a more Central American flavour, replace the oregano with cumin. And try serving this dish with some of our sauce recipes.

- 1 tbsp olive oil
- 1 medium onion, chopped finely
- 2 large cloves garlic, crushed
- 180g/6oz quinoa, rinsed thoroughly through a fine sieve
- 450ml/16fl oz strong vegetable stock (home-made or using 2½ tsp Marigold bouillon in the red tub)
- 100g/3oz of baby broad beans OR peas (frozen work well)

- 1 tbsp chopped oregano OR 1 heaped tsp cumin powder
- 1 medium carrot, grated on the big holes
- Salt and black pepper to taste (but remember the stock will be quite salty)

Optional: substitute some of the stock with a tablespoon or two of dry white wine or sherry. The alcohol burns off so you won't feel its effect, but it does taste good!

1 Place the quinoa in a sieve and rinse thoroughly under the tap in cold water. Set aside.
2 Heat olive oil in frying pan.
3 Add onion and cook until soft – 3-5 minutes.
4 Add garlic and cook for a minute or two, making sure it doesn't burn. Add quinoa, stock (with wine if using), peas or broad beans and oregano/cumin.
5 Bring to boil over high heat then reduce to medium-low. Simmer, covered, for 20 minutes or until liquid is absorbed – if too wet, remove lid and boil fast until reduced.
6 A minute or two before the end, add the grated carrot and cook in.
7 Season then serve.

ALL KITTED OUT

- Chopping board
- Knife
- Garlic crusher
- Scales
- Measuring spoons
- Kettle of hot water for stock
- Measuring jug
- Grater
- Wooden spoon
- Large non-stick frying pan

COOL COMBOS

This adaptable recipe goes well with many of the recipes in this book but here are a handful of suggestions:

- Sautéed Squash with Olive Tapenade & Cannellini Beans, page 114
- Molé Sauce (use cumin option with the quinoa and omit wine), page 149
- Tomato Sauce with Many Options, page 156
- Smoky Black Bean Cakes & Sausages, page 204
- Time-is-Tight Tacos, page 216
- Martin Shaw's Classic Chilli, page 184

make half a batch
use GF flour
reduce oil/use oil spray

Scrambled Tofu

This is our favourite scramble recipe. Adapted from Andy Murray's *Heretic Vegan Cookbook* with thanks.

- 1 tbsp olive oil
- ½ onion
- 1 garlic clove
- 1 tbsp white flour
- ½ cup/120ml soya milk
- 1 block tofu (200g or 250g) crumbled
- ½ tsp dried mixed herbs
- ½ tsp turmeric
- 3 medium vine tomatoes, finely chopped
- 1 dsp Dijon mustard
- Handful of fresh basil leaves
- Salt and freshly ground black pepper

1 Heat the oil. Fry onion and garlic on low heat until soft.

2 Add flour and cook in for a minute or so, stirring well to ensure it doesn't burn. Add the soya milk, stirring to prevent lumps and cook for a minute or two.

3 Add tofu, mixed herbs, turmeric, tomatoes and mustard and stir for 5 minutes. Make toast now if appropriate.

4 Serve with fresh basil leaves and lots of black pepper. If you wish, serve with brown sauce or soya sauce on the side. It's also really nice with added fresh spinach leaves and toasted seeds.

ALL KITTED OUT

- Chopping board
- Knife
- Garlic crusher
- Measuring spoons
- Measuring cups or jug
- Bowl to crumble the tofu
- Heavy-bottomed medium saucepan
- Scissors for basil leaves – or just tear them gently

COOL COMBOS

- Toast, as above
- Part of a big vegan cooked breakfast

£ use rest of packet in a stew or stir-fry
🕐 marinate beforehand for a quick meal
gf wf use tamari soya sauce
😊 reduce soya sauce for young children

Tempeh Rashers

A quick and tangy recipe.

- 1 slab of defrosted or chilled plain tempeh, sliced into long slices or 'rashers'
- ½ tsp smoked paprika
- 2 cloves of garlic, crushed
- 2 tbsp shoyu or tamari soya sauce
- 1 tbsp tomato purée
- 1 tbsp cider vinegar
- 2 tbsp oil – mild olive or plain

1 Steam tempeh slices for 5 minutes to make flavour milder.

2 Make marinade by mixing rest of the ingredients together in a small bowl. Set aside.

3 Remove tempeh pieces carefully from steamer and allow to cool. Coat pieces with marinade, using a pastry brush.

4 Heat oil in frying pan and fry rashers on each side for a minute or two, until they've turned golden. Serve hot.

ALL KITTED OUT

- Steamer
- Chopping board
- Knife
- Measuring spoons
- Small bowl for marinade
- Non-stick frying pan
- Wooden spatula or plastic fish slice

COOL COMBOS

- French Toast, page 91, with tomato ketchup
- On a sandwich as above, plus a bowl of Lentil & Tomato Soup, page 56
- Served with cooked brown rice or quinoa with Greens & Garlic, page 103, and a drizzle of Whizzy Hot Sauce, page 160
- On a roll or sandwich with barbeque/brown sauce, sliced tomatoes and salad

Lunch-out

Lunch, whether home-made, grabbed from a shop or eaten out, is an important meal. Here are some suggestions, depending on your time and budget. Check out Viva!'s *L-Plate Vegan* (details on page 6) for high street meal ideas too!

Eating out

- Specialist veggie/vegan outlets – search the internet or ask around
- Websites such as Happy Cow or Vegetarian Britain identify local health food shops as well as eating places
- Most chains – eateries and supermarkets – offer a vegan alternative or two. If staff aren't sure, ask to see their special diets list. Wagamama and Yo!Sushi are particular favourites of the Viva! team but there are plenty more
- Ethnic restaurants usually offer good choices and many pubs do too
- Encourage a local independent – make friends with them and ask them to provide more options. Here in Bristol, several independent pizzerias now do a good trade in vegan pizza and calzone thanks to locals suggesting they offer vegan melting mozzarella-style vegan cheese. Result! Or just take your own cheese and ask them to use it on the pizza – and to knock a bit off the bill too. For further information see the *L-Plate Vegan* guide – details on page 6

Home-made

Leftovers

These are often even better the next day. Whether the remains of a home-cooked meal or takeaway, they can be reheated in a microwave or heated to go in a food flask.

Wrap filled with chilli leftovers and drizzled with vegan mayo or our Sour Cream, page 35

Soup

Home-made? Try our lovely recipes in Souperb, pages 47-71.

Ready-made? Buy soup in tubs, jars or tins – see page 135.

Wrap it up: sandwiches, subs, pittas and other bread-covered delights

Artichoke & White Bean Dip with Olives

Mash up a tin of butter or cannellini beans with a little olive oil, half a tin of chopped artichoke hearts, a handful of chopped olives, a handful of fresh chopped basil plus salt and lots of black pepper.

Falafel, hummus, tomato and green salad with a drizzle of plain vegan yoghurt or sweet chilli sauce – falafels are widely available and are often vegan, eg Cauldron – just check no egg or dairy has been added.

Hummus with roast veg OR rocket OR tomato OR grated carrot (or all of 'em).

Italian Olive Dip, page 119, fast, easy and rich-tasting. Add crusty bread and sliced tomatoes and salad veg for a Mediterranean treat. Other ideas for dips and sandwich fillings? See pages 118-121.

Pauper's Gourmet Potato & Greens Soup, page 63

Falafels – slice them up in sandwiches, subs, pitta or wraps with salad and all the trimmings

Muffaletta – giant stuffed loaf, round or ciabbatta shaped. For special occasions and to share, page 92.

SLT – cold sliced vegan sausages (Linda McCartney, Fry's, V-Bites) with lettuce, tomato and perhaps a splodge of brown sauce or tomato chutney!

Smoked tofu, Dijon mustard and tomato with rocket – thinly sliced smoked tofu such as Taifun works a treat on sandwiches. Or try smoked tofu with avocado and vegan mayo!

Tofu 'Egg' Mayo, page 120, takes a minute to make. It is very similar to a traditional egg mayo filling.

VLT – veggie rashers, lettuce and tomato in a sub.

White Bean & Roast Garlic Dip, page 121.

Muffaletta Stuffed Loaf, page 92 (picture courtesy of www.flavourphotos.com)

Tofu 'Egg' Mayo Rolls, page 120

VLT sub: vegan rashers, lettuce and tomato with vegan mayo!

White Bean & Roast Garlic Dip, page 121, sandwich with mixed salad

Salads

Wholegrain-based. Use Tropical Rice Salad on page 86 or Quinoa Pilaf, page 124. Alternatively, use any cold cooked wholegrains such as quinoa or brown rice.

Other grains. Couscous and bulghur (cracked wheat) are also so easy – cover in just-boiled water or stock and leave covered for five minutes. Add a handful of grated carrot, chopped tomato, salad greens, cooked pulses or diced smoked tofu, dress with a vinaigrette dressing – and you have an instant feast.

Pulses. Mango Salsa, page 82. Try adding a couple of handfuls of cooked kidney or pinto beans for a more substantial dish.

Cauliflower & Flageolet Bean Antipasto, page 76, or make your own bean salad. Mixed beans are widely available in tins – just add chopped/grated vegetables and a good vinaigrette.

Tropical Rice Salad with Sesame Orange Dressing, page 86

Couscous Salad with fresh mint and coriander plus chopped peppers, tomato, spring onion and cucumber plus a handful of nuts and seeds… drizzled with olive oil and lemon juice

Pinto Bean & Tomato Salad with Herbs and Creamy Dressing

Mango Salsa, page 82

High street

Crispbread and rice cakes – good with lots of things but we particularly like them topped with sundried tomatoes and strips of roasted red peppers from a jar (Aldi and Lidl's are inexpensive).

Hummus, bread or crackers with ready-made salad.

Sushi – many supermarkets stock a vegan one, such as Waitrose Taiko vegetarian or Tanpopo Wholegrain Vegan Vege Mix (Ocado). Just check there is no egg, cream cheese etc. Tesco does not sell a vegan-suitable sushi at the time of writing.

Veg pots – Innocent's range is mostly vegan but check ingredients. Clive's Pots are found in health food shops and most of these are vegan too.

Salads – there is a big range nowadays and they aren't all leaf-based. Try salads based on pulses, grains or pasta too – check nothing non-vegan has been added to the dressing or salad itself. Many M&S and Waitrose salads are particularly good, eg M&S Super Wholefood with Blueberries & Mango or Multigrain Salad with Hummus.

Sandwiches, wraps and subs – some supermarkets are better than others. At best there may be a ready-made hummus or falafel wrap/sarnie. Independent sandwich shops are often the best as they will often make things to order. If they don't have vegan margarine or mayo, ask them to get it in for you if you're a regular! Our local sarnie shop did this and now sells a great range of vegan lunches. Otherwise, rolls with hummus and prepared salad are a good stand-by!

Vegan Sushi with Edamame Beans, page 100, and Pan-seared Tofu

Soup – fresh soups are sold everywhere but check they are vegan (some brands add cream etc). Many of the Co-op's range are suitable as are other supermarket own-brands. Try fresh tomato soup with half a tin of drained beans or whole lentils added in for quality nutrition and extra bulk.

Tins and jars – again, check the labels. Essential's soups in jars are very good and some of them are vegan – try your local health food shop.

Extras

Tomato salsa, fresh or from a jar.

Indian snacks such as samosas and onion bhajis – nicest warmed in the oven but they can be 'nuked' gently or eaten cold too. Even better with some added mango chutney and plain soya yoghurt.

Assorted Indian Snacks with Vegan Raita (Yoghurt Dressing)

Pulses – beans and lentils – in tins or sachets. Great to add to salads and soups for extra nutrition and bulk.

Carrot batons – sold in packets – to dunk in salsa or hummus.

Seeds, eg Munchy pots.

Nuts, preferably unsalted.

Dried fruit.

Fresh fruit.

Mixed Toasted Seeds with Apple

Strawberry & Banana Kebabs

Back to the sauce

Sauces are a simple, tasty way to jazz up good quality, basic ingredients.

Our Cool Combos suggest recipes to use with each sauce. Or just try them with a simple wholegrain dish – see Wholegrain Know-how on page 24. They also work with quick stir-fried or steamed vegetables.

Many of the sauces are made from raw ingredients – if you want them warm, just heat them through gently without boiling. In particular, nut and seed butters thicken a sauce very quickly so gently does it with the heat!

ALL KITTED OUT

Blenders and food processors – many of the sauces need a hand blender or a food processor, but some would work with a whisk.

Grinders – most of the nut-based recipes require a grinder or food processor but some use nut/seed butters instead. If grinding whole nuts, ensure the blades are low enough to do the job well. If you enjoy cooking and do enough of it to justify the cost, check out an electric coffee/spice grinder.

gf wf use tamari soya sauce and ensure the mustard is suitable
make less spicy by reducing the mustard or replacing it with Dijon or French
just whisk up after defrosting

BBQ Sauce

SERVES 4 | GOOD HOT OR COLD. WILL KEEP IN FRIDGE IN AN AIRTIGHT CONTAINER FOR UP TO 2 WEEKS

- 1 shallot OR 1 tbsp red onion, chopped
- 1 garlic clove, roughly chopped
- 2 tbsp soya sauce – preferably shoyu or tamari
- 2 tbsp cider vinegar
- 2 tbsp tomato purée OR tomato ketchup
- 4 tbsp apple or orange juice
- 1 tbsp English Mustard
- 1 tbsp molasses (black treacle)
- ¼ tsp dried thyme
- Black pepper
- ½ tsp smoked paprika

1 Blend everything together until smooth.
2 Use a clean jar or any other airtight container to save leftovers and store in fridge.

ALL KITTED OUT

- Chopping board
- Knife
- Measuring spoons
- Blender (hand or goblet) or food processor
- Container with airtight lid, eg clean glass jar or plastic container

COOL COMBOS

- Vegan sausages and burgers – bought or home-made, eg pages 204 and 219
- Brown rice
- Baked potatoes and steamed greens
- Fried tofu
- Smoked tofu and vegetable kebabs – pieces of onion, pepper and mushroom alternated with smoked tofu cubes

Cheesy Sauce Duo

These sauces are particularly good with pasta, baked potatoes and savoury stuffed pancakes. For an even quicker sauce, see page 8 – Free & Easy Cheese Sauce Mix.

1 Quick Tahini-based

- 180ml/6fl oz water + 2 tbsp
- 6 tbsp tahini
- 4 tbsp nutritional yeast flakes (Engevita brand from good health food shops in a brown or blue tub)
- 1-2 tbsp fresh lemon juice
- 1 medium shallot OR 2 tbsp red onion, finely chopped
- 2 tbsp sweet miso, see page 60

Optional: 1 large pinch smoked paprika for a slightly smoky flavour

1 Combine all ingredients in the pan and blend until smooth.
2 Heat gently without boiling before pouring over your meal.

ALL KITTED OUT

- Chopping board
- Knife
- Measuring jug
- Measuring spoons
- Lemon squeezer
- Blender (hand or goblet) or food processor
- Small saucepan
- Wooden spoon

COOL COMBOS

- Savoury Pancakes, page 36
- Christmas Stuffed Squash with Two-rice, Cranberry & Porcini Mushroom Stuffing, page 180
- Anything which goes well with a cheesy sauce, eg
  - Mac Cheese, page 140
  - Steamed cauliflower
  - Roast root vegetables
  - Baked potatoes
  - Roast vegetable lasagne

2 Creamy Tofu-based

It's easy, tasty and also low-fat. We like it as part of a Mac Cheese dinner – or mixed half and half with ready-made tomato pasta sauce to make Aurora sauce – lovely with pasta or lasagne.

It looks like a lot of ingredients but it isn't complicated. Get all the ingredients and kit out, then measure out the spices and seasonings into a small bowl while the onion and garlic are cooking. Then it's just a matter of blending everything. Heat it gently to boiling point so it thickens and you're done!

- 1 shallot OR ¼ small red onion – finely chopped
- 1 medium clove garlic, crushed
- 2 squirts oil spray

Cheats' tip! – replace the first three ingredients with 1 tsp onion powder and ½ tsp garlic powder!

- 225g/8oz plain tofu, any type (silken or firm)
- 600ml/21fl oz soya milk
- ¾ cup of nutritional yeast flakes

ALL KITTED OUT

- Chopping board
- Knife
- Garlic crusher
- Small pan or frying pan
- Wooden spatula
- Measuring spoons
- Measuring jug
- Small bowl
- Scissors to open tofu packet
- Colander to drain tofu
- Spatula
- Bowl and hand blender or food processor
- Medium saucepan to heat sauce
- Wooden spoon

- 2 tbsp corn flour OR 1 tbsp arrowroot
- 1 tbsp lemon juice
- 1 tbsp cider vinegar
- 2 tsp Dijon mustard
- ½-1 tsp salt, according to taste
- ½ tsp paprika
- ¼ tsp turmeric
- Generous pinch of mild chilli powder
- Black pepper

Optional: 1 tbsp sweet miso

Mac Cheese

Cook sufficient pasta for your diners. Pre-heat the grill a few minutes before the pasta is ready. Drain pasta, place in a flame-proof dish (metal), mix in hot cheesy sauce of your choice and top with fresh sliced tomato and a sprinkling of paprika and/or black pepper.

Grill until the top starts to crispen and serve hot.

1 If using fresh onion and garlic, sauté both in oil spray until onion is softened – otherwise, go to stage 2.
2 Meanwhile, blend tofu until completely smooth – using a spatula to scrape down the sides of the bowl or food processor.
3 Add cooked onion/garlic (or powders) plus rest of the ingredients and blend again until smooth.
4 Heat the sauce gently, stirring continuously until it starts to thicken. Serve hot.

Photo © http://rouxbe.com/plant-based

Coriander Lime Raita

It works well as a dipping sauce with raw vegetable pieces, as a reduced-fat replacement for mayonnaise, with falafel, salad and pitta bread or spooned over most Middle Eastern dishes! See below for an Indian-style alternative.

- 250ml/9fl oz (half a large tub) of plain soya yoghurt (Alpro, Sojade, Tesco etc), bought or home-made, page 32
- 1 tbsp fresh chopped coriander
- 1 tbsp finely chopped spring or red onion
- 2 tsp fresh lime juice
- Salt to taste

Indian-style option. Add these to main recipe:
- ¼ grated cucumber plus
- ½ tsp cumin powder

1 Combine first 4 ingredients.

2 Add salt to taste.

3 Set aside for at least 30 minutes in fridge for flavours to blend.

4 It will keep in the fridge in a sealed container for 2-3 days. Stir before serving.

ALL KITTED OUT
- Chopping board
- Knife
- Measuring spoons
- Lemon squeezer
- Spoon to mix
- Bowl to mix and chill plus plate/saucer to cover
- Air-tight container if storing to use later

COOL COMBOS
- Middle Eastern Spicy Filo Rolls, page 187
- Viva!'s very Moorish Moroccan Stew, page 232
- Quick Aubergine Curry, page 200
- Old School Lentil & Potato Curry, page 191

Creamy Oriental Carrot Sauce

Simple and easy to make, with the ginger and sesame oil adding a lovely twist.

- 110g/4oz silken tofu (about ⅓ of a long-life pack)
- 2 medium-large carrots, grated
- 120-160ml/4-5fl oz water
- 1-2 tsp soya sauce (Kikkoman, Essential, Clearspring brands are good quality)
- 2 tsp toasted sesame oil
- 1 tsp grated fresh ginger OR ginger paste

1 Blend tofu until completely smooth.

2 Add rest of the ingredients and blend until smooth.

3 Adjust seasoning and serve – warm a little if desired but don't boil.

ALL KITTED OUT

- Scissors
- Blender or food processor
- Grater
- Measuring jug
- Measuring spoons
- Small saucepan if heating up

COOL COMBOS

- Joe's Chestnut Rice, page 123
- Vegetable Tempura, page 228
- Gado Gado, page 183 (replace the Satay Sauce)
- Oriental Vegetable Fan Wraps with Spring Onion Tufts, page 192
- Stir-fried vegetables and rice/tofu
- Noodles – rice, soba (buckwheat) or wholemeal

Use leftover silken tofu to make:
- smoothies (whizz with soya milk, banana and/or berries plus agave syrup or other sweetener)
- small quantities of Easy Mayo, page 143, or Sour Cream, page 35

Easy Mayo

A simple, but very nice mayo that is much lower in fat than ready-made varieties or many other recipes. Quantities are easily halved to make less.

- 300-350g firm silken tofu, longlife or fresh
- ¾ tsp salt
- ½ tsp sugar OR 2 tsp agave syrup
- 1 tsp Dijon mustard
- 1½ tbsp lemon juice
- 1½ tsp cider vinegar
- 3 tbsp plain mild-tasting vegetable oil – we've kept this as low-fat as possible but if you want a thicker mayo, increase the oil a little

1 Blend tofu, add rest of ingredients (except oil) and blend again. If using a stick blender, place ingredients into a deep bowl.

2 Once smooth, drizzle in the oil gradually, blending as you do so.

3 Taste and add more sweetener/mustard/salt if desired.

4 Store in an air-tight container in the fridge.

ALL KITTED OUT

- Measuring jug or scales
- Measuring spoons
- Hand blender and bowl OR food processor
- Airtight container

❄ whisk well after defrosting

Fragrant Coconut Sauce

- 2 tbsp ground almonds or almond butter
- 2 large shallots, finely chopped OR 1 small red onion
- 240ml/9fl oz coconut milk
- ½ tsp powdered cardamom – or more, to taste
- 2-3 lime leaves
- 1-2 tsp Thai green curry paste – use a vegan one like Thai Taste or Geo that contains no shrimp/fish sauce
- Salt

1 Blend nuts or almond butter and shallot/red onion into a paste.

2 Add coconut milk and cardamom powder to nut mixture and blend till smooth. Taste and season if necessary.

3 Transfer to a small saucepan, add lime leaves and curry paste and heat gently without boiling. Taste again and add extra cardamom if you wish.

4 Keep warm and remove lime leaves just before serving.

ALL KITTED OUT

- Chopping board
- Knife
- Measuring spoons
- Grinder/food processor or blender
- Tin opener
- Measuring jug
- Small saucepan
- Wooden spoon

COOL COMBOS

- Oriental Vegetable Fan Wraps with Spring Onion Tufts, page 192
- Chinese Red Bean Burgers, page 179
- Joe's Chestnut Rice, page 123
- Most simple noodle and vegetable/tofu dishes

omit or reduce chilli

Fresh Sweet & Sour Sauce

- 3 medium tomatoes, chopped
- 1 large carrot, grated (peel if necessary)
- ½ an onion, roughly chopped
- 60g/2oz dates, chopped (these can be bought ready-chopped)
- 30g/1oz sundried tomatoes, chopped with scissors
- 2 tbsp cider OR white wine vinegar
- 1 tbsp shoyu or tamari soya sauce
- 1 tsp olive oil
- 1cm/half inch piece fresh ginger, grated
- 1 clove garlic, crushed
- Quarter of a red chilli, deseeded (unless you like very hot food) and finely chopped
- A little stock if the sauce is too thick – add a dash at a time

1 In a pan, heat all sauce ingredients but do not boil.
2 Blend to desired consistency – smooth or a bit chunky.

ALL KITTED OUT

- Chopping board
- Knife
- Grater
- Vegetable peeler
- Scissors
- Measuring spoons
- Garlic crusher
- Blender (hand or goblet) or food processor

COOL COMBOS

- Joe's Chestnut Rice, page 123
- Vegetable Tempura, page 228
- Any stir-fried vegetable/tofu combination
- Rice or noodles

gf wf use tamari soya sauce and arrowroot
give it a good whisk while re-heating

Luxury Two-mushroom Sauce (with soup option)

Rich in taste but very low fat. It's also very easy – most of the preparation is done while the porcini are soaking – and it needs only two more ingredients to convert it into a lovely Cream of Mushroom Soup, see page 50.

- 500ml/18fl oz boiling water
- 15g/½oz porcini mushrooms – a small handful
- 120ml/4fl oz dry or medium sherry
- 3-4 tbsp tamari or shoyu soya sauce – add the minimum and increase if necessary
- 2 tsp arrowroot OR 4 tsp cornflour

- 2 medium onions
- 350g/12oz fresh mushrooms
- 1 tsp olive oil
- 1 bay leaf
- 1 tsp dried tarragon OR 1 tbsp fresh tarragon
- ½ tsp salt or to taste

1 Pour boiling water over dried mushrooms and set aside to soak for at least 30 minutes.
2 Mix the sherry with the arrowroot (or cornflour) and set aside.
3 Prepare vegetables. Chop onions into small pieces. Slice fresh mushrooms.
4 In a saucepan, heat the oil. Add onions and sauté on a medium-low heat for 10 minutes, stirring regularly, adding a splash of water if sticking. Add fresh mushrooms, raise heat and stir until they begin to release their juices – about 3 minutes.
5 When dried mushrooms are ready (after the 30 minute soak), remove from soaking liquid with a slotted spoon but keep the liquid. Chop into small pieces with scissors.
6 Add bay leaf, herbs, sherry/arrowroot mixture, salt, reserved porcinis and their soaking liquid to the saucepan. Cover and simmer for about 15 minutes, until mushrooms are tender.
7 Stir sauce occasionally and add a little more stock/water if needed.
8 If sauce hasn't reduced sufficiently by end of the simmering time, uncover and simmer a few more minutes.
9 Discard bay leaf before serving. Taste and season.
10 For a smoother sauce, whizz with a hand blender for a few seconds.

ALL KITTED OUT

- Kettle of hot water
- Measuring jug
- Heat-proof measuring jug for porcini
- Small bowl for arrowroot
- Scissors
- Chopping board
- Knife
- Measuring spoons
- Medium saucepan with lid
- Blender if using

COOL COMBOS

- Roast dinners – use as a gravy
- Over spaghetti and vegetables
- Over rice
- Over vegan sausages, bought or home-made, page 204

Maca Mayo

Using macadamia nuts in this recipe makes a rich, delicious mayo or spread. Use as a thick salad dressing, a dip to accompany raw vegetable chunks or as a rich topping on oat cakes or crostini.

As with any nuts, eat in small quantities. You might also want to experiment with different nuts such as cashews or Brazils.

- 110g/4oz macadamia nuts
- 250ml soya or rice milk
- 1-2 tbsp lemon juice
- 1-2 tsp chopped chives, according to taste
- Salt

1 Grind nuts until powdery for a smooth mayo. Leave a little texture if you want a more textured, cottage cheese-type dish.

2 Blend soya/rice milk with nuts, chives and lemon juice. Add more milk if you want a runnier 'mayo'.

3 Add salt to taste.

4 This will keep in an air-tight container for up to three days.

ALL KITTED OUT

- Scales
- Measuring spoons
- Scissors
- Grinder
- Blender or food processor
- Air-tight container, such as a clean jar with screw-top lid

COOL COMBOS

- Smoky Mexican Mushroom Stroganoff, page 207 – replace Sour Cream with smooth Maca Mayo
- Avocado & Walnut Toast with Tomato & Coriander, page 88 – replace usual vegan mayo with smooth Maca Mayo

Molé Sauce

Pronounced 'Molay', this amazingly-flavoured sauce is based on a traditional Mexican feast-day recipe. Despite the list of ingredients it is easy to make – just get everything ready on a tray, grind the nuts and you're off! Dark bitter chocolate is a common ingredient in Central American savoury recipes and works very well.

- 50g/2oz ground peanuts
- 50g/2oz ground almonds
- 25g/1oz raisins
- 25g/1oz sesame seeds
- ½ tsp ground cinnamon
- ½ tsp fennel seeds
- 4 black peppercorns
- 1 tbsp plain oil (not olive)
- 1 onion, finely chopped
- 2 garlic cloves, crushed

- 1 red chilli, finely chopped – get rid of the seeds unless you love very fiery food
- 1 corn tortilla, shredded into pieces
- 2 tins chopped tomatoes
- 25g/1oz plain dark vegan chocolate (70% minimum but 80% even better)
- 150ml/5oz hot vegan stock
- Salt to taste

1 Grind peanuts and almonds until powdery.
2 Place in a container with raisins, sesame seeds, cinnamon, fennel seeds and peppercorns and set aside.
3 Heat oil in a large saucepan and fry onion, garlic and chilli until soft – about 5 minutes.
4 Add ground nuts, spices etc. Cook for 5 minutes while stirring.
5 Remove from heat and add the tortilla and tomatoes, return to heat and cook for 10 minutes, stirring frequently – preferably use a heat diffuser.
6 Blend with stock until smooth. Add the chocolate and heat gently for about 5 minutes – until it melts and combines with sauce. Taste and season.
7 Stir well and serve.

Adapted from *A Vegan Taste of Mexico* by Linda Majzlik, published by Jon Carpenter, with thanks.

ALL KITTED OUT

- Grinder
- Measuring spoons
- Bowl or plastic container for ground nut and spice mixture
- Chopping board
- Knife
- Garlic crusher
- Tin opener
- Measuring jug
- Heavy-bottomed medium saucepan
- Blender or food processor

COOL COMBOS

- Time-is-Tight Tacos, page 216
- Smoky Black Bean Cakes with plain rice, page 204
- Quinoa Pilaf, page 124

gf wf use suitable curry paste or the curry powder option
☺ use a mild paste and omit chilli

No-cook Curry Sauce

- 1-2 tbsp mild or medium curry paste* OR use 1 tbsp curry powder mixed with 1-2 tsp oil
- 1 tin of plum tomatoes or 8 medium fresh, skins removed
- 10-15 dried apricots – if using the darker, unsulphured type go for the lower amount because they are sweeter. The orange sulphured variety is tarter
- 1-2 large cloves of garlic, according to taste

- 1 pinch chilli powder – OR if you like hot food, quarter to half a green chilli, seeds removed
- 1 small pepper, any colour, roughly chopped
- A little stock or water if the mixture is too thick – or just add a dollop of water and a sprinkle of bouillon powder or Green Oxo!
- * Most of Patak's range is vegan (just avoid those with added cream, yoghurt etc); their lactic acid is from a non-animal source

1 If using fresh tomatoes, dip in boiling water for 10 seconds then peel. Chop roughly.
2 Blend everything until smooth.
3 Warm sauce gently – don't boil.

ALL KITTED OUT

- Measuring spoons
- Tin opener OR boiling water and bowl if using fresh tomatoes
- Knife
- Chopping board
- Blender or food processor

COOL COMBOS

- Quinoa Pilaf, page 124
- Joe's Chestnut Rice, page 123
- Padma Pancakes, page 39
- Any stir-fried rice dish

use ready-roasted peppers

Roasted Red Pepper & Almond Sauce

A special sauce that looks as if you spent hours on it – but in fact it's another 'fast feed', especially if you use ready-roasted peppers.

Roasted red peppers come in two forms: in oil or in brine. If you are using the oily type, omit the olive oil in this recipe. Add oil if using peppers in brine or those you have roasted yourself. (The type in brine will make the sauce taste a bit different.)

- 225g/8oz roasted red peppers – roasted under the grill at home or taken from a jar
- 1 tbsp extra virgin olive oil
- 2 tbsp ground almonds
- 1 tsp dried basil
- 1 tsp crushed garlic (approx 1 large clove)
- ½ tsp salt
- Pinch ground allspice

1 Rinse brine from peppers if using that type.
2 Blend everything until creamy and smooth. Add a little water if it is too thick.
3 Warm sauce through gently.

Home-made Roast Peppers

Skewer each pepper with a wooden chopstick or hold with metal tongs. Hold each pepper over a gas flame for a few minutes, rotating them, until they are blackened. Place in a plastic bag or saucepan with lid and shake around to loosen skins. Peel to remove excess skin.

ALL KITTED OUT

- Grill pan if roasting peppers yourself
- Measuring spoons
- Garlic crusher
- Blender (hand or goblet) or food processor
- Saucepan to warm sauce
- Serving spoon

COOL COMBOS

- Savoury Pancakes, page 36
- Smoky Black Bean Cakes & Sausages, page 204
- Any simple grain dish
- Stir-fried vegetables and tofu (without ginger)
- Cooked pasta and roasted vegetables

basic recipe only
replace flour with 1 dsp arrowroot mixed with a little cold water and add with the stock. Use tamari soya sauce
just whisk well when reheating

Rose's Onion Gravy with Posh Options

A sure-fire gravy recipe adapted from a classic recipe by top cookery writer and Viva! Patron, Rose Elliot. We also suggest a couple of options for special occasions.

- 1 onion, diced
- 2 tbsp oil
- 2 tbsp plain flour
- Clove of garlic (crushed)
- 450ml/15fl oz vegan stock
- 1 tsp yeast extract
- 1-2 tbsp shoyu or tamari soya sauce
- Freshly ground black pepper

Posh options:

- 1 tbsp dried porcini mushrooms soaked in some of the hot vegetable stock
- 2 tbsp red wine or sherry (deduct this amount from the vegetable stock)

1 If using dried mushrooms, soak now.
2 Heat oil in saucepan and fry onion for 5 minutes.
3 Add flour and cook for a further 5-10 minutes until flour and onion are nut-brown and onion is soft and slightly pulpy. Stir frequently.
4 Add garlic then gradually stir in some of the vegetable stock and the wine/sherry if using.
5 Bring to boil and simmer for 10 minutes.
6 If using dried, soaked mushrooms, blend with their soaking stock. Sieve if necessary.
7 Add blended mushrooms, yeast extract, soya sauce and black pepper to gravy.
8 Stir well. Blend if you like or serve as it is.

Recipe adapted with thanks from *Rose Elliot's Vegetarian Cookery*, published by Harper Collins.

ALL KITTED OUT

- Kettle
- Jug
- Chopping board
- Knife
- Measuring spoons
- Garlic crusher
- Saucepan
- Sieve
- Wooden spoon
- Blender or food processor (hand blender is best)

COOL COMBOS

- Chestnut Pâté en Croûte, page 176
- Vegan sausages – bought or home-made as page 204 – plus mash and greens
- Any roast dinner

gf wf use tamari soya sauce

St Clement's Tahini Sauce

Why St Clement's? Oh, oranges and lemons… ask your mum! A simple sauce to cheer up wholegrains and vegetables. It works well cold or warm.

- 4 tbsp orange juice
- 4 tbsp tahini
- 1 tbsp fresh lemon juice
- 1 tsp shoyu or tamari soya sauce

- 1 very small clove of garlic, crushed – about ¼ tsp crushed garlic (add more to taste if you wish)
- 1 tsp agave, maple or date syrup (optional)
- A splash of water or soya milk to thin the sauce if required

1 Combine all ingredients and whisk until smooth.
2 If you want the sauce warm, place everything in a small pan, whisk and heat gently – don't let it boil.
3 If heating, you may need to add more orange juice/water as heating thickens the tahini. Adjust seasoning as necessary.

ALL KITTED OUT

- Measuring spoons
- Garlic crusher
- Lemon squeezer
- Whisk
- Small saucepan if heating up
- Wooden spoon

COOL COMBOS

- Middle Eastern Spicy Filo Rolls, page 187
- Quinoa Pilaf, page 124
- Greens & Garlic, page 103
- Stuffed pitta with salad and falafels (bought or home-made)
- Most vegetable and rice stir-fries

gf wf use tamari soya sauce
omit or reduce the chilli and reduce the soya sauce

Satay (Spicy Peanut) Sauce

A superb and quick way to liven up kebabs, stir-fries, soba (buckwheat) noodles or brown rice.

- Oil spray
- ½ tbsp crushed garlic (about 2 medium cloves)
- 125ml/8 level tbsp smooth peanut butter
- ½ tbsp grated root ginger
- 2 tsp date or agave syrup or a little brown sugar
- 2 tsp tomato purée
- 180ml/6½fl oz hot water
- 2 tbsp cider vinegar
- 1 tbsp soya sauce – shoyu or tamari if possible
- Large pinch chilli powder

1 Get all ingredients ready to go.
2 If you prefer garlic cooked, sauté in 2 tsp plain oil for a minute or two. Otherwise, mix everything in pan until smooth then warm gently until thickened. Use a wooden spoon or balloon whisk.
3 If the sauce is too thick, add more hot water but adjust seasoning to taste.

ALL KITTED OUT

- Kettle of hot water
- Knife
- Vegetable peeler
- Garlic crusher
- Grater
- Measuring spoons
- Measuring jug
- Wooden spoon
- Small saucepan

COOL COMBOS

- Oriental Vegetable Fan Wraps with Spring Onion Tufts, page 192
- Gado Gado, page 183
- Joe's Chestnut Rice, page 123
- Most simple vegetable/tofu stir-fries
- Oriental noodles, eg rice or wholemeal
- Vegetable/tofu kebabs (alternate chunks of veg and smoked tofu on skewers, grilled)

halve the quantities or make a full batch and freeze some

Tomato Sauce with Many Options

Tomato sauce is one of the first sauces most of us learn to make – it's used as a basis for so many dishes such as Spaghetti Bolognese, Chilli and more. It is also great with pasta, wholegrain dishes and so on – but a few simple tweaks can lift it to something much nicer!

Basic Sauce

- 1 medium onion, chopped
- 2-3 large garlic cloves, crushed
- 2 tbsp olive oil (reduce this to 2 tsp if you want a low-fat version)
- 2 tins whole plum tomatoes OR 500g/1lb 2oz fresh, ripe tomatoes
- 1-2 tsp dried basil
- ¼ tsp dried oregano
- Bay leaf
- 1 tbsp chopped fresh herbs other than above, such as parsley or tarragon (or use ½ tsp dried)
- Salt and black pepper to taste
- ½ tsp brown sugar or a tiny drizzle of agave syrup

Optional: 1 tbsp red wine

1 Heat oil in a heavy-bottomed pan. Sauté onion and garlic in oil over a low heat until soft and translucent. Add any options that need to be fried in at this point – see list.

2 Stir to prevent sticking and add a little juice from the tomatoes if necessary.

3 Add rest of tomatoes and chop them in the pan with a knife. They should be chunky but not too large so they retain some texture. Add any options that need to be cooked in at this stage – see list.

4 Stir in herbs, sugar/syrup and red wine if using.

5 Simmer for at least 15 minutes or until sauce has thickened. If you prefer a smoother sauce, blend it partially or entirely. Add other things that you fancy. Blend again if appropriate.

6 Season to taste before serving.

ALL KITTED OUT

- Chopping board
- Knife
- Garlic crusher
- Medium saucepan with lid
- Measuring spoons
- Tin opener
- Small bowl for herbs
- Pepper grinder

COOL COMBOS

- Quinoa Pilaf, page 124
- Savoury Pancakes, page 36
- Christmas Stuffed Squash, page 180
- Middle Eastern Spicy Filo Rolls, page 187
- Smoky Black Bean Cakes & Sausages, page 204

Other options:

- beans or lentils: cooked haricot beans/chickpeas/ whole lentils – you get the picture! These can be blended in to make a smoother sauce. Add a few minutes before serving
- capers: rinsed and drained. Add with the tomatoes

- mushroom: cooked in after the onion and garlic are softened
- olives: add chopped, pitted olives of any colour with the tomato
- pepper: add chopped red, orange or yellow cooked in with the onion and garlic
- rainbow veggie: add a handful each of grated carrot, baby spinach and finely chopped pepper of any colour to the tomatoes

- roast tomato: takes about 30 minutes. Can be frozen in batches. Heat the oven to 200°C (fan oven 180°C)/Gas Mark 6. Put a cross in each tomato, drizzle with olive oil and roast on a baking sheet for 20–25 minutes. Use in the basic recipe, replacing tinned/fresh tomatoes with the roasted ones
- Sicilian or Middle Eastern style: 2 tsp cinnamon, a pinch of chilli powder and a handful of fat raisins. Fry in the

cinnamon and chilli after the onions and garlic are softened; add the raisins with the tomatoes. Blend if you don't like the texture of raisins

- smoky: 1 heaped tsp smoked paprika, fried in after the onions and garlic have softened
- spicy: fry in chilli – ½-1 tsp powder OR 1 large fresh chilli, any colour (deseeded and chopped fine)

gf if you can't find a GF bean sauce: replace it with 1 rounded tablespoon of brown rice miso (Genmai) – available from large branches of Sainsbury's or good health food shops (most misos are fine apart from the barley type, so always read the label)

Viva! Veggie Oyster Sauce

Simple and good.

- 1 vegetable or mushroom stock cube
- 120ml/4fl oz boiling water
- 2 tbsp black or brown bean sauce – just check there is no added dairy – OR brown rice miso (Genmai variety)
- 1 tbsp date or maple syrup
- 1 heaped tsp arrowroot or cornflour dissolved in 1 tbsp cold water

Optional: 1 tsp crumbled nori*

1 Dissolve stock cube in hot water.
2 Mix with brown/black bean sauce and syrup and heat to boiling point.
3 Add dissolved cornflour and stir until thickened. Add nori flakes if using and stir in well.
4 Use hot on stir-fries or cool as a dipping sauce.

*Nori is seaweed sold in flat sheets and used to wrap round sushi. It is also sold as nori sprinkles and used as a condiment but you can crumble toasted whole sheets yourself – hold over a hot cooker ring until it starts to crinkle. If you have leftovers, they will keep in an airtight container for another time – nori tastes great on rice or noodles. If you're in a real hurry, Lee Kum Kee Vegetarian Stir Fry Sauce is the equivalent to oyster sauce! Find it in good supermarkets or Oriental grocers

ALL KITTED OUT

- Kettle
- Measuring jug
- Measuring spoons
- Small bowl to mix arrowroot/cornflour and water paste
- Small saucepan
- Wooden spoon

COOL COMBOS

- Oriental Vegetable Fan Wraps with Spring Onion Tufts, page 192
- Vegetable Tempura, page 228
- Joe's Chestnut Rice, page 123
- Any stir-fried vegetable/tofu dish with rice or noodles

gf wf use GF pasta

Walnut & Parsley Pesto

A lovely variation on the traditional basil pesto – although you can make that, too, using this recipe but replacing the parsley with fresh basil and using pine nuts or cashews instead of walnuts. The pesto is best made in a food processor or a wet & dry grinder, as the parsley stalks need to be blitzed.

- 25g/1oz walnut pieces
- 3 tbsp nutritional yeast flakes. See page 17
- 1 garlic clove
- 50g/2oz flat leaf parsley
- 4-6 tbsp olive oil plus a little water if necessary
- Black pepper
- Salt to taste

1 Blend nuts and yeast flakes with garlic until smooth.
2 Add parsley a little at a time with a little of the oil and blend until smooth. Repeat this process until you have a smooth paste, seasoning it towards the end. Add water as you go if mixture is too stiff.
3 Mix in with hot or cold cooked pasta or vegetables or use as a dip.
4 Pesto will keep for 2-3 days in an airtight container in the fridge.

ALL KITTED OUT

- Chopping board
- Knife
- Measuring spoons
- Grinder for the nuts
- Food processor

COOL COMBOS

- Serve on pasta such as spaghetti, linguine or penne, or on baked/steamed vegetables such as butternut squash

Whizzy Hot Sauce

As spicy or mellow as you want to make it!

- 1 medium-large red onion, roughly chopped
- 1 large red or yellow pepper, roughly chopped
- 1-2 fresh green chillies, deseeded and chopped OR ½ tsp cayenne pepper
- 5 garlic cloves, crushed
- 2 tins plum tomatoes or 8-10 medium fresh tomatoes, chopped roughly
- 1 tsp ground cumin
- 1 tsp ground coriander
- ½ tsp dried oregano
- 2 tbsp fresh coriander, chopped
- Salt to taste

1 In a blender or food processor, combine all ingredients except salt and purée until smooth.

2 Transfer sauce to a medium saucepan and simmer on low heat, uncovered, for about 30 minutes or until sauce has thickened and flavours mellowed.

3 Stir often as it cooks and use a heat diffuser if necessary to prevent sticking.

4 Add salt to taste.

5 This sauce will keep in a screw-top jar in fridge for up to 2 weeks.

ALL KITTED OUT

- Chopping board
- Knife
- Garlic crusher
- Measuring spoons
- Blender/food processor

COOL COMBOS

- Middle Eastern Spicy Filo Rolls, page 187
- Any cooked grains
- Stir-fries
- Pasta and roast vegetables with added pulses – especially butter beans or chickpeas

The main event

Veggie and vegan food is very flexible: it may be just one dish, such as a hearty casserole or pie, or it might comprise several dishes of different flavours and textures – think of an Indian thali, for example. And forget the old stereotype about endless slaving over lentils in clogs – nearly half the recipes in this section alone take 30 minutes or under, many far less. See those dishes marked with the clock symbol. Using ready-made sauces, tinned pulses, ready-cooked wholegrains and so forth will make many of these even faster.

Many recipes stand alone, some need accompaniments and others, in smaller portions, work well as a light meal or brunch.

Every recipe has a Cool Combos section, which will spark your imagination as to the choices and spur you to greater culinary creativity!

African Slow & Sweet Potato Stew with Red Beans

This recipe is hearty, rich and spicy. As with many slow-cooker recipes, it can be turned on in the morning so that the scent of a fragrant, delicious meal welcomes you when you return in the evening. However, it can also be cooked on top of the stove.

- 1 large onion, chopped
- 4 garlic cloves, crushed
- 670g/1½lb sweet potatoes or yams, scrubbed and peeled then cut into medium-small cubes (about 1cm/½ inch)
- 1 tin aduki beans, drained and rinsed OR 200g/7oz home-cooked beans
- 360ml/13fl oz vegan stock
- 1 red pepper, finely chopped
- 670g/1½lb fresh tomatoes, cored, seeded and diced
- 120ml/4fl oz water, plus additional water for sautéing garlic and onions
- 1 tbsp grated peeled fresh ginger
- 2 tsp ground cumin
- ¼ tsp chilli powder, or to taste
- 3 tbsp peanut butter
- 3 tbsp chopped peanuts
- 6 lime wedges
- Salt and pepper to taste

1 Sauté onion and garlic in 3 tbsp water for one minute, then cover and cook for 5 minutes or until tender.

2 **Slow cooker method:** place the onion mixture in the crockpot/slow cooker. Add sweet potatoes and next 8 ingredients (up to, and including, the chilli powder). Cover and cook on low for 8 hours or until vegetables are tender.

Stove-top method: Follow the same procedure but in a medium-large, heavy-based saucepan. Bring to the boil then reduce to a simmer and cover. Cook very slowly, preferably on a heat diffuser. Stir occasionally during the cooking time. It will take about 30 minutes or until the sweet potatoes are tender.

3 Place the peanut butter in a bowl and stir in 1 cup of hot liquid from the stew. Whisk well until the peanut butter has dissolved then return it to the stew and stir in. Taste and season.

4 Top with chopped peanuts and serve with lime wedges.

ALL KITTED OUT
- Chopping board
- Knife
- Garlic crusher
- Measuring jug
- Measuring spoons
- Slow cooker/crockpot OR medium-large heavy saucepan with lid
- Wooden spoon

COOL COMBOS
- Quinoa Pilaf, page 124
- Socca Pizza, page 211, made without the artichokes. Keep it plain or just add a bit of garlic and red pepper
- Greens & Garlic, page 103
- Any other cooked wholegrains such as brown rice or whole-wheat couscous

Replace the peanut butter and nuts with an alternative if you wish, eg cashew, almond or sunflower butter.

easily halved or quartered to serve two or one

Artichoke & Filo Pie with Creamy Butterbeans, Olives & Sundried Tomatoes

This pie looks posh but is actually simple to make. Don't worry about using filo pastry – it will rip a little but all the layers ensure that any holes are covered up and it looks splendid when it's baked. Filo is sold chilled or frozen - just remember to defrost in plenty of time if using frozen. Keep the filo from drying out by covering it with a soaked then well-wrung-out clean tea towel while you are layering the pie.

- 1 medium red onion, chopped plus a little olive oil or oil spray to cook
- 2 tins of butterbeans, rinsed and drained OR 480g home-cooked beans
- 2 tbsp finely chopped flat leaf parsley plus more to taste if needed
- 2 tbsp olive oil (or soya milk if making reduced-fat version)
- 4 tsp lemon juice
- ½-1 tsp salt, according to taste
- Black pepper – freshly ground – to taste
- ⅛-¼ tsp cayenne pepper – start with the minimum, taste and add more if desired
- 1 tin of artichoke hearts, drained OR 240g frozen hearts, defrosted

- 4 tbsp chopped pitted kalamata or black olives
- 6 large sundried tomatoes, chopped very small with scissors – any type, but if using the dried variety, soak in hot water first
- Filo pastry sheets (about ⅓ of a 270g pack, roughly 90-100g)
- Oil or oil spray to coat the filo layers

COOL COMBOS

- Potato Salad, such as our Herby recipe, page 84
- Any greens dish such as Garlic Broccoli, page 103
- Any green or tomato salad
- Mayo, bought or home-made (page 143). Thin down with a little plain vegan yoghurt or plant milk
- Sour Cream, page 35

1 Preheat the oven to 200°C/400°F/Gas Mark 6.

2 In a frying pan, wok or heavy-bottomed pan, heat a little olive oil/oil spray and sauté the onion until tender – add a little water if it starts to dry out.

3 Part-blend/mash two thirds of the butterbeans until smooth and creamy. Mash the rest with a potato masher or hand blender, leaving some texture, and mix in. Add the olive oil/soya milk, lemon juice, parsley, salt, black pepper and cayenne. Mix in well to form a creamy mixture that is stiff but not too dry.

4 Add the chopped artichoke hearts, olives and sundried tomatoes. Mix in gently. Taste the mixture and add more lemon juice/salt/pepper/soya milk if necessary.

ALL KITTED OUT

- 20cm/8 inch dish, round or square: ceramic or better still, a springform tin with removable base
- Chopping board
- Knife
- Frying pan/wok or similar
- Wooden spatula or spoon
- Tin opener
- Potato masher/hand blender
- Large bowl for mashing
- Lemon squeezer
- Rubber spatula
- Measuring spoons
- Fish slice for serving

5 Lightly grease the tin or dish with spray or oil. Line it with several overlapping layers of filo sheets, oiling each layer well. Don't worry if they crumble a bit or have holes – all the layers will make it work! Make sure the sheets overhang the tray so they can be folded back on top of the bake.

6 Spoon half the filling on top of the filo base and smooth out evenly. Fold over some of the filo layers that hang over the edge of the tin. Repeat the folding/spraying process with the second part of the filling. Use a little olive oil to brush the top.

7 Bake for 20-30 minutes or until golden brown. Remove from the oven and allow to cool a little before slicing into portions.

gf wf use tamari soya sauce; use GF stock
replace olive oil with oil spray
for children who don't like beans yet, blend the butterbeans with a little of the stock to make a creamy sauce then return it to the stew

Aubergine & Bean Stew with Red Wine

A simple, classic stew that is full of flavour and tastes even nicer the next day. Lovely with chickpeas or butterbeans but experiment with your favourite bean! This would also work in a slow cooker but add the cooked beans about half an hour before serving.

- 2 tbsp olive oil
- 1 large red onion, chopped
- 1 large aubergine, chopped into medium-small cubes and lightly salted
- 2 medium carrots, diced
- 1 large King Edward or other solid white potato, diced
- 1 medium-large red pepper, chopped into pieces
- 4 cloves garlic, chopped fine
- ½ tsp ground cinnamon
- ¼ tsp allspice
- 2 x 400g tins beans, rinsed and drained OR 480g/17oz home-cooked – see note above

- 1½ x 400g tins chopped tomatoes
- 1 glass red wine – see page 21
- 2-3 tbsp fresh parsley, chopped fine – any type
- ½ tsp dried oregano
- ½ tsp dried basil
- 1 tbsp good quality soya sauce (eg shoyu)
- 85-115ml/3-4fl oz vegan stock – start with less, add more if necessary
- Salt and black pepper

1 Heat the oil and sauté the onions. Add the aubergine pieces to the onions and sauté for another few minutes.
2 Add the rest of the vegetables and the garlic and sauté for a few minutes. Add the cinnamon and allspice and fry for about a minute.
3 Add the beans, tinned tomatoes and the rest of the ingredients. Cook until the vegetables are tender – about 30 minutes. Taste and season if necessary (remember that the aubergines will contain some salt). If a thicker stew is desired, blend a couple of ladles of stew then return to the pan and mix in well.
4 Serve hot.

ALL KITTED OUT

- Chopping board
- Knife
- Vegetable peeler
- Colander to rinse veg
- Bowl to salt aubergines
- Garlic crusher
- Medium-large saucepan with lid
- Wooden spoon
- Tin opener
- Measuring spoons
- Measuring jug

COOL COMBOS

- Quinoa Pilaf, page 124
- Mixed Rooty Mash, page 108
- Mash with Cumin Seeds & Yoghurt, page 107
- Sour Cream, page 35

Modern aubergines don't need salting to remove bitterness – however, salt stops them gulping up all the oil in the saucepan.

easily halved or quartered to serve two or one
gf wf use gluten-free pasta
omit the chilli and reduce the garlic!

Avocado, Fresh Tomato, Garlic & Basil Sauce with Pasta

Genius! The sauce is actually a salad that you add to hot pasta or grains – it melts the avocado a little and warms it all through. Delicious!

- 450g/1lb pasta – spaghetti or linguini work well, but feel free to experiment with other types, eg fusilli, penne, wholemeal noodles or anything with a pretty shape
- 3 tbsp extra virgin olive oil
- 3-4 large cloves garlic
- 2 large ripe avocados
- 2 large ripe tasty tomatoes – eg 'beefsteak' variety
- ½ medium red chilli
- 15 fresh basil leaves, torn – a good handful
- Zest and juice of a lime
- Salt and lots of black pepper

1 Cook the pasta in a large pan of salted boiling water according to the packet instructions – or see our top tip below.

2 While the pasta is cooking, prepare the rest of the dish.

3 If you are cooking the garlic, do so now. Heat 2 tbsp of the oil in a small frying pan and fry the garlic gently for a minute or two, making sure it does not burn. Remove from heat, keeping any remaining oil, and set aside.

4 If using garlic raw, crush and set aside.

5 Peel avocados, remove stones and chop into chunks.

6 Chop tomatoes into chunks.

7 Deseed the chilli and chop finely.

8 Drain the pasta and mix in the prepared vegetables.

9 Add remaining olive oil, lime zest/juice and basil leaves and season well.

10 Serve immediately.

OPTIONS

- For those who prefer larger quantities of garlic, sauté it in some of the olive oil first then just mix it in with the chopped vegetables, herbs and pasta as described.
- Replace avocados with strips of roasted red pepper – home-made or in a jar. You will need at least half a large jar. Roasted peppers are sold either in brine or in oil. If the former, drain well and do not add extra salt to the dish. If they are in oil, omit most of the oil in the recipe.

ALL KITTED OUT

- Chopping board
- Knife
- Medium-large saucepan for pasta
- Measuring spoons
- Garlic crusher
- Wooden spoon
- Small frying pan and spatula (if cooking the garlic rather than using it raw)
- Small container for cooked garlic

COOL COMBOS

- Cauliflower & Flageolet Bean Antipasto, page 76 – or any big beany salad
- Any large green salad

Greener Pasta!

Boil a kettle of hot water, pour it into your saucepan, add the pasta and a little salt. Bring to the boil then switch off the heat and cover the pan with a well-fitting lid. The pasta will continue to cook in the hot water and will be ready in the usual cooking time but without using extra fuel. Stir occasionally to prevent clumping.

Big Puff Pie

A hearty and delicious pie that is fairly quick and easy to make. Basically, it's a stew with a separately baked puff pastry hat!

Choose from ONE of the four protein options below:

- tempeh, 225g pack. Steam for 5 minutes, chop into cubes, fry in a little oil and drizzle with soya sauce
- frozen tofu, 225g pack or thereabouts. Freezing tofu gives it a more solid, chewy texture. Chop it into cubes then freeze in an airtight plastic container. Defrost before using, squeeze out any excess liquid with kitchen paper and fry in hot oil until golden brown. Drizzle a little soya sauce to coat at the end of cooking time
- seitan (wheat gluten). Yakso brand 350g jars from health food shops or Companion brand plain gluten or veggie chicken, 300g tins from Oriental grocers – drain each of these. Any liquid can be incorporated into the pie's gravy
- TVP dried chunks, about 10-15, soaked in hot stock for 20-30 minutes until soft enough to cook

Pie filling

- 2 tbsp olive oil
- 1 medium-large onion, chopped
- 1 clove garlic, crushed
- 200g/7oz mushrooms, chopped if medium or large, left whole if small button variety
- One of the protein options above
- 6 tsp vegan gravy granules (red or green tub Bisto is fine) made up with 300g/12fl oz boiling water
- 1 tbsp porcini mushrooms, soaked in boiled water then chopped into small pieces with scissors. Reserve the soaking water and include it in the 300ml needed for the gravy – see above

(👄)use value mushrooms, use tofu or TVP chunks, omit the porcini and/or the booze and use block puff pastry
(🧍)easily halved or quartered to serve two or one
(❄️)the filling will freeze or else make small individual pies to freeze

- 1 tbsp Dijon mustard
- 1 tsp mixed dried herbs
- 1-2 tsp shoyu or tamari type soya sauce
- 2 tbsp sherry or red wine
- 100g/3oz frozen peas
- Black pepper (gravy granules and soya sauce should provide enough salt)

Pie crust

- 1 pack Jus-Rol puff pastry sheet (sold fresh or frozen in most supermarkets) OR a
- pack of Jus-Rol solid puff pastry, rolled out by hand
- Oil spray or a little vegetable oil
- A little soya milk to brush top of pastry

1 If using tofu, chop it into about 16 cubes and freeze overnight. Remove from the freezer a few hours before you make the pie.

2 If using tempeh, it is sold frozen or chilled. If frozen, it can be chopped before it is needed. Prepare as above.

3 If using TVP chunks, soak them in hot stock for a few minutes while you prepare everything else. Drain and squeeze gently before adding to pie.

4 If using seitan/gluten, drain, reserve liquid and set the seitan aside until ready.

5 Pre-heat oven to 225°C/450°F/Gas Mark 7.

6 Heat olive oil in a medium-large saucepan.

7 Sauté onion and garlic until onion is translucent – about 5 minutes. Add mushrooms and cook for 3-4 minutes.

8 Add the protein option of choice and gently stir in to coat with oil.

9 Make the gravy as above then add the mustard, herbs, soya sauce and sherry/wine and mix well.

10 Add the peas, porcini mushrooms, gravy mixture and all other ingredients to the pie filling (except the pastry and soya milk).

11 Stir carefully to mix in well, taste and season as necessary, turn down heat and leave to simmer.

12 Meanwhile, choose an oven-proof dish (or individual oven-proof dishes) that will hold the pie filling.

13 Use its shape to cut out a pastry lid, or several small shapes if you are making individual pies. Lightly oil a non-stick baking sheet or tray and place the pastry lid(s) on it. If using several lids space them out on the baking tray.

14 Brush with a little soya milk and bake in the hot oven for approximately 20 minutes, or according to the packet instructions – the pastry should be well risen and golden brown.

15 Spoon the stew into dish or dishes, place the pastry lid(s) on top and serve immediately.

ALL KITTED OUT

- Chopping board
- Knife
- Garlic crusher
- Measuring jugs
- Measuring spoons
- Kettle for hot water
- Whisk
- Medium-large saucepan
- Wooden spoon
- Baking sheet for pastry
- Pastry brush
- Medium-large oven-proof dish for the pie (or smaller dishes if making individual pies)
- Knife to cut pastry to size
- Rolling pin if using block pastry

COOL COMBOS

- Greens & Garlic, page 103
- Red Veg, page 113
- Butternut Squash with Garlic-thyme Aduki Beans, page 172
- Mixed Rooty Mash, page 108
- Roasted root vegetables, according to season

As well as Jus-Rol, most major supermarkets stock own-brand puff and shortcrust pastry that is vegan, eg Sainsbury's, Tesco and Waitrose.

easily halved or quartered to serve two or one

Butternut Squash with Garlic-thyme Aduki Beans

This not only tastes extremely good but the orange squash and dark red beans make it a very attractive dish.

- Approximately 450g/1lb butternut squash
- 2 cloves garlic, crushed
- 1 tin aduki beans, drained and rinsed OR 240g/9oz home-cooked

- 1 tbsp olive oil
- 2 tbsp fresh thyme or ½ tsp dried
- One batch of Roasted Red Pepper & Almond Sauce, page 151

1 Peel squash and chop into medium pieces. Steam for 10-15 minutes or until just tender.
2 Meanwhile, make the Roasted Red Pepper Sauce. Heat through gently and keep warm.
3 Heat a frying pan or wok. Add the oil and when hot, sauté the garlic, stirring to ensure it doesn't burn – about 1-2 minutes.
4 Add the cooked squash, thyme and aduki beans. Mix in gently, coating everything in the garlic and oil mixture. Keep warm but don't allow to cook any more.
5 Serve with sauce drizzled over the top.

ALL KITTED OUT

- Chopping board
- Knife
- Vegetable peeler
- Steamer
- Tin opener
- Garlic crusher
- Frying pan or wok
- Wooden or plastic spatula
- Measuring spoons
- Plus equipment to make sauce

COOL COMBOS

- Joe's Chestnut Rice, page 123
- Greens & Garlic, page 103
- Oven-roasted Tofu Mediterranean, page 195

if using pre-cooked grains – home-made or from a sachet | easily halved or quartered to serve two or one
gf wf if gluten-free stock used | cooked rice only, not the entire dish
use plain brown or white rice

Caribbean Coconut Rice

A simple dish with a fresh, zingy taste that also looks pretty. The addition of cooked beans makes it a more substantial meal.

- 150g/5oz long grain raw brown rice + 50g/2oz quick-cook wild rice

  OR use 200g of a mixed grain pack and follow instructions

  OR 400g cooked wholegrains, home-cooked or see the box below

- 650ml/23fl oz hot stock made from 2 tsp vegan bouillon powder/stock cube
- 1 medium onion, chopped
- 4 large peppers, a mix of colours (red and green/yellow and red)
- Half a medium red chilli, deseeded and chopped fine OR ¼ tsp mild chilli powder

- 2-3 garlic cloves, crushed
- 2 large tomatoes (or 4 medium), fresh or tinned
- 2 tsp ground coriander
- 1 tsp Dijon mustard
- 100ml/generous 3fl oz coconut milk
- 1-2 tsp lime zest plus juice of half a lime
- Salt to taste

Optional: 1 tin of kidney or pinto beans, rinsed and drained (240g/9oz home-cooked)

1 Cook wild rice in the hot stock for 10-15 minutes then add the brown rice and cook until both are tender – about 30-40 minutes.

2 Meanwhile, chop the onion and peppers into medium-sized pieces and crush the garlic.

3 Heat oil in a large, heavy-bottomed pan or wok.

4 Add onion and peppers and sauté for several minutes, until onions are translucent.

5 Add garlic and chilli and cook for another 2-3 minutes, then add tomatoes and cook for a minute or two more.

6 Add coriander, mustard and coconut milk and stir well. Set aside until rice is cooked.

7 Mix vegetables with the cooked rice and stir in well.

8 Just before serving, add lime zest and juice.

9 Serve hot.

ALL KITTED OUT

- Scales
- Heavy-bottomed saucepan with lid for wild rice
- Heavy-bottomed pan or wok for rest of dish
- Measuring spoons
- Chopping board
- Knife
- Tin opener
- Garlic crusher
- Zester
- Lemon squeezer

COOL COMBOS

- Mango Salsa, page 82
- Time-is-Tight Tacos, page 216
- Smoky Black Bean Cakes, page 204
- Quesadilla with Guacamole, page 198
- Martin Shaw's Classic Chilli, page 184

For a fast feed, use sachets of ready-cooked brown rice or mixed grains – eg Merchant Gourmet, Tilda, Sainsbury's etc. You'll need just under 1½ packs. You won't need all the stock in the recipe either. Just sprinkle the stock powder/cube into the grains with a splash of water, stir well then heat up the wholegrains.

make half the quantity. Eat part and freeze the rest

Chestnut Pâté en Crôute

Thanks to Rose Elliot, the goddess of veggie food, for this lovely recipe. Some of us at Viva! cook it every Christmas and it is enjoyed by veggies and meat-eaters alike. It also looks fantastic on the dinner table! The recipe is very easy and frees you up to do other things while it bakes. Serve with piles of roast potatoes, butternut squash, parsnips and gravy. It also lends itself to other fillings – try experimenting!

- 4 onions, chopped
- 2 sticks of celery, finely chopped
- 2 tbsp olive oil
- 4 garlic cloves, crushed
- 100g/3½oz mushrooms, sliced
- 435g can unsweetened chestnut purée – OR use a mixture of vacuum-packed chestnuts – chopped roughly – with some purée if you want more texture
- 75g/3oz soft breadcrumbs
- 2 tbsp brandy
- Salt and pepper
- 2 sheets of Jus-Rol chilled ready-rolled puff pastry
- Soya milk to glaze

1 Fry onions and celery in the oil in a large saucepan, covered, for 10 minutes.
2 Add garlic and mushrooms, cook for 2-3 minutes.
3 Mix in chestnut purée (or mixture) plus breadcrumbs, brandy and seasoning.
4 Preheat oven to 230°C/450°F/Gas Mark 8.
5 Place each pastry sheet on a greased baking tray. Divide the chestnut mixture into half and place one portion on each sheet, spooning it lengthways down the middle third. This leaves a piece of pastry on either side from which to make the plait strands.
6 Make diagonal cuts 1cm/½ inch apart on either side of the chestnut mixture on both pastry sheets.
7 Fold these alternately to make a lattice covering the filling and trim the ends – you could make leaves from any leftovers and stick them on top with water.
8 Brush each plait with soya milk.
9 Bake for 5 minutes, then reduce the oven temperature to 200°C/400°F/Gas Mark 6 and bake for a further 20-25 minutes.

ALL KITTED OUT

- Chopping board
- Knife
- Measuring spoons
- Garlic crusher
- Tin opener
- Scales
- Food processor/blender for breadcrumbs
- Medium-large saucepan
- Baking trays, shallow x 2
- Pastry brush

COOL COMBOS

- Rose's Onion Gravy with Posh Options, page 153
- Roasted Red Pepper & Almond Sauce, page 151
- Red Veg, page 113
- Christmas Squash (as a side dish), page 180

easily halved or quartered to serve two or one
use tamari
they aren't very spicy but go easy on the chilli

Chinese Red Bean Burgers

Pretty and flavoursome, these are a great way to use aduki beans and leftover brown rice. If you are pushed for time, use a sachet of cooked rice such as Sainsbury's or Merchant Gourmet.

Sauce: choose from one of these
- Fragrant Coconut Sauce, page 144
- Fresh Sweet & Sour Sauce, page 145
- Veggie Oyster Sauce, page 158
- Creamy Oriental Carrot Sauce, page 142

Burgers
- 2 tbsp olive oil
- 1 small red onion, chopped quite small
- 1 small red pepper, seeded and chopped quite small
- 1 stalk celery, chopped fine
- 1 large garlic clove, crushed

- 1 tsp five spice powder
- ½ tsp paprika
- ½ tsp dried thyme
- ¼ tsp mild chilli powder
- 1 tsp soya sauce – shoyu or tamari
- Salt and black pepper
- 1 tin aduki beans, drained and rinsed OR 240g home-cooked beans (approximately 100g dried)
- 150g/generous 5oz cold, cooked brown rice
- 2 tbsp fresh coriander or parsley, chopped

Optional: 4 tbsp chopped peanuts or cashews

1 Heat 1 tbsp olive oil in a large frying pan.
2 Add onion, red pepper, celery, garlic, five spice powder, paprika, thyme and chilli.
3 Cover and cook, stirring occasionally, for about 10 minutes until softened. Add soya sauce and stir in well.
4 Meanwhile, make sauce of your choice and keep warm if appropriate – this will take approximately 10 minutes.
5 Season the vegetable mixture and set aside to cool.
6 Make the burgers: using a potato masher, mash the beans, cooked rice, coriander or parsley with the cooked veggie mixture. You can use a stick blender or food processor, but don't make the mixture too smooth – retain some texture. Mix in the chopped nuts if using and add salt and pepper to taste.
7 Shape into small burgers and set aside. Chill in the fridge for 30 minutes or more if time allows – this will help them keep their shape.
8 Heat remaining oil in a large frying pan over medium heat. Add burgers and cook, turning once, until browned on both sides – 7-10 minutes. Don't worry if they fall apart, just bash them back into shape with the fish slice/spatula. Alternatively, bake them in a preheated oven at 200°C/400°/Gas Mark 6 for 15-20 minutes, turning once.
9 Transfer bean cakes to a platter, pour sauce over and garnish.

ALL KITTED OUT
- Chopping board
- Knife
- Garlic crusher
- Scales
- Measuring spoons
- Large frying pan, preferably non-stick
- Grinder/food processor
- Spatula
- Fish slice
- Tin opener
- Colander
- Potato masher
- Medium-sized mixing bowl
- Plus sauce equipment

COOL COMBOS
- Oriental Vegetable Fan Wraps with Spring Onion Tufts, page 192
- Tropical Rice Salad with Sesame Orange Dressing, page 86
- Edamame Fuji, page 100

easily halved or quartered to serve two or one
gf wf use GF stock cubes/bouillon
freeze the filling and roasted squash separately. Defrost then reassemble and bake each part together in the oven

Christmas Stuffed Squash with Two-rice, Cranberry & Porcini Mushroom Filling

Lovely – and not just for Christmas.

Squash

- 2 small squashes (eg acorn or small butternut squash)
- 3 cloves garlic
- 2 tbsp olive oil or oil spray
- 1 large sprig of fresh rosemary
- Salt and freshly ground black pepper

Filling

- 1 tbsp olive oil
- 1 onion, finely chopped
- 2 tbsp dried mushrooms (porcini or mixed)
- 70g/2½oz long grain brown rice
- 20g/scant 1oz quick cook wild rice
- 500ml/18fl oz vegetable stock
- ½ tsp chopped rosemary OR ¼ tsp dried
- 2 tsp dried cranberries
- 1 tbsp pine nuts
- 1 heaped tbsp fresh thyme leaves, chopped OR 1 tsp dried

ALL KITTED OUT

- Chopping board
- Knife
- Spoon – metal dessert or tablespoon to scoop seeds
- Scales
- Garlic crusher
- Pastry brush
- Measuring spoons
- Measuring jug
- Medium-large saucepan
- Roasting pan for squash

COOL COMBOS

- Roasted Red Pepper Sauce (Viva!'s favourite), page 151
- Rose's Onion Gravy with Posh Options, page 153
- Luxury Two-mushroom Sauce, page 145
- Cheatin' Cheesy Sauce (either), pages 139-40
- Tomato Sauce with Many Options, page 156

1 Preheat the oven to 200°C/400°F/Gas Mark 6.

2 Cut squashes in half, remove all seeds with a spoon and brush lightly with olive oil or oil spray.

3 Quarter the garlic cloves, place in the hollows and around the edges of each squash half.

4 Add rosemary needles and season with salt and freshly ground pepper.

5 Place in an oiled roasting dish and roast for 45 minutes or until the flesh is soft.

6 While the squashes roast, prepare the filling and sauce (see the Cool Combos list to the left).

7 Sauté onion until translucent and add each type of rice plus the vegetable stock.

8 Bring to the boil, then reduce the heat and simmer for 10 minutes. Add dried mushrooms, rosemary and dried cranberries.

9 Bring to the boil once more, cover and simmer over a very low heat until the stock is absorbed and all the rice is soft (about 20-30 minutes).

10 When rice in the filling mixture is cooked, stir in pine nuts and chopped thyme. Divide rice filling between the four squash halves and return to the oven for 5 minutes.

11 Serve with warm sauce and vegetables of your choice.

easily halved or quartered to serve two or one

gf wf use tempeh or plain tofu. Use tamari soya sauce. If using smoked tofu, make sure it is made without wheat-based soya sauce

Gado Gado

Viva!'s take on an Indonesian classic, Gado Gado, is basically a sumptuous pile of lightly cooked and raw vegetables mixed with a protein source such as tofu and accompanied by delicious satay (spicy peanut) sauce. It's a quick meal that looks impressive and rather beautiful served on a big plate and with a pot of sauce on the side.

Protein

Choose ONE of these

- 1 pack smoked tofu, chopped into small cubes
- 1 pack marinated tofu pieces
- 1 pack tempeh, cubed and steamed for 5 minutes. Lightly fry cubes in oil spray or oil then drizzle with a little soya sauce
- 1 jar seitan or tin of gluten (Yakso or Lima brand seitan in jars from health food shops OR Coronation brand in tins from Oriental supermarkets), drained, lightly fried in oil spray and sprinkled with ½ tsp all-spice powder

Satay sauce

See recipe page 155

Vegetables

- 1 pack bean sprouts, washed and drained

Then choose from at least three of these:

- 1 large carrot, grated on largest holes OR sliced into thin matchsticks
- 2 peppers, any colour, cut into thin strips
- 1 bunch spring onions, sliced lengthways then into long strips
- 100g/3½oz mangetout, lightly steamed for a minute or two then rinsed in cold water and drained
- 100g/3½oz fine beans, prepared like the mange tout
- ½ a small cauliflower, broken into small florets and lightly steamed as above
- Cooked potatoes, diced

1 Make the satay sauce and set aside. See recipe page 155.
2 Prepare all vegetables and steam mange tout, cauliflower and beans – cook so they are *al dente* (still have a bit of bite!) then rinse in cold water and drain.
3 Prepare tofu/tempeh/seitan as necessary – ie chop into cubes if you aren't using the ready-made tofu chunks.
4 On a large serving plate or dish, arrange the vegetables artistically then the protein food of your choice.
5 Re-heat the satay sauce and either pour it over the entire dish OR serve it from a bowl.

ALL KITTED OUT

- Chopping board
- Knife
- Steamer
- Colander
- Large serving plate and spoons
- Plus equipment for satay sauce

COOL COMBOS

- Tropical Rice Salad, page 86
- Vegetable Tempura, page 228
- Joe's Chestnut Rice, page 123
- Cooked plain brown rice or wholemeal noodles (eg Blue Dragon)

In a hurry?

Thai Taste Satay Peanut Sauce is vegan – find in large supermarkets. Check www.thaitaste.co.uk – not everything is vegan but those products that are will be listed on the product page.

easily halved or quartered to serve two or one | **gf wf** if made with lentils (most TVP/veggie mince includes wheat)
adjust the chilli accordingly (hot pepper sauce can be served on the side for the heat lovers amongst you)
replace all oil with oil spray. Use lentil or dried TVP options

Martin Shaw's Classic Chilli

Viva! has cooked and given away literally thousands of portions of this recipe from actor and Viva! Patron, Martin Shaw. It's the best vegan chilli recipe we've found and meat-eaters love it, making it an all-inclusive recipe for most occasions.

Don't omit the magic ingredient (peanut butter) unless you're allergic! It adds a creamy richness that doesn't overpower. Cashew or other nut butters would work too but are more expensive. The chilli is even better the next day so cook it in advance if you can.

- 2 tbsp vegetable oil or oil spray
- 1 large onion, chopped
- 3 cloves of garlic, crushed
- ½ red pepper, chopped
- 1 medium courgette, chopped in half lengthways then sliced into semi-circles
- 100/3½oz mushrooms, chopped
- 1 tbsp peanut butter, smooth or crunchy
- 225g/8oz frozen veggie mince (half a pack). It can be cooked from frozen or defrosted first. See page 16. For other alternatives, see OPTIONS below

- ½-1 tsp mild chilli powder
- 1 tsp paprika
- 1 tsp cumin
- 1 tbsp tomato purée
- 2 x 400g tins of chopped tomatoes
- 1-2 vegan stock cubes (eg Green Oxo) OR 1½ tsp vegan bouillon powder
- 100g/3½oz kidney beans, cooked, rinsed and drained
- 100g/3½oz sweetcorn
- Salt and pepper

1 Fry onion and red pepper in the oil until soft.
2 Add garlic, courgette and mushrooms and cook until mushrooms are golden brown.
3 Add peanut butter and stir in until it melts.
4 Add mince and spices and fry for 4-5 minutes, stirring constantly. If the mixture sticks and needs a bit of moisture, use some of the juice from the tinned tomatoes.
5 Add tomato purée, tinned tomatoes and stock cube/bouillon, then kidney beans and sweetcorn. Bring to the boil, stir well and simmer for 15 minutes. Taste and season if necessary.

ALL KITTED OUT

- Chopping board
- Knife
- Garlic crusher
- Measuring spoons
- Tin opener
- Colander
- Medium saucepan
- Wooden spoon

COOL COMBOS

- Mango Salsa, page 82
- Mash with Cumin Seeds & Yoghurt, page 107
- Quinoa Pilaf, page 124
- Time-is-Tight Tacos, page 216

OPTIONS

- Extra budget: 50g/scant 2oz dried savoury TVP mince (brown in colour, not beige), soaked in a little hot stock before cooking
- OR cooked whole green or brown lentils – about 1 tin, drained and rinsed. Add these a few minutes before serving

halve the recipe and freeze the rolls you can't eat OR make a quarter batch
to cook from frozen, bake in a pre-heated oven at 190°C/375°F/Gas Mark 5 for 20-30 minutes

Middle Eastern Spicy Filo Rolls

These are easy and pretty cheap. For a quicker meal, make the filling the day before. We've given you a choice of vegan minces – or cooked lentils for those of you who don't like the former!

Pastry wrapping

- 1 pack filo pastry (about 270g), defrosted if bought frozen. It is also sold fresh in chiller cabinets
- Oil for filo layers

Filling

- 2 tbsp oil, olive if possible
- 1 onion
- 1 clove garlic
- Half a red chilli, de-seeded and chopped fine
- 1 red or yellow pepper, finely chopped
- 1 small carrot, finely chopped
- 1 tsp dried thyme
- 1 tsp cinnamon
- ¼ tsp allspice
- 1 tbsp raisins
- Half a tin chopped tomatoes (about 200g)
- 50g/1½ oz savoury TVP, soaked in 200ml/7fl oz strong, hot stock OR 110g/4 oz frozen veggie mince, straight from packet (see page 16) OR 1 tin/carton whole lentils, rinsed and drained
- Soya milk to glaze
- Salt & pepper
- 1 tbsp soya sauce (see page 21)

1 Let filo pastry defrost in its bag (read packet instructions beforehand).
2 Meanwhile, make the filling. Heat the oil in a medium saucepan.
3 Sauté onion and garlic for 3-4 minutes. Add chilli, pepper and carrot and cook for a further 3-4 minutes.
4 Stir in thyme, cinnamon and allspice and cook in for about 1 minute, stirring to prevent sticking. Add frozen veggie mince if using – defrosted or straight from the packet. Frozen mince needs no stock.
5 Add raisins, tinned tomato and soaked TVP mince if using.
6 Let this cook on a low heat for about 20-30 minutes. If using cooked lentils, add them a minute or two before the end and stir in well.
7 Pre-heat oven to 180°C/350°F/Gas Mark 4. Lightly oil a baking sheet or two.
8 Open the packet of filo pastry and unroll it carefully. Using a pair of kitchen scissors, cut the sheets into 2 or 4 pieces. Use a damp tea towel to cover the sheets that you aren't using.
9 You will need about 3-4 pieces of filo pastry per roll – oil each piece and overlap them.
10 Put a little of the mince filling in the middle and make a roll – don't over-fill or else they burst. Repeat to make several rolls.
11 Brush with a little soya milk and transfer to the oiled baking sheet. Bake in the oven for about 25 minutes, until golden brown.
12 Good with a minted yoghurt dressing. Simply mix in 1 tbsp fresh chopped mint with 250ml/9fl oz plain vegan yoghurt.

ALL KITTED OUT

- Medium heavy-bottomed saucepan
- Wooden spoon
- Scales
- Tin opener
- Measuring jug
- Measuring spoons
- Chopping board
- Knife
- Pastry brush
- Baking trays

COOL COMBOS

- Viva!'s Very Moorish Moroccan Stew, page 232
- Maca Mayo, page 148
- Spiced Roasties with Lime, page 115
- Greens & Garlic, page 103
- Quinoa Pilaf, page 124
- St Clement's Tahini Sauce, page 154
- Tomato Sauce with Many Options, page 156

easily halved or quartered to serve two or one
gf wf use gluten-free pasta/noodles and white flour. Use Alpro/Provamel cream rather than Oatly. Check that the mustard is gluten-free – some have wheat flour or malt vinegar added, others don't

Mushroom, White Wine & Creamy Tarragon Lemon Sauce with Pasta

Fresh tarragon, mustard and white wine give a gourmet twist to this quick and simple dish.

- Small handful of porcini mushrooms
- 150g/generous 5oz dry spaghetti or noodles
- 2 tbsp vegan margarine, eg Pure, Suma or Biona
- 1 tbsp olive oil
- 400g/14oz chestnut or white mushrooms, wiped with kitchen paper and chopped into quarters or halves so they retain texture when cooked
- 1 clove garlic, crushed

- 4 tsp arrowroot
- 1 glass white wine (approximately 180ml/6fl oz)
- 1½ tbsp wholegrain or Dijon mustard
- 2 tbsp chopped fresh tarragon
- 2 tbsp single dairy-free cream (eg Alpro/Provamel or Oatly)
- 1 tbsp lemon juice
- Salt
- Lots of black pepper, freshly ground

ALL KITTED OUT

- Kettle
- 2 small bowls (for porcini and arrowroot)
- Saucepan
- Colander
- Chopping board
- Knife
- Wok/large frying pan
- Wooden spoon
- Measuring spoons
- Garlic crusher

COOL COMBOS

- Greens & Garlic, page 103
- Luscious Two Pear Salad, page 81
- Large green or mixed salad

1 Boil a kettle of water. Use a little to soak the porcini in a small bowl. Cover and set aside.

2 Pour remaining hot water into a medium saucepan, bring to boil then add the spaghetti or noodles and a little salt. Cook according to the packet instructions.

3 Meanwhile, in a large shallow pan or wok, melt the margarine. Add the olive oil.

4 Sauté fresh mushrooms and garlic together in the margarine/oil mixture for about 3-4 minutes or until the mushrooms start to turn golden brown.

5 Mix arrowroot with the white wine and add to the pan. Stir to prevent lumps. Coat everything well.

6 Cook for a minute or two, stirring continuously. Cook for another minute or two to ensure that the alcohol burns off so you are left with just the flavour of the wine.

7 Add mustard and tarragon and stir in well. Add cream and lemon juice. Add the porcini mushrooms – chop into smaller pieces with scissors if necessary. Keep the soaking liquid and add to the pasta sauce if it is too thick.

8 Add salt to taste and lots of black pepper.

9 Drain the pasta, divide it into shallow bowls or plates and spoon the mushroom sauce over each portion.

easily halved or quartered to serve two or one
replace all oil with oil spray and add a little water to prevent sticking

Old School Lentil & Potato Curry

It's good with the Padma Pancakes recipe (page 39) as pictured – do a bit of multi-tasking! – or use bought chapatis/wraps instead.

Stage I

- 1 tbsp oil or oil spray
- 200g/7oz red lentils, washed and drained
- 1 x ½/1 inch cinnamon stick
- 800ml/28fl oz water
- 2 medium potatoes, raw or cooked

Stage II (done while Stage I is cooking)

- 2 tbsp plain oil or oil spray
- 1 onion, chopped fine
- 1½ tsp cumin seeds
- 1½ tsp ground coriander
- ¼ tsp asafoetida powder OR fenugreek powder
- ¼ tsp mild chilli powder
- 1 tsp salt

1 Wash and drain lentils and place in pan with water, oil and cinnamon stick.

2 Bring to boil and simmer for 15-20 minutes or until tender.

3 While the dahl is cooking, peel and chop potatoes into 1¼cm/½ inch cubes.

4 Add uncooked potatoes to dahl about 15 minutes into cooking time and simmer until soft and tender. If using cooked potatoes, add nearer the end.

5 Heat oil in a small frying pan or wok and sauté onion on a medium heat until softened.

6 Add cumin seeds and fry until they turn brown – keep stirring so they don't catch and burn. Add rest of the spices, stirring in so everything is incorporated.

7 Add this mixture to the dahl, stirring carefully so the potatoes keep their shape. Add salt.

8 If dahl is too thick, add a little hot water before serving.

ALL KITTED OUT

- Chopping board
- Knife
- Vegetable peeler
- Saucepan with lid
- Wooden spoon
- Measuring spoons
- Measuring jug
- Small frying pan
- Plastic or wooden fish slice/spatula

COOL COMBOS

- Padma Pancakes, page 39
- Quick Aubergine & Tomato Curry, page 200
- Joe's Chestnut Rice, page 123 – with or without the chestnuts
- Greens & Garlic, page 103

easily halved or quartered to serve two or one
make the GF version of Padma Pancakes recipe on page 39 (gram flour is already GF), use plain tofu option with added tamari soya sauce (GF)
the pancakes can be made and frozen but the filling won't freeze
replace oil with oil spray and use ordinary tofu or tempeh, not the marinated tofu pieces

Oriental Vegetable Fan Wraps with Spring Onion Tufts

Impress friends and family with this dish – it looks great! Wraps make a good and fast alternative but home-made pancakes are superb, easy and also a pretty yellow colour. Use the full amount in the recipes, just make the pancakes bigger than the wraps.

Choose a sauce:

- Fresh Sweet & Sour Sauce, page 145
- No-cook Curry Sauce, page 150
- Miso Tahini Sauce, page 208
- Satay Sauce, page 155
- Creamy Oriental Carrot Sauce, page 142
- Fragrant Coconut Sauce, page 144
- 4 large thin wraps OR 4 large home-made Padma Pancakes (page 39)
- 1 tbsp plain oil (not olive)
- 2 carrots, cut into thin strips
- 2 red or yellow peppers, cut into thin strips

- 1 small head broccoli, cut into very thin pieces (peel the stalk and use the centre cut into sticks)
- 1 pack of baby sweet corn, sliced lengthways
- 225g/8oz mange tout, halved
- Large bunch of spring onions, washed, trimmed and split lengthways

Plus... choose from

- ½ a pack of smoked tofu, cubed, eg Taifun
- ½ a pack of tempeh, cubed and lightly fried until golden
- 1 pack of Cauldron marinated tofu pieces
- 1 pack plain tofu, pressed, drained, fried in hot oil and drizzled with soya sauce

1 If using home-made pancakes, make now. If using wraps, go to stage 2.

2 Pre-heat oven to 160°C/300°F/Gas Mark 3.

3 Place wraps or pre-cooked pancakes in foil and pop them in the oven to warm through.

4 Make the sauce of your choice if you haven't already done so – takes about 10 minutes. Set aside.

5 If using tempeh or smoked tofu, fry cubes in a little hot oil until golden in a small frying pan or wok – about 5 minutes. Set aside.

6 Heat a wok or large frying pan and add the oil to it.

7 Sauté (lightly fry) carrots and broccoli for 2-3 minutes then add the rest of the vegetables – except for the spring onions – stirring occasionally. Add a little water if vegetables start to stick.

ALL KITTED OUT

- Chopping board
- Knife
- Tinfoil
- Frying pan/wok
- Spatula
- Plus equipment to make the sauce

COOL COMBOS

- Tropical Rice Salad with Sesame Orange Dressing, page 86
- Chinese Red Bean Burgers, page 179
- Vegetable Tempura, page 228
- Spicy Coconut & Lentil Soup (as a starter or sauce), page 68

8 Add tofu or tempeh pieces and warm through.

9 Heat sauce through gently – don't boil.

10 Remove pancakes/wraps from the oven.

11 Place a quarter of the cooked vegetable/tofu mixture inside the wrap/pancake.

12 Place a quarter of the spring onion strips on top of the vegetable mixture so they protrude from the pancakes.

13 Fold the pancakes/wraps in a fan shape so the spring onion tops stick out like feathers.

14 Either serve the sauce in individual tiny bowls/cups alongside or drizzle artistically around each pancake.

use plain tofu as smoked tofu tends to be more expensive
easily halved or quartered to serve two or one
gf wf use plain tofu (or if using smoked, check that it doesn't contain wheat-based soya sauce). Use tamari – wheat-free soya sauce

Oven-roasted Tofu Mediterranean

A really simple recipe that bakes while you prepare other things. We've converted many 'tofu virgins' with this dish!

- 450g/1lb firm tofu, plain or smoked
- 2 tbsp plain soya sauce – preferably shoyu or tamari – if using tamari, reduce to 1-1½ tbsp as it is stronger
- 1 tbsp oil, any kind. Olive oil or leftover oil from a jar of sundried tomatoes is good!
- 2 cloves of garlic, crushed
- 2 tsp grated fresh ginger (or cheat and use ready-grated ginger in a jar)
- ½ tsp dried rosemary
- 1 heaped tsp paprika
- Black pepper
- 6 small-medium tomatoes, eg cherry or plum. A mixture of red and yellow looks particularly pretty

1 Pre-heat oven to 225°C/450°F/Gas Mark 7.
2 Drain the tofu, place a clean cloth on top of it and weigh down with something heavy like tins of baked beans, pressing gently to remove some of the excess liquid. Then cut into medium-sized cubes.
3 Place all the ingredients in a medium oven dish (approximately 20x13cm/8x5 inches). Gently toss everything together with your hands or a spoon so the tofu is evenly coated.
4 Bake in the oven for 15-20 minutes, or until the cubes are brown on top.
5 Gently turn over the cubes so the paler bits get a chance to brown.
6 Return to the oven and bake for another 15-20 minutes.

ALL KITTED OUT

- Chopping board
- Knife
- Garlic crusher
- Vegetable peeler
- Grater
- Measuring spoons
- Oven-proof dish, metal or ceramic
- Fish slice to turn tofu over

COOL COMBOS

- Joe's Chestnut Rice, page 123
- Butternut Squash with Garlic-thyme Aduki Beans, page 172
- Sautéed Squash with Olive Tapenade & Cannellini Beans, page 114
- Greens & Garlic, page 103

Use a teaspoon to peel ginger quickly and easily – better than a knife.

easily halved or quartered to serve two or one
use tamari soya sauce and WF spaghetti or noodles, eg flat rice noodles

Pad Thai with Tofu Triangles

A tasty take on this traditional Thai favourite. Get all your ingredients and equipment ready – then go for it!

Noodles

- 225g/8oz wholemeal noodles, wholemeal spaghetti, soba (buckwheat) or rice noodles
- Pan of boiling water

Tofu triangles

- Oil spray or oil for frying
- 1 block plain tofu (approx 225g/8oz)
- 1 tsp soya sauce (shoyu or tamari)

Sauce

- 6 tbsp natural peanut butter, smooth or crunchy
- 2 tsp agave or date syrup OR 2 tsp brown sugar
- 4 tbsp fresh lime juice – plus more to taste

- 1-2 pinches chilli pepper flakes or powder
- 5-6 tsp tamari or shoyu soya sauce, or more to taste

Stir-fry

- 2 tbsp oil
- 1 small onion, sliced thinly
- 2 cloves garlic, crushed
- 1 red or yellow pepper, chopped into medium pieces
- 2cm/1 inch piece of ginger, grated
- Packet bean sprouts
- A little water or extra lime juice if needed
- Roasted peanuts for garnish – 1-2 tbsp
- Chilli flakes to serve for those who like hot food!

1 Put hot water on for noodles. Use the packet instructions to time cooking so they are ready just as the rest of the dish is completed.

2 Meanwhile, prepare the tofu by weighing down to remove excess moisture (see page 22). Then cut it into triangles or cubes. Heat a good non-stick frying pan or wok until hot then add 1 tbsp oil or 3 squirts of oil spray. Fry each side until golden brown (about 5 minutes) using a chopstick or fish slice to gently move the pieces around and prevent them from breaking up. Sprinkle in the soya sauce, remove from pan and set aside.

3 Mix peanut butter, sugar/syrup, soya sauce, lime juice and chilli in a small bowl. Set aside.

4 Heat frying pan or wok again, add oil and stir fry onion, garlic and red pepper until cooked. Add ginger. Stir fry for two minutes.

5 Add peanut sauce mixture, bean sprouts and noodles. Stir fry until everything is hot and the sauce has thickened – a minute or two. Add the tofu pieces, taste and add a little water or extra lime juice/soya sauce if necessary.

6 Serve immediately with roasted peanuts on top and chilli flakes on the side if desired.

ALL KITTED OUT

- Chopping board
- Knife
- Large saucepan
- Frying pan or wok
- Spatula
- Chopstick
- Colander
- Garlic crusher
- Lemon squeezer
- Grater
- Measuring spoons
- Small bowl
- Fork or whisk

COOL COMBOS

- Joe's Chestnut Rice, page 123
- Vegetable Tempura, page 228
- Edamame Fuji, page 100
- Greens & Garlic, page 103
- Spinach Citron, page 116

Use Thai Taste Satay Peanut sauce if in a hurry! Details page 183 (Gado Gado).

Quesadillas with Guacamole & Lime Sour Cream Dip

A Quesadilla (pronounced 'Kesadeeya', hombres!) is a stuffed or filled tortilla which is then fried. Inspiration for this dish came from a Sophie Dahl recipe, which we promptly veganised by using dairy-free sour cream and cheese. One of the Viva! team served this to a mixture of vegans, veggies and meat-eaters and it went down a storm.

Each of the different layers and dips are easy, it just takes a little time to make.

- Have all your ingredients ready before you start
- Make the two dips first: Guacamole and Lime Sour Cream
- Make the Cheesy layer by grating vegan cheese and carrot then mixing with the coriander
- Make the two fillings: Tofu Scramble and Refried Beans

NB: buy a large bunch of fresh coriander as it is used in the guacamole, grated cheese mix and the garnish.

COOL COMBOS

- Quinoa Pilaf, page 124
- Molé Sauce, page 149
- Mango Salsa, page 82
- Smoky Mexican Mushroom Stroganoff (as a side dish), page 207

Guacamole

- 2 medium-large ripe avocados, skinned and mashed with a fork
- 1 lime, zest and juice
- 1 medium tomato, seeds removed, finely chopped
- ½ red onion, peeled, finely chopped
- Large handful fresh coriander leaves, finely chopped
- Few drops Tabasco or other hot pepper sauce
- Salt and freshly ground black pepper

Lime sour cream dip

- 6 tbsp Sour Cream, page 35
  OR 3 tbsp each of plain vegan yoghurt and vegan mayo
- 1 lime, zest and juice
- Sea salt and freshly ground black pepper

Cheesy layer

- 150g/5oz strongish-tasting melting vegan cheese, see page 17
- 3 medium carrots, grated
- 1 small bunch fresh coriander, roughly chopped (about 2 good handfuls)

Tofu scramble layer

- 2 tbsp plain oil
- 300g/11oz firm tofu, crumbled
- ¼ tsp turmeric
- ½ tsp ground cumin

- ½ tsp smoked paprika
- 1 dsp Dijon mustard
- 2 spring onions, finely sliced
- 1 red chilli, seeds removed, finely chopped
- 2 garlic cloves, peeled, finely chopped

Refried beans layer

- 2 tbsp oil
- 400g tin black beans in water, drained
- 2 large roasted red peppers from a jar, sliced
- few drops hot pepper sauce or Tabasco

Plus

- 4 plain tortillas or wraps – Discovery and Old El Paso brands are vegan
- A little plain oil or low-cal spray
- Any leftover fresh coriander, chopped, for garnish

1 **Guacamole.** Place all the ingredients in a bowl and season to taste with salt and freshly ground black pepper. Leave one of the avocado stones in it, cover and set aside.

2 **Lime Sour Cream Dip.** Mix together all ingredients and season to taste with salt and freshly ground black pepper. Cover and set aside.

3 **Cheesy Layer.** Grate the cheese and mix with the grated carrot and chopped coriander in a container. Set aside.

4 Preheat oven to 150°C/300°F/Gas Mark 2-3.

5 **Tofu Scramble.** Heat oil in a frying pan over a medium heat and fry the tofu with turmeric, cumin and smoked paprika for 4-5 minutes, then add mustard, spring onion, chilli and garlic and continue to cook for a further 2-3 minutes. Set aside in a separate container and wipe the frying pan with kitchen towel ready for the quesadillas.

6 **Refried Beans.** Heat oil in a small saucepan, stir in black beans, peppers and Tabasco/hot pepper sauce and cook over a low heat for 6-8 minutes, or until warmed through. Mash slightly but retain some texture. Season to taste with salt and freshly ground black pepper and remove from the heat.

7 To assemble the quesadillas, heat a non-stick frying pan with oil or spray and place one of the tortillas in it over a low heat for 1-2 minutes to warm through. Spoon some bean mixture on half the tortilla, top with tofu mixture followed by cheese and coriander. Fold over and gently press down. Repeat with another tortilla. Place in oven to keep warm while cooking another.

8 Fry each for 2-3 minutes on either side, or until golden-brown and crisp. If some of the filling protrudes when you turn them – simply shove it back in again! Repeat with the other two tortillas.

9 To serve, cut each quesadilla into two or three pieces and arrange on a serving plate. Serve with guacamole and lime sour cream dip on the side.

easily halved or quartered
if oil spray is used

Quick Aubergine & Tomato Curry

Simple and delicious! Particularly good with something mellow to offset its slight tartness, such as lentil dahl or a potato and chickpea curry. Also nice with a tin of chick peas or black-eyed beans added.

- 675g/1½lbs aubergines
- 2 tbsp plain oil or oil spray
- 1 heaped tsp turmeric powder
- 4 cloves
- 1 heaped tsp cumin powder
- 1½ tsp coriander powder
- 6 black peppercorns
- 2½cm/1 inch piece fresh ginger, grated or finely chopped
- ½ tsp paprika
- ½ tsp chilli powder
- 3 tomatoes, chopped
- 1 tsp salt
- Juice of half a lemon
- 2 tbsp fresh coriander, chopped

1 Cut aubergines in 2cm/1 inch cubes and soak in cold water.
2 Assemble all the spices. Heat oil and fry spices and ginger for 2 minutes.
3 Drain the aubergines. Add them, the salt and tomatoes.
4 Cook, stirring occasionally, for 5 minutes. Add lemon juice, cover and cook slowly until tender – about 20 minutes. Taste and adjust seasoning if necessary.
5 Add chopped fresh coriander just before serving.
6 Serve hot.

ALL KITTED OUT

- Chopping board
- Knife
- Bowl to soak aubergines
- Measuring spoons
- Large saucepan with lid
- Spatula
- Wooden spoon

COOL COMBOS

- Padma Pancakes, page 39
- Old School Lentil & Potato Curry, page 191
- Coriander Lime Raita, page 141
- Boiled rice: white or brown – Basmati is nicest
- Chapatis

Quick Thai Vegetable Curry with Tofu

You can make this curry red or green, according to preference. The heat can also be adjusted, depending on how much curry paste is used – but remember that the rice will dilute some of its fieriness! We also offer three protein options, with instructions about how and when to cook them.

if ready-cooked rice and ready-prepared veg used | easily halved or quartered to serve two or one
use plain tofu and check the curry paste | if it is made pretty mild!

Rice

- 330g/12oz brown or white rice
- 1 tsp bouillon powder or ½ a stock cube

  OR 2 sachets ready-cooked rice, eg Tilda, Merchant Gourmet etc

Protein options

- 1 pack of plain tofu, approximately 225g

  OR 1 handful of TVP chunks, soaked in hot stock then drained

  OR 1 pack of Cauldron Marinated Tofu Pieces (add just before serving)

Curry

- 1 tbsp oil
- 2 large packs of suitable ready-prepped veg OR
- 1 medium onion – any colour – chopped
- 1 aubergine, cut into medium-small cubes

- 700g/1½lbs assorted veg – a selection of these works:
  - fine green beans (frozen work well)
  - red, orange or yellow pepper, chopped into strips
  - carrot sticks
  - broccoli florets, quite small
  - baby sweetcorn
  - mangetout
  - OR equivalent ready-prepped stir-fry mix
- 1-2 dsp red or green vegan Thai curry paste, eg Thai Taste. (Many contain fish/shrimp sauce so check labels or Viva!'s *L-Plate Vegan* guide (see page 6 for details). If using a sauce, it is weaker than paste
- 4 lime leaves
- 1 tin coconut milk OR half a block of creamed coconut, grated – add a little hot stock if using block
- Salt and black pepper
- Juice of half a lime or more
- Handful of chopped coriander leaves
- 2-3 tbsp roasted cashews for garnish

1 If using pre-cooked rice, go to stage 2. If cooking brown or white rice from scratch, see notes below.

2 If frying tofu, do this next. Press and drain (see page 22) then pat dry and cube. Heat oil in a non-stick frying pan or wok then fry tofu until all sides are golden brown. Drain and set aside.

3 If using TVP chunks, put to soak now in hot stock, cover and set aside. Drain and squeeze out a little before using.

4 Prepare vegetables.

5 Heat oil and sauté onion and aubergine until soft, adding garlic and curry paste nearer the end, allowing it time to cook. About 5-10 minutes total cooking time. Add TVP chunks now, if using. If using ready-prepped veg, cook the hard types first then add the softer ones last.

6 Add coconut milk/grated block and lime leaves and cook for a further 5 minutes.

7 Add rest of vegetables and cook until just tender. Add tofu chunks or marinated pieces if using.

8 Add lime juice, season and taste. Stir in coriander just before serving, reserving a little for garnish. Top with the cashews and serve with the rice.

ALL KITTED OUT
- Chopping board and sharp knife
- Measuring spoons
- Measuring jug
- Scales
- Wooden spoon
- Colander
- Sieve
- Tin opener
- Medium-large saucepan for rice
- Frying pan for tofu pieces
- Fish slice or wooden spatula
- Medium-large saucepan for curry

COOL COMBOS
- Pad Thai, page 196, minus tofu triangles

With Thai food, white rice is traditionally served more sticky than Indian so you may want to factor in extra cooking time – normal time is about 11 minutes so plan for 12-13 minutes. Brown rice invariably takes considerably longer (25-30 mins) so start it cooking while you prepare the curry. Jasmine rice is another option – follow packet instructions if using.

easily halved or quartered to serve two or one | gf wf (check the vegan mayo ingredients) | go easy on the chilli
form into burgers or sausages, place in airtight plastic boxes, separating each layer with greaseproof paper/baking parchment
use oil spray

Smoky Black Bean Cakes & Sausages

Bean Cakes

- 70g /2½oz (about ⅓ tin) cooked black beans or kidney beans
- 250g/9oz cooked brown rice
- ¼-½ tsp mild chilli powder
- ¾ tsp smoked paprika
- 1 tbsp soya sauce (GF tamari or regular)
- Salt and black pepper
- 1 tbsp olive oil OR a few squirts of low-cal spray

1 Partly mash the beans.
2 Mash most of the rice.
3 Add spices and soya sauce.
4 Mix everything well together and form into 3-4 burgers.
5 Chill in the fridge for at least 30 minutes.
6 Heat a non-stick frying pan and add the oil/low-cal spray.
7 Cook burgers for 2-3 minutes or until brown – if they fall apart, squidge them back together with the fish slice. Turn and repeat the process.
8 Serve in lettuce leaves or a bun with a dollop of one (or two) of these:
- Vegan mayonnaise – bought or Easy Mayo, page 143
- Tomato Salsa or Mango Salsa, page 82
- Guacamole, page 198
- Tomato Sauce with Many Options, page 156

ALL KITTED OUT

- Bowl
- Scales
- Potato masher
- Measuring spoons
- Frying pan – non-stick
- Hand blender

COOL COMBOS

- Spiced roasties with lime, page 115
- Any coleslaw recipe, pages 78-80
- Any mash, pages 107-108

Sausages

- 1-2 tbsp oil or a couple of squirts of spray
- ½ red onion
- 2 large cloves of garlic, crushed
- ¼ tsp chilli powder
- ¾ tsp smoked paprika
- 1 small carrot, grated on the small holes
- 220g/7oz cooked black or kidney beans
- 100g/3½oz oats, porridge or jumbo (GF or regular)
- 1 tbsp soya sauce, GF tamari or regular shoyu
- 1 tbsp Dijon mustard OR tomato purée
- Flour for coating (GF or regular)
- Oil for frying

1 In a frying pan or wok, heat the oil. Fry the onion until it starts to soften then cook in the garlic, stirring for another minute or so.
2 Add the carrot and spices and fry in for about a minute, stirring well.
3 Transfer to a bowl, add the beans, soya sauce, Dijon mustard/tomato puree and mix together well.
4 Mash with a potato masher or hand blender. The mixture should not be completely blitzed – it needs to be quite creamy but with a bit of texture. Stir in the oats and mix with a spoon to integrate.
5 Form into sausages and let them chill in the fridge for 20-30 minutes.
6 Roll gently in a little flour to coat.
7 Heat 2-3 tbsp oil in the non-stick frying pan/wok and fry the sausages gently until golden on all sides. Keep them warm in a low oven if necessary.

Smoky Mexican Mushroom Stroganoff

If you haven't discovered the joys of chipotle chillies, now's the time. This dish is rich, creamy and taste-dazzling. It needs little by way of accompaniment other than a cooked grain and a green salad.

✻ can be made in around half an hour if you use quinoa or long grain brown rice and put the grains on to cook first. The stroganoff itself is quick to make

⚘ easily halved or quartered to serve two or one. Use leftover silken tofu to make smoothies or vegan mayo

gf use gluten-free stock cubes/bouillon

- 200g/7oz brown rice OR quinoa OR mixed grains (see box below)
- 1 tsp bouillon powder or Green Oxo cube
- 1 tbsp vegan margarine
- 1 tbsp olive oil
- 1 large red onion, halved, peeled and thinly sliced
- 1 chipotle chilli (reduce this to half if you are very intolerant to hot food and increase the smoked paprika by at least ½ tsp)

- 1 tsp smoked paprika
- 1 batch of Sour Cream, page 35, OR 1 tub vegan cream cheese such as Sheese, Tesco or Tofutti mixed with 5 tbsp plain vegan yoghurt
- 2 tbsp white wine
- 700g/generous 1½lbs large mushrooms – chestnut are very good – sliced
- 1 bunch chives, chopped into small pieces with scissors. Reserve about a tablespoon for garnish
- Salt

1 Put the grains on to cook with bouillon/Green Oxo. Brown rice takes 25-30 minutes as will the mixed grains, quinoa about 20.

2 Meanwhile, make the stroganoff.

3 Using scissors, cut the stalk from the chipotle. Soak in just-boiled water, cover and set aside for at least 10 minutes. Snip off the bottom – the thick, woody bit – and scrape out the seeds. They are very hot, so throw them away!

4 Now cut remaining chilli into very small pieces with scissors.

5 In a large frying pan, wok or heavy-bottomed large saucepan, heat margarine until melted. Add olive oil and fry onion and chipotle pieces until onion is soft and translucent. Add smoked paprika and fry in, stirring well.

6 Add mushrooms and coat with the oil mixture. Sauté until golden brown. Add white wine.

7 Sauté on a low heat until mushrooms are tender, stirring occasionally. Add 1-2 tbsp water if they start to dry up.

8 Add sour cream and chives just before serving, stirring in well. Taste and season if necessary.

9 Serve with the rice and garnish with remaining chives.

ALL KITTED OUT

- Kettle of hot water
- Medium saucepan with lid
- Scissors
- Measuring jug
- Measuring spoons
- Chopping board
- Knife
- Large frying pan, wok or large, heavy-bottomed saucepan
- Wooden spoon

COOL COMBOS

- Martin's Classic Chilli, page 184
- Quinoa Pilaf, page 124
- Maca Mayo minus chives, page 148 – to replace the Sour Cream
- Green Salad of your choice with a light dressing if using as a main course

- Chipotles have a hot, deep and smoky taste that is unique. They can be bought from larger branches of Tesco or from a good deli. Otherwise hunt online for Mexican food specialists. Failing all else, try using a fresh, de-seeded red chilli with extra smoked paprika
- Serve with one of these – check the packet instructions or see pages 24-25 (Wholegrain Know-how):
  - Quinoa
  - Brown long grain rice
  - Mixed grains – those packs of mixed brown and wild rice for example, which look lovely and taste good too – preferably a quick-cook type

easily halved or quartered
gf wf use a gluten-free grain such as rice or quinoa and use plain tofu; if using smoked tofu, check it isn't flavoured with a wheat-based soya sauce

Smoky Stuffed Cabbage Leaves with Miso Tahini Sauce

Main dish
- 100g/3oz dried wholegrains OR 220g/8oz cooked: choose from
  - brown rice
  - quinoa
  - barley
  - wild rice or mixed grain combos
  - cooked grains can also be bought in sachets, eg Merchant Gourmet and Sainsbury's
- 4 large cabbage leaves – the large, central veins removed with a sharp knife
- 2 tbsp olive oil
- 1 medium-large onion, chopped
- 2 cloves garlic, crushed or chopped
- 1 pepper, any colour, chopped
- 1 medium carrot, grated
- 1 pack smoked tofu, diced
- 1 tsp smoked paprika

Miso tahini sauce
- 200ml/7fl oz water
- Generous 5 tbsp light miso
- Generous 5 tbsp tahini
- 2 tbsp rice vinegar OR 1 tbsp cider vinegar mixed with 1 tbsp water
- 1 small clove garlic, crushed
- Pinch of dried tarragon

1 Put grains on to cook if not already prepared.

2 Steam cabbage leaves for 12-15 minutes, or until tender. Remove from heat and set aside.

3 Pre-heat oven to 200°C/400°F/Gas Mark 6.

4 Heat olive oil and sauté onion until translucent. Add garlic and pepper slices – cook until starting to soften. Add carrot, smoked tofu and smoked paprika. Stir in the cooked grains and heat through thoroughly.

5 Spread out each cabbage leaf. Divide the cooked grain and smoked tofu mixture into four portions. Fold each leaf carefully and place on baking tray with the seam underneath.

6 Heat through in the oven for 5-10 minutes.

7 Serve with the sauce – make it while the stuffed leaves are baking.

8 Combine all sauce ingredients and blend or whisk until smooth. Heat gently in a small pan – don't let it boil. Add a little water if necessary as tahini thickens when heated.

9 Serve the hot stuffed rolls with sauce on the side or drizzled over.

ALL KITTED OUT
- Scales or pre-measured cooked grains if cooking from scratch
- Kettle
- Steamer
- Saucepan for grains if necessary
- Small saucepan
- Whisk or hand blender
- Wooden spoon
- Serving spoons
- Measuring spoons
- Chopping board and knife
- Garlic crusher
- Baking pan or oven-proof dish

COOL COMBOS
- Spinach Citron, page 116
- Cheesy Sauce I or II, pages 139-140 – instead of the Miso Tahini sauce

Socca Pizza with Cream Cheese, Sundried Tomatoes & Artichoke Hearts

Nothing to do with football… rather, it is a cross between a pizza and a crêpe. Made from gram flour (chickpea flour), Socca is traditional street food from Nice and there is a similar dish from Genoa called Farinata. We have given it a modern twist.

omit artichoke hearts and substitute red pepper | easily halved or quartered to serve two or one
gf wf ● use gluten-free baking powder such as Dove's Farm ● use gluten-free stock cube or bouillon ● Tofutti and Sheese cream cheese are gluten-free, as are chickpea flour and Fry-Lite spray

Socca batter

- 100g/4oz chickpea flour (also sold as gram or besan flour), available from large supermarkets, health food shops, delis and ethnic grocers
- 1 tsp vegan bouillon powder or crumbled stock cube
- ½ tsp freshly ground black pepper
- ½ tsp baking powder
- 250ml/9fl oz warm water
- 3 tbsp virgin olive oil
- ½ tsp dried mixed herbs or any Mediterranean herbs of your choice such as oregano, rosemary or thyme
- Low-cal spray

Topping

- 125g – half a tub – of vegan cream cheese (eg Tofutti or Sheese), any flavour – or home-made recipe, page 34
- 1 medium onion, finely chopped
- 6 sundried tomatoes, chopped in pieces with scissors (use the ready-to eat variety)
- 4 artichoke hearts, halved – from a tin, jar or defrosted from frozen

1 Sift chickpea flour into a large mixing bowl and add bouillon powder/crumbled stock cube, pepper and baking powder. Don't omit the sifting process as gram flour is often lumpy.

2 Pour in water gradually, whisking well to avoid lumps.

3 Slowly mix in 2 tbsp olive oil and mix thoroughly until a runny batter has formed.

4 Add rosemary and any of the herb options.

5 Cover and set aside while the oven heats up. It's even better if you can prepare the batter a few hours beforehand or overnight.

6 Preheat the oven to 220°C/430°F/Gas Mark 7-8.

7 Pour batter into pizza dish or baking tray, squirted with a little oil spray.

8 Cook for 7 minutes.

9 Remove from oven and drizzle on the remaining tablespoon of oil. Spoon on small dollops of cream cheese and scatter the other ingredients evenly across the socca.

10 Return to the oven for about 5 minutes, making sure the edges don't burn. Serve hot and eat immediately.

ALL KITTED OUT

- 28cm/11 inch long shallow baking tray or a medium pizza pan, preferably non-stick – the batter should spread quite thinly. If using a pizza pan, ensure it has no holes!
- Scales
- Measuring spoons
- Measuring jug
- Sieve
- Large mixing bowl
- Whisk
- Wooden spoon
- Knife or pizza cutter to serve from the baking tray

COOL COMBOS

- Sautéed Squash with Olive Tapenade & Cannellini Beans, page 114
- Avocado, Fresh Tomato, Garlic & Basil Sauce with Pasta, page 168
- Cauliflower & Flageolet Bean Antipasto (Chilled Marinated Salad), page 76
- Marinated Mushroom Salad, page 83

gf wf use GF stock
replace oil and margarine with oil spray

Spanish Chickpea & Potato Stew

Serve this simple, aromatic stew with a big green salad or lightly steamed greens such as kale or cabbage – plus hunks of bread.

Note – the flavour and thick gravy depend on the release of starch from the potatoes. To achieve this, cut long potato slices then snap them in half as uneven surfaces release starch more effectively. Similarly, grating the tomato adds to thickness and flavour and removes the need to skin it.

- 4 medium-large potatoes – partly cut, partly broken
- 1 small potato, grated and set aside separately
- 1 large ripe tomato, beefsteak type
- 1 large onion, chopped
- 2 large cloves garlic
- 1½ tins chickpeas, drained and rinsed
- 1 tbsp olive oil
- 2 tsp vegan margarine
- Sea salt and freshly ground black pepper

- 1 tbsp fresh or freeze-dried parsley
- 2 level tsp paprika – plain or smoked
- Small glass of red wine
- 1 Green Oxo or 1-2 tsp vegan bouillon such as Marigold red or purple tub
- 1 tbsp tomato purée

Optional vegetables: peppers, courgettes, celery or green beans would all work well individually or together

Other options: chunks of Spicy Seitan Sausage (page 44) or a bought vegan spicy sausage, eg V-Bites Chorizo, Sheese Deli or Vegusto

1 Heat a little olive oil and soften onions and garlic. Add margarine and wine. Add parsley, salt and pepper.

2 Grate tomato into the mixture and add paprika, plus a little water to prevent burning. Cook for a couple of minutes.

3 Add chickpeas and large sliced potatoes, stock cube/bouillon powder, tomato purée, optional vegetables and enough water to cover. Simmer for about 45 minutes then grate the small potato into the stew to help thicken gravy.

4 Cook for another half hour, until cooked and gravy is nice and thick. Alternatively, leave to cook for about 8 hours on lowest setting of a slow crockpot.

5 Serve with fresh crusty bread. This stew is even better cooked the day before you need it, giving flavours plenty of time to develop.

ALL KITTED OUT

- Chopping board
- Knife
- Garlic press
- Measuring spoons
- Grater
- Tin opener
- Medium-large slow cooker/ crockpot or ordinary, heavy-bottomed saucepan with lid

£ ✎ ⓥ gf wf ☺

easily halved or quartered to serve two or one
gf use GF flour. Tofutti and Sheese cream cheese are gluten-free
wf use WF (eg spelt) or GF flour

Speedy Pizza

This is a really easy way to make pizza – it's a bit like a scone base rather than the traditional bread dough variety.

Pizza scone base

- 250g/9oz self-raising flour (we used white but experiment with half and half wholemeal self-raising and white if you want more of a wholefood taste)
- 3 tbsp olive oil
- ¾ tsp salt
- 100ml/3fl oz water plus a little more if necessary

Topping

- 100ml/3fl oz tomato purée OR tomato-based pasta sauce
- ½ tub Tofutti or Sheese plain vegan cream cheese
- 1 small red onion, sliced very fine
- ½ a small red pepper, sliced thinly
- 50g/scant 2oz mushrooms (about 5-6 medium mushrooms)
- 1½ tsp dried mixed herbs (or use ½-1 tsp rosemary)
- 100g/3oz melting vegan cheese. See page 17
- Salt and black pepper
- Olive oil to drizzle over the top

Options: replace the mushrooms or pepper pieces with halved artichoke hearts or olives

1 Preheat the oven to 230°C/450°F/Gas Mark 8.
2 In a bowl, sieve flour and salt and add oil. Mix in water gradually and knead until all the flour is incorporated. You may need to add more water, a teaspoon at a time, if necessary.
3 Roll pizza dough out thinly on a lightly floured surface. You can make it square and put on a large non-stick baking sheet or use a pizza base – the large ones with holes are good.
4 Bake in the oven for 5 minutes.
5 Remove from oven. Spread tomato purée or pasta sauce evenly on the base, then top with cream cheese.
6 Spread onion, red pepper and mushroom pieces evenly across pizza.
7 Sprinkle herbs and vegan cheese over everything, plus a little salt and lots of black pepper.
8 Return to oven and bake for 10-15 minutes, checking after 10. Vegetables should be just cooked. Drizzle with a little olive oil and serve hot.

ALL KITTED OUT

- Chopping board
- Knife
- Scales
- Measuring spoons
- Measuring jug
- Sieve
- Mixing bowl
- Pizza baking sheet or rectangular non-stick baking sheet
- Rubber spatula or similar to spread tomato sauce on pizza base

COOL COMBOS

- Oven-roasted Tofu Mediterranean, page 195
- Italian Olive Dip, page 119
- Cauliflower & Flageolet Bean Antipasto (Chilled Marinated Salad), page 76

If you have a favourite yeasted pizza dough recipe, use that instead. Make it by hand – or use the dough programme on a bread maker. Roll out dough on to a pizza pan and bake with the topping – no need to pre-bake the base.
  Alternatively, use a ready-made vegan pizza base, eg Waitrose stone-baked pizza bases, Napolina, Sainsbury's Italian Pizza Base Twinpack or Thin & Crispy Twin Pizza Base or Jus-Rol Bake It Fresh Pizza. There are also gluten-free bases but check labels – some contain milk or egg derivatives so ask customer services if you're not sure. If the packet says 'may contain…' this information is for allergy sufferers not vegans.

reduce quantities to suit your appetite. Store the rest of the taco shells in an airtight container for future meals

gf wf Discovery and Old El Paso taco shells are gluten-free. Most tomato salsa is GF but check the label | go easy on the chilli

Time-is-Tight Tacos

- 4-8 taco shells (Discovery and Old El Paso brands are vegan)
- 1 tin pinto or kidney beans, rinsed, drained and slightly mashed
- 115ml/4fl oz ready-made tomato salsa (available in jars or fresh in tubs)
- 1 red pepper, finely diced
- ¼-½ tsp chilli powder, according to taste (or use a dash of Tabasco/hot pepper sauce)

- 1 small clove garlic, crushed
- 1 tsp ground cumin
- 1 avocado, peeled and chopped into chunks
- 1 large tomato, chopped into small pieces
- 1 tbsp fresh lime juice
- Green leaves of your choice, finely shredded – approximately one small handful per person. A mixture of rocket, cos and lamb's lettuce or similar is nice

1 Pre-heat the oven to 200°C/400°F/Gas Mark 6.

2 Warm taco shells in the oven for 5-10 minutes.

3 Meanwhile, mix all ingredients together except for taco shells and leaves.

4 Divide mixture into four and place inside taco shells – if there is too much, place the shells on top of the extra.

5 Decorate with shredded leaves round the edges.

ALL KITTED OUT

- Baking tray
- Chopping board
- Knife
- Measuring spoons
- Garlic crusher
- Tin opener

COOL COMBOS

- Mango Salsa, page 82
- Ready-cooked rice or quinoa - home-made or from a pouch, eg Tesco, Sainsbury's, Merchant Gourmet etc

much cheaper than commercial tofu burgers
easily halved or quartered to serve two or one. Alternatively, make the whole recipe and freeze some | **gf** use GF oats and tamari soya sauce
reduce oil for frying onion mixture to 1 tsp and fry the burgers in oil spray

Tofu Burgerettes

These are simple to make and delicious (and you can of course make them bigger!)

- 1 tbsp olive oil
- 1 medium onion, finely chopped
- 1 clove garlic, crushed
- 225g/8oz firm plain tofu
- 3 tbsp oats – jumbo is best but porridge will work
- 2 tbsp gram flour – also known as chickpea or besan flour – available from big supermarkets, ethnic food shops or health food shops

- 1-2 tbsp shoyu or tamari soya sauce. Start with 1 tbsp and taste mixture first
- 1 tsp paprika
- 1 tsp mixed herbs
- ½ tsp allspice
- Plain oil or oil spray to fry burgers

1 In a medium saucepan, heat oil and sauté onion and garlic until onion is translucent.
2 Turn off heat, place onion mixture into a bowl, add tofu and mash mixture with a potato masher until soft.
3 Add all other ingredients except for frying oil.
4 Mix in until everything is thoroughly integrated.
5 Divide the mixture into 8 and make burgers – use a cookie cutter or the lid of a small jar.
6 If you have time, chill burgers for about 30 minutes to make cooking easier.
7 In a frying pan – preferably non-stick – heat oil or spray. Gently fry burgers for a few minutes until golden brown on each side.

ALL KITTED OUT

- Scissors
- Chopping board
- Knife
- Mixing bowl
- Frying pan, preferably non-stick
- Medium bowl
- Fork or potato masher
- Fish slice or spatula
- Burger press if using

COOL COMBOS

- Carrot & Beetroot Slaw, page 80
- Celeriac & Seed Slaw, page 79
- Herby Potato Salad, page 84
- Lentil & Tomato Soup, page 56
- Potato Salad with Creamy Wholegrain Mustard Dressing, page 85
- Serve in a roll or pitta bread with salad, vegan mayo and other things such as:
  - Sweet chilli sauce, English or Dijon mustard, tomato ketchup, pickle, tomato salsa

A simple burger press makes regular-sized burgers. They cost about a fiver from good kitchen or hardware stores. It's a great investment if you make a lot of bean/tofu burgers as they compress and firm up the mixture, making cooking (and freezing) easier.

easily halved or quartered to serve two or one
gf wf use tamari soya sauce
replace oil with oil spray

Tofu Frittata with Curly Kale

This delicious and easy frittata uses protein and calcium-packed tofu instead of the traditional eggs. Not only does it taste good but using tofu means it is cholesterol-free and the entire recipe is low-fat and healthy. Try adding a handful or two of chopped, cooked potatoes if you have leftovers.

This works with lots of sides but we particularly liked baked or microwaved sweet potato wedges and a soya yoghurt dip on the side – which can all be prepared while the frittata is baking.

- 1 tbsp olive oil or 3 squirts oil spray
- 6 cloves garlic, roughly chopped or crushed
- 1 bunch of Swiss chard – any colour, chopped with woody parts of stem removed
  OR 1 bag ready-chopped curly kale
- 2 tsp dried oregano
- 400-450g/14oz-1lb firm tofu
- 1 tbsp soya sauce
- 1 tbsp Dijon mustard
- ¼ tsp turmeric

- ½ cup nutritional yeast flakes (see page 17)
- 1 tbsp cornflour mixed with a little cold water to a smooth paste
- 1 tbsp flax meal (ground flaxseeds) mixed with 2 tbsp hot water and left for 5 minutes
- Freshly ground black pepper
- Salt to taste

Optional:
- ¼ tsp allspice
- ½ tsp paprika
- 1 pinch mild chilli powder

1 Pre-heat oven to 200°C/400°F/Gas Mark 6. Lightly oil a good non-stick 20cm/8 inch shallow cake tin – round or square.

2 Unwrap tofu and place it in a colander over the sink. Press as much water out as possible and set aside.

3 Meanwhile, heat a wok or heavy-bottomed large pan over a medium heat. Add olive oil/spray and gently sauté the garlic for a minute or two, stirring so it doesn't burn. Add a tiny splash of water or two if it begins to stick.

4 Turn up heat and add the greens and oregano. Cook for 3-5 minutes, or until the greens are wilted – if using kale, make sure it is tender. Add a splash of water if it starts to dry out.

5 Now make the frittata base. Crumble tofu so that it looks like cottage or ricotta cheese. Add rest of the ingredients and stir in well.

6 Add tofu mixture to cooked greens and mix together well. Keep it dry. Taste and season as necessary.

7 Press mixture firmly into the greased cake tin, using something heavy to press it down.

8 Bake for 20 minutes or until lightly browned. Cool for 3 minutes before turning upside down carefully on a plate. Cut into slices and serve.

ALL KITTED OUT

- 20cm/8 inch cake tin, preferably springform or with a removable base
- Colander
- Kitchen paper or clean tea towel
- Wok or large frying pan
- Measuring spoons
- Spatula
- Garlic crusher
- Bowl
- Plate to weigh down tofu
- Weights (from scales or tins of food) to go on top of plate

COOL COMBOS

- Quinoa Pilaf, page 124
- Mixed Rooty Mash, page 108
- Mash with Cumin Seeds & Yoghurt, page 107
- Plain vegan yoghurt (eg Alpro/Provamel)
- Hot pitta bread
- Rice – brown or white
- Roasted butternut squash or sweet potatoes
- Mash with olive oil and fresh herbs
- Sour Cream, page 35

Tony's Leek & Almond Pie

This delicious creamy pie is very easy to make and looks lovely, too. Thanks to Tony Wardle – Viva!'s Associate Director and super-cook – for the recipe!

- 3 medium-large leeks, cut lengthways and then sliced into 2cm/1 inch long pieces
- 2 tbsp olive oil
- 2 medium onions, cut in half lengthways then sliced thinly
- 2 cloves garlic, crushed
- Oil spray or a little oil
- 1 sheet of ready-rolled vegan shortcrust pastry (eg Jus-Rol or Sainsbury's)

- 4 heaped tbsp nutritional yeast flakes (see page 17)
- 25g/1oz ground almonds
- A pinch of ground nutmeg
- Soya cream, ½ carton (125ml/generous 4fl oz) – Alpro or Provamel brand
- ½ tsp salt
- Lots of black pepper
- 2-4 tbsp flaked almonds

ALL KITTED OUT

- Chopping board
- Knife
- Large bowl to wash leeks
- Colander to drain them
- Garlic crusher
- 1 large wok or deep frying pan
- Wooden spoon
- 1 metal or ceramic baking dish, preferably non-stick – about 22cm/9 inch square and 3cm/1½ inch deep
- Baking parchment/ greaseproof paper
- Fork
- Baking beans or a small handful of any dried beans
- Measuring spoons
- Scales
- Knife
- Fish slice

COOL COMBOS

- Spinach Citron, page 116
- Tomato salad with red onion, fresh basil and a drizzle of vinaigrette

1 Preheat oven to 200°C/400°F/Gas Mark 6 – about 10-15 degrees less if fan-assisted.

2 Soak leeks in a bowl of cold water for a few minutes. Shake vigorously to get rid of grit, rinse and drain in a colander. Set aside.

3 Heat olive oil and sweat onions and garlic for 2-3 minutes, until onions start to soften. Add leeks and continue to cook gently until soft enough to eat – 5-10 minutes. Add a small splash of water if they start to stick and stir occasionally.

4 Meanwhile, grease oven dish with oil spray or a little oil and gently place the sheet of pastry into dish, distributing evenly. Trim off top edges with a knife. Pierce pastry base a few times with a fork and cover the dish with baking parchment so it bakes evenly. Scatter baking beans over the parchment to weight it down evenly if possible.

5 Cook the pastry in the hot oven for 10 minutes. This is called 'blind baking' and it prevents the pastry base from going soggy. Remove from oven and set aside.

6 Reduce the oven temperature to 190°C/375°F/Gas Mark 5 (10-15 degrees less if fan-assisted).

7 Add yeast flakes, ground almonds, nutmeg, salt and pepper to onion/leek mix. Stir in soya cream and mix well. Taste and adjust seasoning as necessary.

8 Spoon filling into pastry dish and distribute evenly. Scatter flaked almonds over top and bake for 15-20 minutes. Check after 15 minutes to ensure almonds are not burning. They should be a light golden brown.

9 Serve hot or warm.

gf wf use GF pasta and check pesto ingredients

Tony's Sundried Tomato & Asparagus Pasta with Pesto

Another one from Tony W – this simple and superb recipe has been a mainstay at the Incredible Vegan Roadshows for years! It works well as a salad, too.

- 50g/scant 2oz sundried tomatoes, chopped into small pieces with scissors. Prepare according to type:
  - original dried – soak in hot water
  - in oil – need no soaking but reduce amount of olive oil in the recipe
- 1 bunch asparagus
- 250g/8oz fusilli or penne pasta (about half a regular pack)
- 2 tbsp extra virgin olive oil

- 4 garlic cloves, finely chopped but not crushed
- Half a jar vegan pesto, eg Meridian or Zest
- Handful of finely chopped fresh coriander OR 1 tsp dried herbs such as basil or oregano
- Freshly ground black pepper
- Salt

1 Boil two kettles of hot water – most of this is to cook the pasta.
2 Prepare sundried tomatoes as stated and set aside.
3 Snap off woody ends of asparagus and chop remainder into 2cm/1 inch pieces and steam until just tender – keep an eye on it as it only needs a few minutes.
4 Cook pasta in a pan of boiling water for 10 minutes or according to packet instructions/personal taste.
5 Meanwhile, heat the olive oil, add chopped garlic and fry gently until lightly browned. Set aside.
6 Drain pasta and mix in the cooked asparagus pieces.
7 Add cooked garlic, vegan pesto and herbs.
8 Add sundried tomato pieces to pasta mixture. Any soaking water can be kept and used for stock or soup.
9 Add salt and lots of freshly ground black pepper.

ALL KITTED OUT

- Kettle
- Jug or bowl to soak sundried tomatoes
- Lid or plate to cover
- Saucepan
- Measuring spoons
- Chopping board
- Knife
- Colander
- Scissors

COOL COMBOS

- Socca Pizza, page 211
- Oven-roasted Tofu Mediterranean, page 195

Vegan Chick'n Caesar Salad

A vegan variation on a North American classic – the tangy, creamy Caesar dressing is addictive! It goes down well with meat-eaters and just about everyone else. If you haven't come across vegan 'chicken', give it a go, it's really good. If you don't like faux meat products, use smoked tofu instead.

Caesar salad dressing

- 5 tbsp vegan mayo
- 2 tbsp soya or rice milk
- 1 tbsp lemon juice
- 1 clove garlic, crushed
- 2 tsp tahini
- Salt and pepper, to taste
- 1 tsp Dijon mustard
- 1 tsp capers
- 1 tbsp olive oil
- 1 tbsp finely chopped fresh parsley
- 1 tbsp olive oil

Faux chicken: choose from ONE of these

- 1 pack VBites Vegideli Chicken-style Pieces (ready to eat)
- half a pack of Realeat's Meat-free Chicken-style Pieces OR Fry's Vegetarian Chicken-style Strips. Each variety needs to be fried quickly first – just follow the packet instructions
- 1 pack smoked tofu, cut into strips and lightly fried
- 200g home-made seitan pieces, lightly fried, page 43
- 1 tbsp vinaigrette dressing – bought or home-made
- Salt and pepper, to taste
- 1 cos lettuce, shredded – or other leaves of your choice
- 1 tbsp chopped parsley
- 4 spring onions, sliced, including the greens
- 4 tbsp croutons – if using shop-bought, check they are vegan. Some are, some aren't

1 Make Caesar Salad dressing by mixing all its ingredients together. Refrigerate in the jar until needed.
2 If using 'chicken' strips, seitan or tofu, cook them: heat olive oil in frying pan and sauté over a medium heat until golden brown.
3 If using VBites Pieces, go to no. 4.
4 Add vinaigrette, salt and pepper. Mix well, remove from heat and set aside.
5 Mix lettuce in with the Caesar Salad dressing. Add 'chicken' strips and mix in parsley and spring onions.
6 Top with the croutons and serve.

ALL KITTED OUT

- Chopping board
- Knife
- Measuring spoons
- Jar or other container with well-fitting lid
- Garlic crusher
- Frying pan
- Spatula
- Serving bowl

COOL COMBOS

- Tofu Burgerettes, page 219
- Big Mushroom Burger, page 89
- Muffaletta Stuffed Loaf with a Choice of Two Fillings, page 92
- Smoky Black Bean Cakes, page 204
- Celeriac & Seed Slaw, page 79

use a proper deep-fat fryer for speed!
gf gluten-free self-raising flour option and use tamari in the dip
wf use WF flour and tamari

Vegetable Tempura

This is based on a traditional Japanese dish and is fantastic as an occasional treat. If you've got a deep fat fryer it makes the dish extra simple and quick to make. It can also be made using mushrooms only – in that case, serve them with garlic mayo. Add 1-2 cloves of crushed garlic to bought vegan mayo or add to our Easy Mayo recipe (page 143).

Batter

- 180g/6oz fine wholemeal self-raising flour or gluten-free equivalent
- 180g/6oz gram flour (also known as chickpea or besan flour)
- 275ml/10fl oz water – sparkling mineral water works particularly well
- Pinch salt

Vegetables to fry

- Main course: 8-10 pieces of assorted vegetables per person
- Starter: 4-5 pieces per person

- Use a mixture of vegetables: mushrooms, red pepper rings, onion rings, carrot pieces (thin, cut on diagonal) and cauliflower all work well, as do plain tofu chunks
- To fry – fresh plain vegetable oil

If using a deep-fat fryer, follow manufacturer's instructions

If not, use a deep pan and fill ⅓ with oil – use at least 1.5L oil

Dip

Mix together:

- 2 tbsp soya sauce – shoyu or tamari
- 2 tbsp cold water
- ½ tsp grated root ginger

ALL KITTED OUT

- Chopping board
- Knife
- Scales
- Measuring spoons
- Whisk or hand blender
- Mixing bowl
- Deep-fat fryer or large saucepan
- Chip basket or slotted spoon
- Toothpick or small sharp knife
- Oven tray
- Kitchen paper
- Grater
- Small bowl for dip

COOL COMBOS

- Joe's Chestnut Rice, page 123
- Butternut Squash with Garlic-thyme Aduki Beans, page 172
- Oven-roasted Tofu Mediterranean, page 195

1 Sieve the flours into a large bowl. Make a well and add water gradually, using a balloon whisk or stick blender to ensure there are no lumps. Set batter aside.

2 Prepare vegetables. Pieces need to be small enough to cook quickly in the batter but not so small or thin that they disintegrate – a piece of cauliflower should be about 3cm/1½ inches wide at the 'flower' part.

3 Pre-heat oven to a medium-low heat (160°C/325°F/Gas Mark 3). Have an oven tray ready, lined with kitchen paper.

4 Heat oil and do the batter test: drop in a little dollop of batter and if it floats, the oil is hot enough, if it sinks it isn't. Quickly make the dip while oil is heating. Set aside.

5 Fry vegetables in batches of eight pieces. Dip in the batter, making sure all are coated. Give a quick shake to get rid of any excess and, using the basket/slotted spoon, place carefully into the hot oil.

6 Fry each batch, tossing gently to ensure the pieces don't stick together. Fry until golden brown – use a toothpick or knife to test if vegetables are tender – carrots will take longer than mushrooms.

7 Drain and transfer vegetables to oven tray – use a chip basket or slotted spoon. Place in oven and repeat the process, making sure the oil stays hot enough during the cooking process – if it loses heat the tempura will be soggy. Do the batter test again to ensure it is hot! You may need to skim the surface of the oil to remove bits of cooked batter.

8 Serve hot with the dip and other dishes of your choice.

Viva!'s Green & Wild Tahini Noodles

This is a nutritional knock-out – tasty too. Make it as raw or cooked as you want – we offer both alternatives. For a hot/warm version, prepare sauce and vegetables before noodles are cooked. For a cold dish, follow the instructions to the right.

half or quarter the quantities to serve two or one
gf wf use rice or other gluten-free noodles, use tamari and use only plain or home-cooked tofu pieces (the bought marinated pieces contain wheat)
for those kids who like greens

- 225g/8oz wholemeal spaghetti OR other noodles, eg rice or soba
- 2 large carrots, grated on the big holes
- 2 handfuls of finely shredded dark green leafy vegetables. Use cabbage, curly kale, chard – even shredded Brussels sprouts work well. Remove the big central vein from cabbage-type greens before shredding.
- 1 head of broccoli, cut into very small florets
- Handful of fresh mint, chopped – or coriander or fresh basil if you wish
- 4 tbsp toasted sesame seeds plus more mint for garnish

Tahini sauce

- 4-5 tbsp tahini

- 2 tbsp tamari or shoyu soya sauce
- 3 tbsp water
- 1 tbsp brown sugar or agave syrup
- 1 tbsp rice vinegar or 2 tsp cider vinegar
- 1 tsp hot chilli sauce or 1 chopped fresh chilli, seeds removed
- 1 tsp Dijon mustard
- Fresh black pepper
- 1 pinch salt, if needed

Optional extras

- Ready-made marinated tofu pieces (eg Cauldron) OR plain tofu, cubed and fried
- Chopped red pepper
- Shredded rocket or other dark green salad leaves
- Lime or lemon wedges

1 Boil the kettle and cook noodles in boiling water according to packet instructions. You can eat the dish warm – see text under picture.
2 If eating cold, cook noodles then rinse under cold water. Drain and set aside, coating lightly with oil to prevent noodles from sticking – can be done in advance.
3 While noodles are cooking, toast sesame seeds. Heat a dry wok or frying pan, add seeds and stir continuously to prevent burning. Keep stirring until they stop 'popping' ensuring they don't catch. Remove from heat and set aside.
4 Chop broccoli into small florets the size of small grapes.
5 If you want to steam the broccoli and cabbage for a couple of minutes, do so now – otherwise set aside.
6 Toss all vegetables together and add noodles.
7 Make tahini sauce by putting the dressing/sauce ingredients in a jug or bowl and mixing with a fork or whisk. Taste and adjust seasoning if necessary.
8 Add sauce to the noodles and vegetables. Toss, coating everything evenly.
9 Add chopped herbs and any optional extras you choose.
10 If using lime or lemon wedges, squeeze one over each portion.
11 Garnish with more mint and sesame seeds.

COOL COMBOS

- Edamame Fuji, page 100
- Marinated Mushroom Salad, page 83
- Chinese Red Bean Burgers, page 179

use frozen spinach | use GF stock cubes/bouillon
omit chilli/cayenne
use oil spray and sundried tomatoes in a packet (ie not in oil). If you can only get the type in oil, rinse off and reduce oil/oil spray in recipe

Viva!'s Very Moorish Moroccan Stew

We couldn't leave this recipe out as it's a relatively new dish from our Incredible Vegan Roadshows which is extremely popular – and no wonder, it has a gorgeous, deeply-spiced and fragrant taste.

- 12 sundried tomatoes, chopped into pieces with scissors (see note above)
- 1L hot vegan stock, made with a veggie stock cube or 3 tsp Marigold red tub bouillon powder
- 2 tbsp extra-virgin olive oil (plus more for garnish if desired) OR oil spray
- 1 large onion, medium chopped
- 6 cloves garlic, crushed
- 2 tsp ground cinnamon
- 2 tsp ground cumin

- ¼ tsp cayenne pepper or chilli
- 2 heaped tsp paprika
- 1 tin (400g) plum or chopped tomatoes
- 2 tins (400g each) chickpeas, drained and rinsed well
- 2 tbsp raisins
- 140g/5oz washed baby spinach (or use a few lumps of frozen spinach)
- Salt and black pepper
- Fresh coriander, chopped – 2-3 tbsp

1 Soak sundried tomato pieces in a quarter of the hot stock and set aside. If using the type in oil, go to step 2.
2 Heat olive oil/spray in a large pot over medium-high heat.
3 Add onion and sauté until it begins to turn translucent. Add a little water/stock if it starts to stick.
4 Add garlic to the onions and lower heat if it starts to brown.
5 Add cinnamon, cumin, cayenne and paprika and sauté for a minute or so.
6 Add tinned tomatoes, chickpeas, sundried tomatoes, raisins and stock.
7 Stir well. If using whole plum tomatoes, chop up in the pan with a knife.
8 Chickpeas should be slightly covered with liquid. If too low, add water to bring it just above the chickpeas.
9 Bring mixture to boil, reduce heat and gently simmer for 30-40 minutes.
10 Remove stew from heat. Use a potato masher to mash some of the chickpeas in the pot – or put about a third of the stew in a bowl and mash with a hand blender. Return to the pan.
11 Stir in spinach and heat through until wilted or melted (if using frozen) – a few minutes. Adjust seasoning.

Sweet thing

Yes, you can have your cake and eat it. Not to mention cookies, ice cream and many other delights. Long gone are the days when a fresh but worthy fruit salad or fruit crumble was the only vegan dessert on offer. We hope you enjoy these recipes – and if your local eaterie is lagging behind the times, feel free to wave these recipes under the owner's nose!

Baking tips

Some like it hot

Unless you are familiar with your oven's variations, think about spending a fiver or so on an oven thermometer. They save wasted time and money – some ovens are too cool, others too hot. Try a good hardware or kitchen shop, department store or online store, eg Lakeland.

Well-oiled

Most cakes work well made with oil – and oil is better for the environment and biodiversity than margarine (which usually contains palm oil). But a few tips…

- Oil doesn't work well in icing or pastry
- Mix the oil with other liquids rather than trying to cream it with dry ingredients
- Most cold-pressed oils are too strongly flavoured for baking. However, Clearspring Light Sunflower oil for frying is mild and less refined. Otherwise just use regular, cheap vegetable oil (refined rapeseed)
- If converting recipe from marg to oil… Oil is 100% fat whereas margarine is around 80% fat:20% water so adjust accordingly. Eg if a recipe calls for 100g marg, use 80ml oil and an extra tablespoon (tbsp) of water or plant milk. See the Sumptuous Sponge Cake page 252 and Magic Muffins page 251 for examples of how to use oil in a recipe

Gently does it – baking vegan-style

- Don't overmix. Unlike egg-based cakes, vegan baking doesn't need electric beaters! Just mix in gently and thoroughly
- Once you've got the liquids mixed in to the dry ingredients, tap the mixing bowl hard on the work surface to get rid of air bubbles. Pour the batter into the tin and tap hard again. This will ensure lighter cakes
- Now get the cake in the pre-heated oven immediately – that way the raising agents get to work properly
- Let the cake sit and cool properly before you decorate and/or slice
- Store at room temperature in an air-tight container, not the fridge

A bunch of flours

Use plain flour only (white and/or fine wholemeal) and add your own baking powder. This not only saves cupboard space and money but ensures that the raising agents work better in your cakes. Self-raising flour often loses its freshness over time. 150g/6oz/1 cup plain flour:2 tsp baking powder OR 110g/4oz:1½ tsp.

Gluten-free? Follow the same rule – either buy plain GF flour mix such as Doves Farm and add GF baking powder. Alternatively, make your own – it's not difficult. See **www.allrecipes.co.uk** and search for 'gluten-free baking and cooking'.

Eggsit eggs

Flax meal (ground up flaxseeds/linseeds) is one of several egg alternatives in vegan baking. Make it yourself or buy it in a pouch, eg Virginia Harvest brand. For more advice about egg alternatives, visit **www.veganrecipeclub.org.uk/replacing-eggs-vegan-baking-delicious-easy**.

SERVES 6-8 | 60 MINUTES: 10 MINUTES PREPARATION, 40-50 MINUTES BAKING TIME

freeze half of it for another time | use GF self-raising flour
use WF self-raising flour | this cake is relatively lower in fat and sugar than most

Banana Cake

Is it a loaf, is it a cake? You decide. Whatever, it's quick to whizz up – although you'll need to hang around while it cooks. Set your timer or mobile alarm and do useful things or put your feet up!

- 3 large, very ripe bananas
- 60g/2oz vegan margarine OR scant 50ml plain oil
- 100g/generous 3oz soft brown sugar
- 250g/9oz plain flour – preferably half white + half fine wholemeal. All white will work but isn't so nice
- 3½ tsp baking powder
- 1 tsp vanilla essence
- 5 tbsp soya milk or other non-dairy milk (4 tbsp if using oil instead of margarine)
- 2-3 tbsp chopped dates or other chopped fruit of your choice. NB Ready-chopped dates are on sale in larger supermarkets and many health food shops

Optional: chopped walnuts, pecans, Brazil nuts or sunflower seeds

1 Preheat oven to 180°C/350°F/Gas Mark 4 – about 10-15° lower if using a fan-assisted oven. Grease large non-stick loaf tin with oil spray or light coating of margarine/oil.
2 In a large bowl, mash bananas with a fork or potato masher. Add margarine if using and cream together well.
3 Add sugar and mix in well.
4 Sieve flour and baking powder, add banana mixture and stir well.
5 If using oil, mix it with the soya milk and vanilla essence. Stir liquid in to cake mix a little at a time, mixing well.
6 Add dried fruit and nuts/seeds if using.
7 Spoon batter into loaf tin and cook for 40-50 minutes until cooked through and golden brown on top. Test after 45 minutes, using a toothpick or sharp knife – it should come out clean if ready. If not, return to the oven for a further 5-10 minutes.
8 Leave to cool for a few minutes then turn out onto a wire rack and let it cool completely.

ALL KITTED OUT

- Large loaf tin, non-stick
- Scales
- Sieve
- Measuring spoons
- Large mixing bowl
- Smaller bowl to mash bananas etc
- Whisk
- Wooden spoon
- Rubber spatula

COOL COMBOS

- Blueberry Orange Sauce, page 284
- Dairy-free cream – see page 17-18
- Vegan ice cream – see page 18

Top Tip

Double the quantities and make two cakes – you can freeze one and it uses the oven more economically.

gf if GF biscuits used – see below
wf if WF biscuits used
❄ (without chocolate topping)

Boozy Chocolate Tiffin with Optional Chocolate Topping

This is very rich and even richer with the topping! It's essentially a fridge cake so there is little cooking involved.

- 225g/8oz vegan margarine. See page 18
- 75g/3oz natural unrefined brown sugar
- 3 tbsp date or golden syrup
- 5 tbsp cocoa powder
- 50g/2oz each of
  - dates or apricots, chopped finely (scissors are quickest)
  - glacé cherries, quartered
- 350g/12oz vegan biscuits, crushed*

- 30-45ml/2-3 tbsp whisky, rum or brandy

Optional chocolate topping
- 225g/8oz vegan chocolate – dairy-free milk or plain/dark. See page 19

* Digestives – Co-op own brand, Tesco Value or McVitie's Light (not regular)

Oat – ordinary HobNobs or supermarket own brand oat biscuits are usually vegan

GF – eg DS Digestives or Sunstart Golden Crunch

1 Crush biscuits by whizzing in a food processor until they turn into small crumbs. Alternatively, place in a clean plastic bag and batter enthusiastically with a rolling pin to break them up.
2 Put margarine, syrup, sugar and cocoa powder in saucepan and heat slowly until melted, stirring occasionally.
3 Stir in dates, cherries, biscuits and booze of choice.
4 Mix well then spoon into greased non-stick tin.
5 Level and put in fridge to chill for approximately 20 minutes. If not using chocolate topping, slice into fingers.
6 If using chocolate topping, melt chocolate in bowl over a pan of simmering water or in a microwave on low-medium setting. (Go carefully if using a microwave as the heat can burn chocolate if left in too long.)
7 When chocolate has melted, spread it over chilled biscuit base and refrigerate until just slightly soft – about 15 minutes. Cut into fingers then return to fridge to set completely – this helps to stop cracking.

f) use cheaper nuts and berries OR omit one or both altogether
gf) use GF flour and baking powder
wf) use WF flour

Chocolate Berry Cake

One of the best chocolate cakes ever! It's slightly squidgy in the middle and is lovely served warm, with ice cream…

- 55g/2oz hazelnuts or flaked almonds (omit if unsuitable). Buy ready-roasted nuts if possible
- 250g/9oz self-raising flour or see page 237
- 85g/3oz cocoa powder
- 3 tsp baking powder
- 250g/9oz caster sugar
- 1½ tsp vanilla extract
- 120ml/4fl oz mild-tasting plain oil
- 340ml/12fl oz soya milk – use 50ml less if you want a firmer cake
- 125g/4½oz frozen raspberries or frozen mixed berries (don't use fresh – they are too soft to bake)

Optional: extra roasted chopped hazelnuts or roasted flaked almonds to decorate

1 Grease a 20cm/8 inch loose-bottomed cake tin and line base with greaseproof paper.
2 Preheat oven to 180°C/350°F/Gas Mark 4 (reduce by 10-15 degrees if using a fan-assisted oven).
3 If using unroasted nuts, gently roast in a non-stick frying pan until golden brown. Cool, then – if using whole hazelnuts – chop into small chunks.
4 Sift flour, cocoa powder and baking powder into bowl. Mix in sugar, vanilla extract, oil and soya milk. Beat gently until everything is mixed to a thick batter and stir in berries – and nuts, if using. Tap the bowl hard once on the work surface.
5 Pour mixture into cake tin, tap firmly on the work surface then place in the oven immediately and bake for 35-40 minutes or until cooked. Test with a sharp knife or toothpick. The middle should be slightly gooey.
6 Decorate with flaked nuts if desired.
7 Allow to cool in the tin then transfer to a wire rack – or serve it warm. It is especially nice with dairy-free cream/ice cream or vanilla soya dessert.

ALL KITTED OUT

- Cake tin, 20cm/8 inch round springform with loose bottom
- Pencil/pen
- Scissors
- Greaseproof paper
- Measuring spoons
- Scales
- Sieve
- Large mixing bowl
- Hand whisk
- Small frying pan
- Wooden spatula
- Wooden spoon
- Sharp knife or toothpick
- Cooling rack (a clean one from a grill pan is fine)

4 tbsp apple sauce, eg a value brand in a jar

Chocolate Brownies

Topping
- 60g/2oz margarine
- 4 tbsp/60g cocoa powder
- 4 tbsp soya milk
- 160g/scant 6oz brown sugar
- 1 tsp vanilla essence

Batter
- 1 small banana, mashed well OR 1 small sweet potato OR 4 tbsp apple sauce
- 125g/4½oz white flour
- 2 tsp baking powder
- 4 tbsp cocoa powder

- 100g/scant 4oz caster sugar
- ½ tsp salt
- 120ml/generous 4fl oz soya milk
- 2 tbsp vegetable oil

Optional:
- 50g/2oz chopped nuts, eg walnuts – reasonably sized, not crumbs!
- 50g/2oz vegan chocolate chips – ready-made or just break some dark vegan chocolate into pieces with a rolling pin (see page 19)

1 If using sweet potato, peel and chop into small pieces. Steam until tender for a few minutes, mash to a purée and set aside. Otherwise, use apple sauce or mashed banana option.

2 While cooking, pre-heat oven to 180°C/350°F/Gas Mark 4.

3 Grease cake tin and cover base with baking parchment. Use a pencil to draw around the base of the cake tin to obtain correct size of baking paper.

4 Make topping first by combining topping ingredients in a saucepan. Slowly bring to boil and simmer for a minute, stirring well.

5 Remove from heat and place in a bowl of cold water to reduce temperature. Beat with a fork to thicken and cool then add vanilla essence. Set aside.

6 Make the batter: combine sifted flour, baking powder, cocoa, sugar and salt in a bowl with nuts and choc chips.

7 Stir in soya milk, sweet potato purée, banana or apple sauce and oil. Mix well.

8 Spread batter inside cake tin with a palette knife – it's quite stiff but will spread in the oven – then pour topping over evenly.

9 Bake for 30 minutes. Insert a sharp knife or toothpick into the centre. If it comes out clean the cake is ready – if not, return to the oven for another 5 minutes or so. Leave to cool then cut into 12 or 16 squares.

Funky Chocolate Fudge

For those with a criminally sweet tooth! This is nice served with coffee after dinner or just as a treat.

- 1 tub Tofutti Original dairy-free cream cheese or other brand eg Tesco Free From or Sheese – OR home-made, page 34
- 450g/1lb icing sugar
- 1 tsp vanilla essence
- 175g/6oz vegan chocolate (dairy-free milk chocolate, plain dark chocolate or half and half – see page 19)

Options

- A handful of chopped walnuts, macadamias or almonds
- A handful of shredded coconut
- A handful of dried blueberries or cherries

1 Blend cream cheese until smooth. Add icing sugar and vanilla.
2 Melt chocolate in a double boiler – heat up about 5cm/2 inches of water in a pan. Place a bowl over the top – it shouldn't touch the base of the pan or the water.
3 Add chocolate to the bowl, stirring until dissolved. Blend melted chocolate with cream cheese/sugar mixture until completely integrated.
4 Add any options, stirring in well.
5 Pour into 8 inch square pan lined with non-stick baking paper.
6 Refrigerate until firm. Pull baking paper out of pan. Cut fudge into bite-size pieces. Store in fridge in an airtight container.

ALL KITTED OUT

- Scales
- Measuring spoons
- Hand blender or food processor
- Large bowl if using hand blender
- Saucepan and bowl to fit over the top of the pan
- Wooden spoon
- 20cm/8 inch square baking pan
- Non-stick baking parchment/paper
- Knife
- Air-tight container

COOL COMBOS

- Vegan vanilla ice cream, see page 18
- Espresso coffee

gf wf use GF flour and GF baking powder. It will make a slightly heavier cake but will still taste good

Lemon Drizzle Slices

Really nice!

Cake
- 100g/scant 4oz vegan margarine, see page 18
- 150g/5oz self-raising flour – or see flour tips page 237
- 1 level tsp baking powder
- 150g/5oz caster sugar
- 175g/6oz silken tofu, see page 22
- 60ml/4tbsp soya milk
- 1 lemon, zested or finely grated
- 1 tbsp lemon juice

Glaze
- Juice of 1 lemon
- 100g/scant 4oz granulated sugar

1 Preheat oven to 180°C/350°F/Gas Mark 4.

2 Grease and line bottom of cake tin with greaseproof paper or baking parchment.

3 Place all the ingredients in food processor and mix for 10 seconds. Scrape down the sides and mix for a further 5 seconds. If you don't have a food processor, whizz the mixture with a stick blender, or mix very vigorously with a whisk or wooden spoon.

4 Pour mixture into the prepared tin and bake for 25-30 minutes or until pale golden and springy. Test with a sharp knife or toothpick – it should come out clean. If not, return to the oven for a few more minutes.

5 While cake is baking, stir together lemon juice and sugar for the icing.

6 Remove cake from oven. Immediately spoon lemon juice and sugar mixture over whilst still hot – spread evenly.

7 Leave until cold then cut into slices.

ALL KITTED OUT
- Baking tin: EITHER 18cm/7 inches x 23cm/9 inches by 2.5cm/1 inch OR 20cm/8 inch square
- Oil and pastry brush to grease tin OR low-calorie spray
- Greaseproof paper or baking parchment
- Pencil and scissors
- Scales
- Measuring spoons
- Sieve
- Food processor and rubber spatula OR mixing bowl and wooden spoon
- Lemon squeezer
- Small mixing bowl for sugar and lemon juice glaze

COOL COMBOS
- Good on its own but try a drizzle of Oatly or other non-dairy cream, see pages 17-18
- Or vegan vanilla ice cream, see page 18

gf use GF flour plus 1 large, well-mashed banana and a drizzle more soya milk to thin the batter a little
wf use WF flour plus banana and soya milk as above
❄ cakes freeze well without icing

Magic Muffins

These are really easy and have been fed to hundreds of people, including those sceptics who believe you can't make cakes without eggs. Our picture shows naked muffins but it is very easy to remedy this – see icing recipe below!

- 330g/12oz self-raising flour (best results from 165g wholemeal self-raising and 165g white self-raising) – or see flour tips page 237
- 225g/8oz caster sugar
- 1½ tsp bicarbonate of soda
- 4 tsp soya flour OR egg replacer (soya flour works just as well and works out much cheaper) – buy from either a good health food shop or large supermarket
- 290ml/scant 11fl oz soya or other plant milk
- 110ml/4fl oz plain vegetable oil (not olive)
- 1 tsp vanilla essence

PLUS whatever flavourings you like – see options below

ALL KITTED OUT

- Scales
- Measuring spoons
- Measuring jug
- Sieve
- Mixing bowl
- Whisk
- Wooden spoon
- Muffin tins and cases – large
- Sharp knife or toothpick

OPTIONS

- Chocolate and cinnamon – substitute some of the flour with cocoa powder and 1 tsp cinnamon powder
- Blueberry – a handful of any frozen or dried berries
- Apple and cinnamon – apple chunks and 1 tsp cinnamon
- Pear and cinnamon – as the apple variation
- Carrot – 1 medium grated carrot – also nice with lemon zest added
- Maple and pecan – replace some of the sugar with maple syrup and add a handful of pecan pieces
- Banana – 1 well-mashed ripe banana (add 1-2 tbsp extra liquid if mixture is too dry)
- Lemon and poppy seed – zest of 1 lemon, 2 tbsp juice and 1 tbsp poppy seeds
- Orange and cranberry – zest of 1 orange, 2 tbsp juice and 1-2 tbsp dried cranberries
- Mixed berry – frozen or dried berries are best because they keep their shape whilst baking but fresh will do at a pinch

- White chocolate and berry (use vegan white chocolate eg Organica or Vantastic) and frozen berries, eg blueberries or raspberries
- Triple vegan chocolate chip or else use broken pieces from a bar of vegan chocolate – Organica's dark chocolate or their Couverture bar (which tastes rather like Galaxy). If you have a good health food store they may sell vegan chocolate chips

Or try just about any dried fruit (chop if large, like apricots)

ICING

- 150g/generous 5oz icing sugar, sieved
- 25g/1oz hard white vegetable fat (Trex is vegan) OR 25g/1oz creamed coconut, slightly melted + 25g/1oz vegan margarine, eg Pure
- Flavouring, eg vanilla essence, lemon essence and zest, cocoa powder etc

1 Pre-heat oven to 200°C/400°/Gas Mark 6. Get muffin tins and cases ready.
2 Sift together flour, sugar, bicarbonate of soda and egg replacer/soya flour. Mix well.
3 Mix soya/rice milk, oil and vanilla essence together then whisk into dry ingredients. Add flavourings of your choice.
4 Mix together until just combined (try not to over-mix). Spoon batter into muffin cases placed in muffin tins and bake for 17-20 minutes, until a toothpick inserted into the middle comes out clean. Check after 17 minutes.
5 While muffins are baking, make icing by creaming vegetable fat OR creamed coconut/margarine then mixing in icing sugar and flavourings until everything is amalgamated. Chill in fridge or freezer until you want to serve the cooled muffins. Use a fork or piping bag to ice.

gf wf use GF or WF flour and baking powder and see page 237

Sumptuous Sponge Cake with Three Variations

The basic recipe makes a vanilla sponge and a vanilla 'buttercream' filling and topping. We also give options to make a lemon cake or a fresh strawberry-filled cake.

Vanilla icing
- 85g/3oz vegan margarine
- 200g/7oz icing sugar
- 2 tsp vanilla essence

Vanilla cake
- 175g/6oz vegan margarine OR 140ml plain vegetable oil + 2 tbsp plant milk or water
- 175g/6oz caster sugar
- 330g/12oz white self-raising flour. For a plain flour alternative and adjusted baking powder quantities, see page 237

- 4 tsp baking powder
- Pinch salt
- 330g (⅔ large tub) plain vegan yoghurt
- 1 tbsp flax meal (ground flaxseed) mixed with 3 tbsp hot water
- 2 tsp vanilla essence
- A little plant milk (eg rice, soya) if batter too thick
- Raspberry or strawberry jam

1 Make icing: cream margarine with icing sugar, mix in vanilla essence and chill in fridge or freezer until cake is cooled.

2 Preheat oven to 180°C/350°F/Gas Mark 4. Reduce by 10-15 degrees if using a fan-assisted oven.

3 In a saucepan, warm margarine/oil and caster sugar until melted. Leave to cool.

4 Grease the cake tins and line bases with greaseproof/baking paper.

5 Sieve flour and baking powder into bowl and add salt.

6 Pour margarine/oil and sugar mixture, yoghurt, flax meal mix and vanilla extract into the flour mix plus extra soya or other plant milk if using oil option or if mixture is just too thick.

7 Mix well until you get a soft, dropping consistency. The batter will look slightly curdled – this is just the cake's raising agents doing their work!

8 Add a little more soya milk if necessary.

9 Spoon cake mix equally into tins and bake for 30-40 minutes until risen and golden.

10 If using an ordinary oven, make sure you space cake tins in oven so bottom cake is overshadowed as little as possible by top cake. After 25 minutes you may need to swap them over to ensure each cake is cooked evenly.

Variation II: Lemon Cake with Lemon Icing

Lemon icing
- 45g/1½oz Trex and 45g/1½oz vegan margarine eg Pure, Vitalite, Biona or Suma
- 200g/7oz icing sugar
- Zest of one lemon
- 2 tbsp lemon juice
- 1 tsp lemon essence

Lemon cake

Ingredients same as for vanilla version EXCEPT omit vanilla essence and ADD:
- zest of one lemon
- 2 tbsp lemon juice
- 1-2 tsp lemon essence

1 Cream icing ingredients thoroughly. Chill before you start making the cake.
2 Make cake as in first recipe.
3 When cake is ready, spread half the icing on bottom half and place the second half on top.

Variation III: Strawberry Cake Variation

Strawberry filling
- 400g/14oz strawberries, hulled* and sliced
- 1 tsp orange flower water
- 1 tbsp caster sugar

Optional: 1 tbsp orange liqueur, eg Cointreau or Grand Marnier

*To hull strawberries, use a small sharp knife to remove the stalk and attached white pithy bit

1 Set aside about one third of fruit; marinate remainder in orange flower water, sugar and liqueur, if using.
2 Leave in fridge for at least one hour, but chill overnight if easier.
3 Before serving, fill cake with marinated fruit and decorate top with unsoaked strawberries.

11 When cooking time is up, the centre of cakes should feel springy. Test with a cocktail stick – it should come out cleanly if cooked. Leave cakes to cool completely before placing on a cooling rack.
12 Carefully remove greaseproof paper from bottom.
13 Spread jam and half the icing on bottom cake. Place second cake on top and ice that.

make a batch and freeze what you can't eat for another time
use GF flour and GF baking powder. The scones will be a bit heavier but still nice
use WF or GF flour | Freezable – see above

Sweet Scones

Good served with dairy-free whipping cream and jam!

- 250g/9oz self-raising flour – or see page 237 for plain flour:baking powder ratios
- 1 tbsp flax meal mixed with 3 tbsp warm water. Set aside. OR 3 tsp soya flour
- 1 tsp baking powder
- 45g/1½oz vegan margarine plus more for greasing eg Pure, Vitalite, Biona, Suma

- 3 tbsp caster sugar
- 100ml soya milk if using flax meal option OR 150ml/5floz if using soya flour. Plus a little extra for glazing

To Serve:
- Thick dairy-free cream, see page 18
- Strawberry or other jam of choice

1 Preheat oven to 220°C/425°F/Gas Mark 7.
2 Sift flour, baking powder (and soya flour if using) into large bowl and rub in margarine until mixture resembles breadcrumbs.
3 Add sugar and mix together thoroughly.
4 Make a well in middle of the mixture and slowly pour in soya milk, stirring with a metal spoon. Add the flax mixture if using now also. Bring mixture together until it forms a dough.
5 On a large chopping board (well-scrubbed to avoid onion overtones!), knead dough for five minutes. Roll out to a thickness of about 2.5cm/1 inch and, using a fluted 9cm/3 inch cutter (or drinking glass of same size), cut rounds from dough.
6 Place rounds on greased and floured, non-stick baking tray and brush tops with soya milk.
7 Bake for 12-15 minutes. Leave to cool on a rack.

ALL KITTED OUT

- Scales
- Measuring jug
- Measuring spoons
- Mixing bowl
- Sieve
- Metal spoon
- Scone/cookie cutters or an appropriately-sized glass if you don't have them
- Baking tray
- Pastry brush

but chilling time is 1 hour minimum
use plain GF biscuits – see page 240

Chocolate Peanut Butter Pie

Simple, quick and very nice!

- 200g/7oz vegan biscuits – see page 240 (Tiffin recipe)
- 75g/scant 3oz vegan margarine. See page 18
- 1 pack firm silken tofu (about 350g/12oz). See page 22
- 125g/generous 4oz smooth peanut butter
- 2 tbsp soya milk
- 100g/scant 4oz vegan chocolate – dairy-free milk, plain dark or a mixture. See page 19

1 Crush biscuits into crumbs using either a food processor OR a clean plastic bag and rolling pin.
2 Melt margarine in a saucepan.
3 Mix biscuit crumbs into margarine, stirring thoroughly to ensure the fat gets well integrated.
4 Press mixture into a 20cm/8 inch flan tin, using the back of a wooden spoon, then place in fridge to chill.
5 Blend silken tofu until it is very creamy – ie not grainy. Add peanut butter and soya milk and whizz again.
6 Heat a little water in a saucepan. Place a bowl over the pan, making sure it doesn't touch the bottom.
7 Add chocolate pieces and stir with a wooden spoon until melted.
8 Add melted chocolate to tofu mixture, stirring well. Add a little more soya milk if it is too stiff.
9 Pour the mixture onto biscuit crust and chill until firm – at least one hour.

ALL KITTED OUT

- Knife to open biscuit packet
- Wooden spoon
- Food processor to crush biscuits OR plastic bag and rolling pin
- Food processor or blender for tofu and other filling ingredients
- Small-medium saucepan to make base
- Same or another saucepan to melt chocolate
- A glass or ceramic bowl to fit pan that doesn't touch the bottom
- Rubber or silicone spatula
- 20cm/8 inch flan tin with removable base
- Scales
- Measuring spoons
- Scissors to open tofu packet

COOL COMBOS

- Good on its own but you may want to try it with vegan ice cream and fresh banana slices
- Boozy Chocolate Sauce for Grown-ups, page 285

gf wf use GF vegan biscuits (eg Tesco Free From Digestives or Golden Crunch)

Creamy Baked Cheesecake with Three Variations

This baked cheesecake is lovely. It is lightly flavoured with rosewater and raisins, making it fragrant and creamy without being sickly. It can also be made as individual servings using small, loose-bottomed tins.

- 200g/7oz vegan biscuits, eg ordinary HobNobs (ie not chocolate-coated!) or ginger nuts
- 75g/2½oz vegan margarine. See page 18
- 1 pack firm silken tofu, with liquid, see page 22
- 1 tub of plain/original vegan cream cheese, eg Tofutti, Sheese or Tesco. See page 17
- 1 tbsp vegetable oil

- 2 tbsp golden syrup
- ½ tsp vanilla essence
- 4 tsp rosewater
- 3 tsp arrowroot or cornflour
- 2 tbsp raisins

Topping
The baked cheesecake looks good on its own but you might want to sprinkle some shelled pistachio nuts on top

1 Preheat oven to 180°C/350°F/Gas Mark 4.
2 Grind biscuits until lump free. Use a food processor or place in a strong plastic bag, tie up and crush with a rolling pin.
3 Melt margarine in a saucepan and add biscuit crumbs. Mix well so the fat is completely absorbed.
4 Spread crumb mixture in lightly-oiled, loose-bottomed or springform non-stick cake tin and press down firmly. Bake in the oven for 5 minutes.
5 Meanwhile, blend tofu until very smooth. Add remaining ingredients – except the raisins – and blend well. Stir in raisins.
6 Remove biscuit crumb base from oven. Using a rubber spatula, spoon the cream cheese mixture over top of the base. Check that it has set and isn't too wobbly. Return to oven for a further 5-10 minutes if necessary.
7 Remove from oven, cool before serving.

Versatile variations

Fruity: omit the rosewater and raisins and add 1 tsp of vanilla essence. Top with fresh fruit of your choice.

Ginger & Lime: omit rosewater and replace with zest and juice of 1 lime. Add 2 tsp fresh grated ginger. Replace raisins with chopped, unsulphured apricots.

ALL KITTED OUT

- Scales
- Measuring spoons
- Food processor or rolling pin and plastic bag
- Small-medium saucepan
- 18cm/7 inch or 20cm/8 inch loose-bottomed/springform cake tin OR 6-8 individual loose-bottomed tart tins
- Blender/food processor for cheesecake filling
- Rubber spatula

use value vegan dark chocolate eg Aldi Dairyfine (!) dark or Tesco Everyday Value plain
quarter the quantities. This will give you at least two servings, but it will keep for a few days in the fridge
the half vegan milk with plain version might be more suitable than the version made with all dark chocolate

Juliet's Luxury Chocolate Mousse

This quick and simple recipe from Viva!'s founder and director looks – and tastes – fantastic! We offer two versions – one all dark, the other a mix of dark and vegan milk chocolate. You might also like to vary the flavouring – orange liqueur, mint essence, coffee flavouring…

- 1 pack firm silken tofu (approximately 300-350g). See page 22
- 150g/generous 5oz vegan chocolate – EITHER dairy-free dark chocolate OR use half dark and half vegan milk chocolate such as Moo-free. See page 19
- 2 tbsp maple, date or agave syrup – or just use 1 tbsp of fine brown sugar
- ½ tsp vanilla extract – or other flavourings of your choice. See above
- Pinch of salt

Optional
- 1-2 tbsp brandy
- Fresh raspberries or strawberries to decorate

1 Blend tofu and salt until completely smooth and creamy, scraping sides of the bowl to ensure everything is blended properly.
2 Melt chocolate in a double boiler. This means that you heat a couple of inches of water to boiling point in a saucepan. Turn the heat down and place a thick glass or ceramic bowl over the pan of water, making sure that the bottom of the bowl doesn't touch the base of the pan. Break chocolate into chunks and place in the bowl with syrup and vanilla extract.
3 Stir gently with a spatula until chocolate has completely melted.
4 Add chocolate mixture and any flavourings to the tofu and blend again, using the spatula to scrape down sides of the bowl, as before. Taste, add more syrup or sugar if necessary and blend again. Add the brandy if using, according to taste.
5 Refrigerate in individual serving dishes for an hour or so – little espresso cups look lovely, or nice glasses.
6 Just before serving, decorate with whipped dairy-free cream and/or fresh raspberries/strawberries if using.

ALL KITTED OUT

- Scissors
- Mixing bowl if using hand blender
- Hand blender or food processor
- Rubber spatula
- Measuring spoons
- Wooden spoon
- Saucepan
- Glass or ceramic bowl to fit on saucepan without touching the bottom
- Serving dishes – see suggestions in the recipe

COOL COMBOS

- Cashew Shortbread, page 273
- Dairy-free/vegan single or whipped cream, see pages 17-18
- Dairy-free/vegan ice cream, see page 18
- Blueberry Orange Sauce, page 284

Medjool Dates with Cream Cheese & Sherry Vanilla Sauce

Medjool dates are very large dates sold in large branches of supermarkets or good greengrocers. They have a beautiful butterscotch-type flavour and are much nicer than the traditional, smaller variety. Alternatively, use fresh figs cut in half. This would also go well with the Cashew Shortbread recipe on page 273 or other nice vegan biscuits.

- 1 pack of medjool dates (approximately 2-3 medjool dates per person)
- 1-2 generous tsp plain vegan cream cheese per date, eg Tofutti Original, Sheese Original or Tesco Free From Original Style Spread

Sauce
- 60ml/4 tbsp sweet or medium sherry made up with water to 250ml/8fl oz (many sherries – including most of Harvey's – are vegan but check first)
- 1 tsp arrowroot
- 1 tbsp dark brown sugar
- ½ tsp vanilla extract

1 Mix arrowroot into sherry/water, whisking well.
2 Bring to boil, stirring continuously.
3 Add sugar and vanilla extract and simmer for a few minutes, until sugar is dissolved.
4 Allow to cool – you want sauce to be just warm.
5 Split dates with a sharp knife, remove stones if necessary and spoon cream cheese into each. Place dates on a serving plate, drizzle sauce artistically around them and serve.

ALL KITTED OUT
- Measuring jug
- Measuring spoons
- Small saucepan
- Balloon whisk
- Chopping board (well-washed so no onion/garlic odours!)
- Knife
- Small spoon
- Serving spoon
- Serving plate

COOL COMBOS
- Cashew Shortbread, page 273 (pictured)

easily halved or quartered to serve two or one
gf wf see biscuit notes in recipe

Mocha Yoghurt

- 4 tsp instant coffee granules
- 1 tbsp boiling water
- 2 tsp cocoa powder mixed with 2 tsp caster sugar plus a little extra for dusting
- 3 tbsp brown sugar

- 250ml (half a large tub) of plain soya yoghurt – try to have this as cold as possible to speed up the process

Optional: small pieces of ginger nut biscuits or walnut pieces for garnish. Orgran GF and vegan Biscotti Amaretti Italian-style almond biscuits would also go well

1 Dissolve coffee granules and sugar in boiling water – add a little more if necessary but take care it doesn't make the yoghurt too watery.

2 Allow mixture to cool a little then whisk it, together with the cocoa/sugar mixture, into the yoghurt.

3 Taste for sweetness and coffee strength – if needed, dissolve a further tsp of coffee with 2 tsp sugar in a little boiling water and add.

4 Add biscuit pieces if using.

5 Divide mocha mixture into individual serving bowls, cover and chill for at least half an hour.

6 Decorate with a light dusting of cocoa powder/sugar and a walnut piece or two if using. Serve biscuits on side.

ALL KITTED OUT

- Kettle of hot water
- Measuring spoons
- Mixing bowl
- Whisk
- Individual serving dishes – eg ramekins, espresso cups

COOL COMBOS

This works nicely on its own as a light dessert but if you want to push the boat out a bit, try with
- Cashew Shortbread, page 273
- Chocolate Brownies, page 244

Speedy Chocolate Pudding

This makes a simple, quick and cheap dessert which can easily be jazzed up with something crunchy, such as our Cashew Shortbread recipe – see below – or even chopped fresh fruit. It can also be made with an orange or mint flavour.

- 1 pack firm silken tofu, crumbled (300-350g, depending on pack). See page 22
- 100ml/6 generous tbsp agave or date syrup – OR caster sugar to taste
- 125g/4oz cocoa powder, sieved
- 1-2 tsp vanilla extract OR try a drop or two of peppermint or orange flavouring
- Pinch of salt

1 Blend tofu until creamy.
2 Add rest of ingredients and blend until everything is completely amalgamated. Taste and add extra syrup/sugar if desired.
3 Chill before serving.

ALL KITTED OUT

- Scissors
- Hand blender or food processor
- Sieve
- Measuring spoons

COOL COMBOS

- Cashew Shortbread, page 273
- Chocolate Brownies, page 244
- Berry fruits – raspberries or other
- Ice cream, see page 18
- Baked bananas

Strawberry Tarts

These look the business! The pastry is the kind you press in with your fingers so it's very easy and quick to do. Whichever size tart you go for, use the loose-bottomed type tins as they are much easier to serve. And enough of the Carry-on jokes already.

The Vanilla Custard is also easy (but you can cheat and use bought vanilla soya dessert or custard if you're in a hurry. Shh, we won't tell…)

Vanilla Custard Filling
- 2 tbsp plain flour
- 4 tbsp cornflour
- 6 tbsp water
- 65g/generous 2oz caster sugar
- 315ml/11fl oz soya milk
- 2 tsp vanilla extract

Pastry
- 110g/scant 4oz vegan margarine. See page 18
- 30g/1oz icing sugar
- 125g/scant 5oz plain flour

Topping
- 1 large punnet of strawberries
- 3 tbsp redcurrant jelly or other red seedless jam + 1 tbsp water

ALL KITTED OUT
- Scales
- Measuring spoons
- Sieve
- Small bowl
- Mixing bowl
- Wooden spoon
- 23cm/9 inch loose-bottomed

- tart tin, 6 deep individual tartlet tins OR a silicone 6 hole tray
- Small saucepan (used twice so wash after making the filling)
- Small whisk
- Chopping board
- Colander
- Knife

1 Make the pastry using either a food processor or mixing bowl. Cream the sieved icing sugar with the margarine. Then add the sieved flour a third at a time.
2 If pastry too crumbly, add 1 tbsp+ ice-cold water, a little at a time but not too much! Mix it in, then form the pastry into a ball and place in a plastic bag. Chill for at least 30 minutes.
3 Make the vanilla custard filling by mixing the flour and cornflour together with water, beating vigorously until creamy.
4 Gently heat sugar and soya or creamy coconut milk in a medium saucepan. Add cornflour/flour mixture and bring it to the boil, stirring continuously. Add the vanilla essence, remove from heat, place in a bowl and chill.
5 Preheat the oven to 180°C/350°F/Gas Mark 4. Grease the tin(s).
6 If making individual tarts, divide pastry into six pieces. Otherwise, place all the pastry into one 23cm/9inch loose-bottomed tart tin.
7 Press the pastry in so that the bottom and sides are completely covered. Keep the base thin. If the pastry is a bit sticky, coat your hands in a little flour.
8 Place the tart(s) in the oven and bake for 15-20 minutes or until pastry is light golden brown and not too crisp.
9 Remove and let cool for a few minutes. Carefully remove the pastry from the tin(s) and place on a rack. Let pastry cool completely.
10 Just before serving, hull the strawberries (remove stalk and with the knife, remove the white pith just inside the top). Slice thinly.
11 Spoon the vanilla custard carefully into the tartlet case(s), making sure they are evenly filled.
12 Arrange sliced strawberries neatly on top.
13 Make the glaze. Heat the jelly and water together in a small pan, mix well, cool just a little then drizzle carefully over the tarts. Let the glaze set before serving.

the dessert is quick to make but needs fridge time
for an even cheaper version use smooth peanut butter and value dark chocolate, eg Aldi or Lidl

Tiramisu

This is an easy and relatively economical way of making tiramisu – delicious yet far less fatty than the traditional variety. Adapted from Robin Robertson's recipe in *Vegan on the Cheap* (John Wiley & Sons) with thanks.

Base

- 4 slices of bread taken from a good quality, unsliced white loaf – it can be slightly stale. Slices need to be just under 2cm/1 inch
- 85ml/3fl oz soya milk
- ½ tsp vanilla essence (use best quality you can afford)
- 60g/2oz caster sugar
- 2 tbsp brandy or Amaretto liqueur (optional but very nice!)
- 1 tsp cocoa powder – not drinking chocolate

Mocha Crème Topping

- 110g/4oz unsalted cashew pieces (blanched almonds also work) – ground to a fine powder. OR 6 tbsp cashew or other nut butter

- 1 pack of firm silken tofu (preferably 350g but smaller size will work), drained and pressed down to get rid of excess liquid. See page 22
- 110g/4oz caster sugar
- 3 tsp instant coffee dissolved in a little just-boiled hot water to make a smooth syrup
- 1 tsp vanilla essence – see above
- 1 tbsp cocoa powder – see above

Optional

- 50g (half a large bar) dark vegan chocolate – grated. See page 19

1 Remove crusts from bread and cut into large triangles. Arrange on the bottom of a square, lasagne-type dish.
2 Heat soya milk and 60g/2oz of caster sugar in small saucepan until sugar has dissolved. Add half teaspoon of vanilla essence, plus brandy/Amaretto if using, mix well then turn off heat.
3 Pour milk mixture over bread – pierce lightly with a fork to ensure liquid soaks all bread pieces. Sieve the teaspoon of cocoa powder over evenly. Set aside.
4 Now make the Mocha Crème. Grind cashews to a fine powder if you haven't already done so. Set aside.
5 Make coffee mixture by mixing hot water and coffee granules in saucepan. Set aside.
6 Blend ground nuts with drained silken tofu until smooth and creamy. Use spatula to scrape sides and avoid lumps.
7 Add sugar, vanilla essence and coffee mixture and blend again thoroughly.
8 Spoon mixture evenly over bread base then sprinkle rest of the cocoa powder over evenly.
9 Chill for at least an hour then top with grated chocolate before serving, if using.

gf wf most vegan ice cream is suitable but always check the label carefully!

Viva!bocker Glory

The ultimate in old school desserts. I used to make these many years ago when I was a waitress. They sold like hot cakes – as soon as one came out of the kitchen, the entire restaurant would start ordering.

- 4 tbsp jam thinned with a little water (strawberry or raspberry probably work best)
- 2 scoops of vegan ice cream, see page 18
- Fresh fruit of your choice, eg banana, raspberries, strawberries, blueberries, pineapple chunks, mango

- Vegan whipping cream, see page 18
- 2 tsp grated vegan chocolate, see page 19
- 1 tsp toasted slivered almonds or hazelnut pieces

1 Drizzle one third of fruity sauce at bottom of sundae glass or other dish.
2 Place one scoop of ice cream, followed by a layer of fruit.
3 Repeat process until you reach the top – leave enough fruity sauce for the topping.
4 Squirt or pipe cream on top, add grated chocolate, another squirt of fruity sauce and sprinkle with nuts.
5 Eat immediately.

ALL KITTED OUT

- Sundae glasses, preferably tall
- Long spoons if possible
- Chopping board
- Knife
- Measuring spoons
- Small bowl to thin the jam
- Grater
- Small frying pan if toasting nuts yourself

COOL COMBOS

- Serve with ice cream wafers, eg Eskal gluten-free Wafer Rolls with Chocolate Cream (HFS), Giannis Ice Cream Cones (Aldi), Tesco Ice Cream Wafers. (Many wafers are inherently vegan but check for hidden whey etc)

use value salted cashews, shake off excess and omit salt from recipe
try GF flour and GF baking powder

Cashew Shortbread

These are easy to make and absolutely delicious. The cashew nuts add a buttery, rich taste. They are particularly nice with the rhubarb option but there are other good options in Cool Combos – see below.

- 115g/4oz vegan margarine, see page 18
- 60g/2oz brown sugar (granulated or soft)
- 75g/scant 3oz raw cashew pieces or whole cashews

- 125g/scant 5oz self-raising or plain flour, preferably half fine wholemeal and half white
- Baking powder: ¼ tsp if using plain flour, ⅛ tsp if using self-raising
- Small pinch of salt

1 Preheat oven to 190°C/375°F/Gas Mark 5.
2 Cream margarine with sugar until smooth.
3 Grind cashews to a fine powder and add to margarine/sugar mixture.
4 Sieve flour, baking powder and salt into mixture and mix until well amalgamated.
5 Place dough on a large sheet of greaseproof paper and place another sheet on top – this makes it easier to roll. Roll out to about 6mm/¼ inch thick, remove the top layer of greaseproof paper then press out biscuits using cookie cutters. Hearts are nice!
6 The dough will be quite sticky so use a fish slice or metal palette knife to slide it under each rolled-out biscuit.
7 Place on ungreased, non-stick baking tray and bake for 10-12 minutes. Allow to cool a little before carefully sliding fish slice/palette knife beneath each biscuit and transferring to a wire rack – they are quite delicate.
8 Allow biscuits to cool completely before transferring to an air-tight container.

ALL KITTED OUT

- Scales
- Measuring spoons
- Sieve
- Mixing bowl
- Fork
- Rolling pin
- Greaseproof paper
- Cookie cutters
- Fish slice or metal palette knife
- Non-stick baking tray
- Wire rack
- Air-tight container

COOL COMBOS

- Speedy Chocolate Pudding, page 265
- Stewed Rhubarb (made with dark brown sugar and grated fresh ginger) served with vegan ice cream – plain or ginger, see page 18
- Juliet's Luxury Chocolate Mousse, page 260
- Mocha Yoghurt, page 264

gf use GF bread or GF/WF breadcrumbs OR GF porridge oats. If using oats, double the quantity of margarine

Raspberry & Banana Bake with Crunchy Topping

This makes a nice alternative to the usual fruit crumble. The contrast of raspberries and banana works well together.

- 1 pack frozen raspberries or mixed berries (about 350g/12oz)
- 3 bananas, sliced
- Brown sugar or agave syrup to taste
- 150g/5oz fresh white or wholemeal breadcrumbs
- 2 tbsp vegan margarine. See page 18
- 4 tbsp dark brown sugar
- Vegan ice cream to serve. See page 18

1 Preheat oven to 180°C/350°F/Gas Mark 4.

2 Lightly grease oven-proof dish.

3 Put raspberries and bananas into the dish, adding the sugar or agave syrup to taste.

4 Mix margarine, 4 tbsp brown sugar and breadcrumbs together.

5 Cover the fruit with the crunchy topping mixture and bake for 20-30 minutes.

6 Serve hot with the ice cream.

ALL KITTED OUT

- Scissors
- Knife
- Food processor to make breadcrumbs
- Measuring spoons
- Oven-proof dish
- Serving spoon

with home-made custard and no brandy

Bread & Butter Pudding with Marmalade Pudding Variation

An excellent recipe that is good as a budget version or with a little brandy luxury!

- 100g/scant 4oz raisins or sultanas, preferably large Lexia raisins
- 3 tbsp brandy (optional)
- Custard*, made with
  - 850ml/1½ pints soya milk
  - 3 tbsp custard powder
  - 4 tbsp caster sugar
  OR use 2 x 500ml packs of Alpro/Provamel ready-made vegan custard
- 10-12 pieces of medium-thick sliced white bread
- Vegan margarine, see page 18

Optional
- 2 tsp soft brown sugar
- Nutmeg to sprinkle – about ¼ tsp

* Custard powder: Birds and supermarket own brands in tubs (NOT packets) or Just Wholefoods brand. Cartons of instant vegan custard sold by Alpro and Provamel

1 Preheat oven to 180°C/350°F/Gas Mark 4.
2 If using brandy, soak raisins in brandy in a small bowl. Set aside.
3 If making custard from scratch, place a little soya milk with the custard powder in a pan and mix to a paste. Add the rest of the soya milk and the sugar, whisking. Bring to boil, stirring. Set aside when thickened.
4 Grease oven-proof dish. Spread bread with margarine, remove crusts and cut each slice into triangles.
5 Put layer of bread – margarine side up – on the edges and bottom of the dish. Sprinkle with handful of raisins. Add layer of custard. Repeat process, ending with custard.
6 If using nutmeg/brown sugar topping, mix together then sprinkle over top of pudding.
7 Bake in hot oven for about 30 minutes, or until golden brown.
8 Serve on its own or with vegan vanilla ice cream or dairy-free cream – see pages 17-18.

Marmalade Pudding Variation

1 Use Bread & Butter Pudding recipe as above – omit raisins if preferred.
2 Spread bread with margarine and liberal amounts of bitter, thick-cut marmalade.
3 Bake according to instructions above.

gf wf use GF or WF flour

Chinese Banana Fritters

Batter

- 100g/3½oz white self-raising flour – or see page 237 for plain flour and baking powder option
- 1 tbsp gram flour (chickpea or besan flour, available from large supermarkets, ethnic grocers and health food shops – GF)
- 2 tbsp caster sugar
- 1 tsp Chinese five-spice powder: Bart spices, large Tesco, Waitrose, HFS, Oriental stores or online, eg Ocado. It's also delicious used in stir-fries

- 140ml/5fl oz soya milk
- 140ml/5fl oz cold water
- ¼ tsp salt
- 2 tbsp sesame seeds

Other ingredients

- 5-6 firm bananas, halved lengthways and chopped into three
- Plain vegetable oil to shallow fry
- Icing sugar to dust

1 Preheat oven to 150°C/300°F/Gas Mark 2.
2 Sieve the flours and sugar into mixing bowl with the salt and five-spice powder.
3 Add liquid a little at a time until a smooth batter forms.
4 Add sesame seeds and mix in by hand.
5 Heat about half to an inch of oil until very hot – a drop of batter or water should sizzle.
6 Dip banana pieces in batter and fry in small batches (4-6 pieces at a time) until golden and crispy – too many will cool the oil and make them soggy.
7 Keep each batch warm in oven while you fry the rest.
8 Serve with dusting of sieved icing sugar and accompaniments of your choice, as below.

ALL KITTED OUT

- Mixing bowl
- Sieve
- Measuring spoons
- Scales
- Whisk or electric beater
- Frying pan, deep wok or deep-fat fryer
- Slotted metal spoon
- Oven tray or dish
- Kitchen paper

COOL COMBOS

- Booja Booja Ginger Ice Cream (Feisty Rollercoastery Ginger flavour!)
OR Swedish Glace Vanilla ice cream mixed with 2 tbsp chopped crystallised ginger

Individual Hot Citrus Puddings

These little sweet yet tangy hot desserts are a winner: delicious, cheap and easy and they look lovely too. Read the recipe carefully before you start – especially the sauce and lemon juice/hot water part at the end – then get everything weighed out and ready. Now go, you vegan chef...

Batter: dry ingredients
- 125g/4½oz plain white flour
- 150g/5oz light brown sugar
- 1 tsp baking powder
- ½ tsp bicarbonate of soda
- ¼ tsp salt

Batter: wet ingredients
- 120ml/4fl oz soya milk
- 2 tbsp mild vegetable oil

- 3 tsp lemon or lime zest
- Juice of 1 lemon

Dry Sauce
- 150g/5oz light brown sugar
- 30g/1oz plain white flour

Wet Sauce
- Juice of 2 lemons or 2-3 limes
- Boiling water added to juice to make up to 250ml/9fl oz

1 Preheat oven to 180°C/350°F/Gas Mark 4 for at least 10 minutes. If a fan-assisted oven, reduce heat by about 10-15 degrees.
2 Put kettle on to boil.
3 Lightly oil 6 individual ramekin dishes (8 or 9 cm).
4 In a medium bowl, mix together dry batter ingredients.
5 In a jug or smaller bowl, whisk together wet batter ingredients then add to the dry batter ingredients and mix well.
6 Place in ramekins.
7 Make dry sauce by first whisking together flour and sugar. Sprinkle mixture quickly and evenly over batter in each ramekin.
8 Quickly make wet sauce: mix lemon/lime juice with boiling water and pour evenly over each ramekin. Yes, really! DO NOT STIR.
9 Bake for 20-25 minutes until tops are golden and puddings are still slightly gooey inside – test with a toothpick. If using fan-assisted oven, check after 15 minutes. If too gooey, return to the oven for another 5-10 minutes.

ALL KITTED OUT
- Scales
- Measuring jug
- Measuring spoons
- Kettle
- 6 individual ramekin dishes
- Medium mixing bowl
- Jug or smaller bowl
- Whisk

COOL COMBOS
- Vegan single, whipping or ice cream – see pages 17-18

gf use GF flour and GF baking powder + ½ cup apple sauce; reduce liquid by 120ml
wf use WF flour

Warm Apple Upside-down Cake

A simple, satisfying, old-fashioned pudding like Mum or Gran might have made. For a real nostalgia-fest, replace apple with peach halves or pineapple rings – fresh or tinned. Drizzle agave or golden syrup over the fruit before spooning the batter over it. Retro heaven!

- 300g/11oz self-raising flour (white or half and half wholemeal self-raising with white self-raising) or see plain flour details page 237
- Egg replacer options: 4 tbsp soya flour OR 4 tbsp apple sauce (eg value) OR 1 tbsp flax meal (ground flaxseeds) dissolved in 3 tbsp hot water
- 1½ tsp baking powder
- 200g/7oz caster sugar

- 1 tsp cinnamon (optional)
- 85ml/3fl oz plain vegetable oil (just under 6 tbsp)
- 1 tsp vanilla essence
- 2 tsp cider or white wine vinegar
- 300ml/11fl oz equal parts soya milk and water. If using a thinner plant milk (eg rice), don't water it down
- 4 large eating apples, peeled, cored and sliced thinly

1 Pre-heat oven to 190°C/375°F/Gas Mark 5.
2 Prepare cake tin by oiling lightly – especially the base.
3 Sieve dry ingredients into mixing bowl: flour, soya flour option if using, sugar, baking powder, cinnamon if using.
4 Whisk all wet ingredients together in a jug: oil, soya milk/water, vanilla essence and vinegar, plus flax meal mixture or apple sauce option if using.
5 Pour liquid slowly into flour mixture and stir well.
6 Place sliced apple at bottom of tin and cover with batter.
7 Bake for about 35-40 minutes, until a toothpick or sharp knife comes out clean from the middle of the cake.
8 Let the cake cool a little then place a plate or shallow baking tray on top of the tin. Carefully turn the cake upside down onto the plate/tin. Slide the palette knife gently under the base to remove it and reveal the apple (or pineapple or peach) topping.
9 Serve while still warm.

ALL KITTED OUT

- 20cm/8 inch springform tin
- Greaseproof paper
- Scissors and pencil
- Oil spray OR pastry brush and oil/margarine
- Scales
- Measuring spoons
- Measuring jug
- Sieve
- Mixing bowl
- Whisk
- Wooden spoon
- Toothpick or sharp knife
- Palette knife

COOL COMBOS

- Custard, home-made – see page 277 – or from a carton, Alpro or Provamel
- Oatly Cream or any other dairy-free cream, see pages 17-18

use frozen blueberries or mixed berries
eat sparingly if you are a diabetic

Blueberry Orange Sauce

Nice drizzled on pancakes, cake, ice cream... whatever you fancy!

- 110g/4oz blueberries, frozen or fresh
- 240ml/8fl oz fresh orange juice
- 1 tsp orange zest
- 1 tsp arrowroot
- 1 tsp fresh ginger, grated (optional)

1 Mix arrowroot with orange juice with a small whisk.

2 Place all ingredients in a saucepan.

3 Cook over medium heat, stirring occasionally, for 5-10 minutes, stirring well to ensure the arrowroot doesn't go lumpy. You want the blueberries to be fairly soft.

4 Serve warm over pancakes or ice cream – or see below for ideas.

ALL KITTED OUT

- Scales
- Measuring jug
- Measuring spoons
- Bowl or jug to mix arrowroot with orange juice
- Whisk
- Medium saucepan
- Wooden spoon

COOL COMBOS

- Pancakes, page 36
- Banana Cake, page 239
- Warm Apple Upside-down Cake, page 282
- Juliet's Luxury Chocolate Mousse, page 260

if you have leftover alcohol
whisk up well after defrosting and heat through gently
gf wf use arrowroot

Boozy Chocolate Sauce for Grown-ups with Sober Option

So quick, so nice, so moreish... this makes a dark, sophisticated sauce which works well with a number of things.

- 4 tbsp agave syrup or caster sugar. Add more according to taste
- 2 tbsp sieved cocoa powder NOT drinking chocolate
- 120ml/4fl oz liquid. Choose from 90ml/3fl oz water + 2 tbsp whisky or brandy OR 120ml plant milk such as almond or soya OR 120ml tinned coconut milk for a really rich, creamy treat. If you want booze in these versions, great, just reduce milk to 90ml/3floz

- 1 tsp cornflour or arrowroot
- 1 tsp vanilla essence

1 Mix cocoa powder with a little of the liquid option to form a smooth paste. Add cornflour/arrowroot, using a whisk if necessary to get rid of any lumps. Add the rest of the liquid, sugar/agave syrup and vanilla essence.
2 Mix well and cook over medium heat until thickened, stirring constantly – use a small whisk if necessary.
3 Taste to see if sweet enough – add more sugar or syrup as necessary, ensuring it dissolves properly.
4 Serve hot.

ALL KITTED OUT

- Small saucepan
- Sieve
- Measuring spoons
- Measuring jug
- Wooden spoon
- Whisk

COOL COMBOS

- Pancakes, page 36, filled with banana and/or raspberries
- Chocolate Brownies (oh, go on), page 244
- Vegan ice cream – preferably vanilla or chocolate – page 18

Intelligent indexes

We have tried to make this book as accessible and appropriate for your individual needs as possible. The ingredients index is especially useful if you've got bits and pieces of food that need using up. The themed indexes are aimed at specific needs, eg budget, child-friendly, gluten-free etc.

Index by ingredient

We hope this index will help you to search by ingredients you already have – eg a batch of tomatoes that need using up, some leftover brown rice or a tin of beans near their use-by date etc. Cooking by ingredients saves money and food wastage.

- What this index includes: core ingredients such as vegetables, fruit, pulses (beans, lentils, peas), rice, other grains and cereals, nuts and seeds, plant milks, yoghurt and cream, speciality flours (eg chickpea/gram), pasta and noodles, tempeh, tofu, condiments, herbs and spices (fresh and dried), vegan condiments such as nutritional yeast flakes, miso, tamari or shoyu soya sauce – and the occasional commercial meat and dairy alternative
- What it *doesn't* include: basics like oil or oil spray, plain flour, cornflour, vegan margarine, sugar, salt, pepper, bicarbonate of soda or baking powder
- Ingredients in listed recipes may be an integral part of a dish, an optional extra or just a serving suggestion
- Soya milk is usually specified in recipes using milk but most recipes are interchangeable so feel free to experiment with other types. It's best to use unsweetened varieties, especially in savoury dishes – sugar or syrup can always be added where necessary
- Allergens or foods you don't like? If you are searching the index for either of these, don't be put off by the inclusion of an ingredient, eg nuts. Always check the main recipe – some items will be an optional extra or may be omitted from the dish without too much effect. Or try an alternative, eg cashews instead of peanuts, tahini instead of peanut butter. Get creative!
- On a budget? We've listed the cookbook's budget recipes (page 301). See also **www.veganrecipeclub.org.uk/eating-well-budget**. This has lots of ideas, including links to ingredient cost-cutting and replacements

Themed indexes

💷 Cheap as chickpeas – budget dishes

For lots of useful tips about eating well and cheaply, see www.veganrecipeclub.org.uk/eating-well-budget

Fast feeds – 30 minutes or less
Desserts & cakes

Blueberry Orange Sauce 284
Boozy Chocolate Sauce for Grown-ups with
   Sober Option 285
Boozy Chocolate Tiffin with Optional
   Chocolate Topping 240
Cashew Shortbread 273
Chocolate Peanut Butter Pie 256
Funky Chocolate Fudge 247
Juliet's Luxury Chocolate Mousse 260
Magic Muffins 251
Medjool Dates with Cream Cheese & Sherry
   Vanilla Sauce 263
Mocha Yoghurt 264
Speedy Chocolate Pudding 265
Sweet Scones 255
Tiramisu 269
Viva!bocker Glory 270

Mains

Avocado, Fresh Tomato, Garlic & Basil Sauce with
   Pasta 168
Big Mushroom Burger 89
Butternut Squash with Garlic-thyme Aduki Beans 172
Caribbean Coconut Rice 175
Chinese Red Bean Burgers 179
Coconut Parsnip with Red Beans, Lime & Ginger 104
Gado Gado 183
Martin Shaw's Classic Chilli 184
Muffaletta Stuffed Loaf with a Choice of
   Two Fillings 92
Mushroom, White Wine & Creamy Tarragon
   Lemon Sauce with Pasta 188
Old School Lentil & Potato Curry 191
Oriental Vegetable Fan Wraps with Spring Onion
   Tufts (wraps or cooked pancakes) 192
Pad Thai with Tofu Triangles 196
Pancakes, Basic Batter Savoury 36
Pancakes, Padma Indian-style 39
Quick Aubergine & Tomato Curry 200
Quick Thai Vegetable Curry with Tofu 203
Quinoa Pilaf 124
Smoky Black Bean Cakes & Sausages 204
Smoky Mexican Mushroom Stroganoff 207
Socca Pizza with Cream Cheese, Sundried
   Tomatoes & Artichoke Hearts 211
Speedy Pizza 215
Time-is-Tight Tacos 216
Tofu Burgerettes 219
Tony's Sundried Tomato & Asparagus Pasta
   with Pesto 224
Tropical Rice Salad with Sesame Orange
   Dressing (pre-cooked rice) 86
Vegan Chick'n Caesar Salad 227
Vegetable Tempura 228
Viva!'s Green & Wild Tahini Noodles 231

Sauces

BBQ 138

Cheesy, Quick Tahini-based 139
Cheesy, Creamy Tofu-based 140
Coriander Lime Raita 141
Creamy Oriental Carrot 142
Easy Mayo 143
Fragrant Coconut 144
Fresh Sweet & Sour 145
Luxury Two-mushroom 146
Maca Mayo 148
Miso Tahini 208
No-cook Curry 150
Roasted Red Pepper & Almond 151
Rose's Onion Gravy with Posh Options 153
St Clement's Tahini 154
Satay (Spicy Peanut) 155
Sour Cream 35
Tomato with Many Options 156
Viva! Veggie Oyster 158
Walnut & Parsley Pesto 159
Whizzy Hot 160

Sides, bread-based

Avocado & Walnut Toast with Tomato
   and Coriander 88
Big Mushroom Burger 89
French Toast 91
Savoury Scones 95
Scrambled Tofu 126
Tofu 'Egg' Mayo 120

Sides, dips

Cheese, Cream 34
Italian Olive Dip 119
Guacamole 199
Grilled Aubergine & Coriander Chutney 118
Sour Cream 35
Tofu 'Egg' Mayo 120

Sides, grains

Joe's Chestnut Rice 123
Quinoa Pilaf 124

Sides, hot

Cabbage with Sesame & Marmalade 97
Cauliflower Dijon 98
Edamame Fuji 100
Garlic Broccoli 103
Green Beans with Tomatoes & Herbs 101
Greens & Garlic 103
Joe's Chestnut Rice 123
Mash with Cumin Seeds and Yoghurt 107
Mixed Rooty Mash 108
Mustard Glazed Carrots 112
Quinoa Pilaf 124
Red Veg 113
Sautéed Squash with Olive Tapenade &
   Cannellini Beans 114
Spiced Roasties with Lime (with
   leftover potatoes) 115
Spinach Citron 116
Tony's Asparagus Gratinée 117

Sides, protein-packed

Avocado & Walnut Toast with Tomato
   and Coriander 88
Cheese, Cream 34
Cheese, Soft Ricotta-style 33
French Toast 91
Quinoa Pilaf 124
Tofu Burgerettes (as a snack in a roll) 219
Tofu 'Egg' Mayo 120
Scrambled Tofu 126
Tempeh Rashers (pre-marinated rashers) 127
Sour Cream 35

Sides, salads

Avocado, Fennel & Grapefruit Salad 75
Carrot & Beetroot Slaw 80
Cauliflower & Flageolet Bean Antipasto 76
Coleslaw, Carrot & Beetroot 80
Coleslaw, Celeriac & Seed 79
Coleslaw, Traditional 78
Herby Potato Salad 84
Italian Olive Dip 119
Luscious Two Pear Salad with Balsamic Dressing 81
Mango Salsa 82
Potato Salad with Creamy Wholegrain
   Mustard Dressing 85

Soups

Cheesy Broccoli 48
Chilled Avocado 49
Cream of Mushroom (pressure cooked) 50
Cream of Tomato (pressure cooked) 51
Harira, Middle Eastern Aromatic
   (pressure cooked) 52
Jerusalem Artichoke (pressure cooked) 55
Lentil & Tomato with Herbs 56
Miso 60
Quick Cream of Watercress 64
Spicy Coconut & Lentil 68
Thai Banana 71

Going solo – cooking for one
Desserts & cakes

Banana Cake (slice and freeze leftovers) 239
Blueberry Orange Sauce 284
Boozy Chocolate Sauce for Grown-ups with
   Sober Option 285
Bread & Butter Pudding with Marmalade
   Pudding Variation 277
Cashew Shortbread 273
Chinese Banana Fritters 278
Chocolate Peanut Butter Pie 256
Juliet's Luxury Chocolate Mousse 260
Mocha Yoghurt 264
Raspberry & Banana Bake with Crunchy Topping 274
Speedy Chocolate Pudding 265
Sweet Scones 255
Viva!bocker Glory 270

Mains

African Slow & Sweet Potato Stew with
   Red Beans 163

gf Gluten-free

Individual recipes give specific gluten-free alternatives, eg tamari soya sauce, plain tofu, gluten-free bread. See also page 237 for gluten-free baking tips

Wheat-free

Individual recipes suggest wheat-free alternatives, eg tamari soya sauce, plain tofu, wheat-free bread. See also page 237 for baking tips

Kid–friendly
Children, like adults, have different tastes and preferences about food and will also go through phases about what they do and don't like. It may feel like a struggle sometimes but everything we've heard suggests it's important to keep offering new foods, including those they may have rejected previously. It can take over twenty goes before they might take to some things (their taste buds change all the time). Also, getting kids to cook or help with preparation is a great way for them to try new foods – they're more likely to eat something they have ownership of!

Freezable, (all or part of the dish)

Freeze items like pancakes, savoury rolls and burgers in layers of greaseproof paper/baking parchment to keep them whole. Large cakes or substantial savoury loaves can be wrapped in cling film or foil but make sure they are as airtight as possible. Soups, sauces, stews etc are fine in airtight plastic tubs and boxes. Remember to label and date.

Another useful tip is to keep a list of what's in the freezer on the fridge door, preferably with dates – have a look before you head off to the shops! Try and plan meals around what's in your cupboards, fridge and freezer – it saves money, time and means less food is wasted.

Low-fat/diabetic-friendly

See also Viva!Health's Big D Diabetes Guide for scientifically sound health tips and nutritional tips as well as more recipes and food ideas. Buy it from www.vivashop.org.uk/vvf or phone 0117 944 1000 (Mon-Fri, 9-5) to order. Alternatively, download free www.vivahealth.org.uk/campaigns/diabetes/guide

End quotes

American Dietetic Association's Position on Vegetarian Diets

'It is the position of the American Dietetic Association that appropriately planned vegetarian diets, *including total vegetarian or vegan diets**, are healthful, nutritionally adequate, and may provide health benefits in the prevention and treatment of certain diseases. Well-planned vegetarian diets are appropriate for individuals during all stages of the life cycle, including pregnancy, lactation, infancy, childhood, and adolescence, and for athletes.

'The results of an evidence-based review showed that a vegetarian diet is associated with a lower risk of death from ischemic heart disease. Vegetarians also appear to have lower low-density lipoprotein ('bad') cholesterol levels, lower blood pressure, and lower rates of hypertension and type 2 diabetes than non-vegetarians. Furthermore, vegetarians tend to have a lower body mass index (they are slimmer) and lower overall cancer rates.

'Vegetarian diets in childhood and adolescence can aid in the establishment of lifelong healthful eating patterns and can offer some important nutritional advantages. Vegetarian children and adolescents have lower intakes of cholesterol, saturated fat, and total fat and higher intakes of fruits, vegetables, and fibre than non-vegetarians. Vegetarian children have also been reported to be leaner and to have lower serum cholesterol levels.

'Vegetarian diets appear to offer some nutritional advantages for adolescents. Vegetarian adolescents are reported to consume more fibre, iron, folate, vitamin A, and vitamin C than non-vegetarians. Vegetarian adolescents also consume more fruits and vegetables, and fewer sweets, fast foods, and salty snacks compared to non-vegetarian adolescents.'

Craig, W., Mangels, A.R., American Dietetic Association, 2009. Position of the American Dietetic Association: Vegetarian Diets. *Journal of the American Dietetic Association*. 109 (7) 1266-1282

Medical Journal of Australia on Vegetarian Diets

'Research has shown that a well planned vegetarian diet can meet nutritional needs for good health and may reduce the risk of cancer, cardiovascular disease, metabolic syndrome, insulin resistance, type 2 diabetes, hypertension and obesity. Choosing plant based meals is also environmentally beneficial. Vegetarian diets are generally lower in saturated fat and cholesterol and higher in dietary fibre, antioxidants and phytochemicals than non-vegetarian diets. It is likely that the combination of these factors provide vegetarians with a significant health advantage.'

Reid, M.A., Marsh, K.A., Zeuschner, C.L., Saunders, A.V., Baines, S.K., 2012. Meeting the Nutrient Reference Values on a Vegetarian Diet. *Medical Journal of Australia Open*. 1 Suppl 2: 33-40

* Our emphasis